Aquarius Revisited

AQUARIUS REVISITED

SEVEN WHO CREATED THE SIXTIES COUNTERCULTURE THAT CHANGED AMERICA

William Burroughs Allen Ginsberg Ken Kesey
Timothy Leary Norman Mailer Tom Robbins
Hunter S. Thompson

PETER O. WHITMER

WITH BRUCE VanWYNGARDEN

MACMILLAN PUBLISHING COMPANY
New York

Macmillan Publishing Company
866 Third Avenue, New York, N.Y. 10022
Collier Macmillan Canada, Inc.

Library of Congress Cataloging-in-Publication Data
Whitmer, Peter O.
Aquarius revisited.
Includes index.
Contents: William Burroughs—Allen Ginsberg—
Ken Kesey—[etc.]
1. United States—Popular culture—History—20th
century.   2. United States—Social conditions—
1960-1980.   3. United States—History—1961-1969.
I. VanWyngarden, Bruce.   II. Title.
E169.12.W48   1987   973.92   87-16195
ISBN 0-02-627670-4

Permission acknowledgments appear opposite Contents.

Macmillan books are available at special discounts for bulk purchases
for sales promotions, premiums, fund-raising, or educational use.
For details, contact:
Special Sales Director
Macmillan Publishing Company
866 Third Avenue
New York, N.Y. 10022

10 9 8 7 6 5 4 3 2 1
PRINTED IN THE UNITED STATES OF AMERICA

For the Great Habeeb, Big Blue,
and the view to the West
—POW!

For Frances
—B.V.

Contents

Acknowledgments

Aquarius Revisited was begun years ago as the biography of one man, Timothy Leary, and grew through three *Saturday Review* articles, a newspaper article, and a deep curiosity over what really happened during the years I was a student at Berkeley. It was necessary to get out of the forest to see the trees. Along the way, many people helped show me the path to daylight.

A special note of thanks to Bruce Van Wyngarden, who shared the vision and whose perservering editorial eye crafted the final manuscript: no surrender; to Kevin McShane at Fifi Oscard Agency for creating the title and for doing what only agents can do; to Frances FitzGerald and George Butterick for their articulate and significant feedback, and, of equal importance, their encouragement; to Dominick Anfuso at Macmillan for putting up with me.

To the seven people in this book, a heavy debt is owed for their cooperation. A special debt is owed to Timothy Leary for his duration over the long haul: he held the keys of introduction; and to Tom Robbins for his continued assistance in thinking through concepts, his support, and his sincere interest in the success of this project.

Also, my appreciation to the staffs of the libraries at the University of California, Berkeley, the University of Connecticut, Columbia University, and Worcester, Massachusetts Public Library; to Elisa Goldberg, my research assistant; and to the entire crew at Advanced Word Processing.

Last, and most, to Candace, my family, for her tolerance.

Peter Whitmer
May 1987

Aquarius Revisited

Prologue

The Fast Track to Yestermorrow

THE DAY I PICKED up the Ferrari was overcast, a combination of clouds, fog, smog, and other unidentifiable components that is produced only in L.A. Given the poor lighting, the precise color of the car was difficult to determine. I had ordered a black 308 GTS, and it was clear something was wrong.

Taking off my sunglasses, which while functionally unnecessary, were certainly *de rigueur* while taking delivery of a seventy-thousand-dollar Italian sports car, I approached the manager, appropriately dressed in worn tennis shoes, no socks, Levi's, and a Primo Beer T-shirt.

"Uh, say, now . . . Just what color would you say this little beauty is? It's sorta tough to see . . . must be the light. Would you say it's bronze? Or uh . . . copper?

"*Bronze!?*" he screamed as if ordering a sculpture from a near-deaf artisan.

"*Copper?!*" he rasped just as loud, but with more anger, as if I had just mistaken his car for a Fiat. His shouts had heads turning to see what was going on with the commodities market. One more time, as if his message needed an encore, he screamed, *"Bronze!? Copper?! My good fucking God, man! This car is not only gold . . . it's Ray Charles Gold!!!*

I responded by putting my sunglasses back on. "Of course," I said quietly, in a futile attempt to make him think it was all just a little test. "Keys?" I said, simply, and held my hand up as he fastballed them to me right over the car's hand-rubbed Pinafarina body.

I caught them left-handed and tossed them back to him in a high, looping arch destined to land in the middle of the hood, just beyond his grasp. "I ordered the *black* Ferrari," I snapped. "I'm Dr. Whitmer."

He dove for the keys like a beer-league touch footballer and managed a spectacular catch, as the contents of his T-shirt pocket went flying. "Dr. Whitmer! Of course! Your car is all prepared. It's in the back of the garage. I thought you were from one of the TV studios; they send over such jerks. Here, follow me."

The car was washed, waxed, and polished. It shimmered like a streak of obsidian on chrome spoke wheels. It spoke silently of menace and mystery. "Yes, this is yours," the manager chirped. "And so far as the color goes, it's pretty obvious." I added that it *certainly* had nothing to do with Ray Charles.

There may still be two giant S-shaped black marks on the pavement of the agency's parking lot. It was partially anger, partially the simple fact that the first time you get behind 420 horsepower, something noisy and indelicate is sure to happen.

Scanning the sleekness of the Ferrari, it occurred to me that spending a huge chunk of a publishing contract advance on an outrageously expensive foreign toy might well induce a few facial tics among conservative New York publishers. Only a few months before, over a scratchy international telephone connection, my editor in New York kept repeating to me, "Our editorial board wants to offer you a contract, but they have two big doubts: the vehicle and connective tissue. How can you write a book about seven men who made the 1960s unless you have the right vehicle? And further," he proceeded as the telephone hookup clicked, faded, buzzed, ". . . problem is . . . one of . . . boardmembers was going on and on . . . *sounds* like . . . great idea . . . *fascinated* . . . know just how . . . decade actually got put together . . . nothing quite like . . . 1960s before . . . since. But can he find enough *connective tissue?* And," he added, with an echo that was irritating me as much as the static on the line, "how can he ever find The Right Vehicle?"

Now here it is only ninety days after that garbled phone conversation and The Right Vehicle purrs its twelve cylinders, sounding like a jungle cat poised to leap. Finding the "right vehicle" had certainly taken less time and effort than collecting the connective tissue that bonded together the seven people I had been tracking down. It seemed I was very near the end of a long dig back through forty years of cultural history, of today's and tomorrow's America in the making. The Ferrari in front of me was the maximum machine, the only fitting vehicle to play out my idea of a five-speed, dual-exhaust, chrome-spoke update of *On the Road.* I was to start in Los Angeles with Tim Leary, and move north, up the entire west coast, visiting places and people—Berkeley and Esalen, the former haunts of Allen Ginsberg and William Burroughs and Hunter Thompson, and Ken Kesey and Tom Robbins. And as a last-minute update on counterculture in the 1980s, in between Kesey's farm in Oregon and Tom Robbins's place in La Conner, Washington, I was going to visit the Yuppie dropout commune of Rajneeshpuram.

———————◇◆◇———————

MY OWN ARCHEOLOGICAL EXPEDITION had larky beginnings: in 1969 I picked up Timothy Leary as he was hitchhiking through Berkeley, (and kept in contact with him over the intervening eighteen years). This was after he was fired from Harvard and before his imprisonment and subsequent escape to Algeria and Switzerland for marijuana possession. At that time, he was smack in the middle of enjoying life as one of the very few people over thirty years of age that American youth could trust: the Grand Panjandrum of counterculture was in the process of running for governor of California. In a brazen attempt at hippie alchemy, he was attempting to turn Flower Power into political clout.

I met the long-haired, bell-bottomed, slightly stoned Timothy Leary only months after I had read his doctoral dissertation, which had been required reading for my undergraduate class in Personality. The two experiences did not mesh. It was as if someone very different had done the academic research and writing, certainly not this bubbly fifty-year-old, mindlessly chattering next to me, thumbing his way through the university town like a goofy gypsy.

On the ride down the Berkeley Hills from where I had found Leary, I asked him about some of the specifics of his dissertation. He took time out from flashing the peace sign to admiring students and turned to me, saying, "Like psychology, man!"

"I know, I know," I sputtered incredulously. "I've read it; I just can't remember all of it." Leary's smile vanished, and he bent toward me and launched into a detailed and articulate monologue on his original research in testing Harry Stack Sullivan's theories of interpersonal psychology. "It was the first good, clean research done in the area of transactional analysis—Eric Berne then used it in *Games People Play*," he concluded with a touch of resentment, referring to the recent bestselling book.

Lecture finished, he stuck his head out the window of my yellow University pickup truck and shouted, "Peace . . . love . . . peace!!" The driver and his silly curiosities had been dealt with; it was back to the carnival.

I made a pact with myself at that moment to look into the matter more thoroughly, to try and find out what lay behind this transformation—not just Leary's change from Harvard professor to international guru—but the finger-snap change of a generation of dull brown caterpillars into a nation of gaudy butterflies. How could so many be changed so drastically, so quickly? There must be a plot!

A seemingly harmless avocation turned into a rampaging obsession.

An occasional evening of digging through the dusty, dark bowels of libraries, reading letters, soon became weekends, then entire summers of reading, phoning, and interviewing. And yes, by God, there *was* a plot; a logical and orderly progression connected it all. Pieces became parts of patterns; randomness evolved into an intricate interlocking of human relationships. It was as if that jumbled pile of colorful rocks inside the kaleidoscope was, as my investigation went on, slowly but surely transformed into a precise, symmetrical radial design.

Nothing I ever uncovered pointed to a single cataclysmic event to mark the beginning—no big bang, no golden plates, no great fireballs in the sky, just a small pocket of individuals who, although different in many ways, shared a like-mindedness. Each experienced that time-honored feeling that there must be something more to life than the tedium of socially acceptable gainful employment, stable family life and predictable conformity. And each did something about it. But what provided structure and direction and synergy was, incredibly, a series of encounters that, more often than not, was as quirky and serendipitous as my initial meeting with Leary.

In 1943, William Burroughs was living in New York City. Through a mutual friend who knew Burroughs growing up in St. Louis, and whose musical tastes happened to pique the curiosity of another Columbia undergraduate living on the same dormitory floor, Burroughs was introduced to Allen Ginsberg.

In 1957, Norman Mailer wrote a long essay, *The White Negro,* in which he described and explored a revolution of consciousness that was afoot in America. It was written partly in response to the growing restlessness of youth, and partly in response to a challenge from William Faulkner, who felt that Mailer did not know what he was talking about. Both Ginsberg and Burroughs knew what Mailer was saying; it was essentially the same message that was contained in Ginsberg's poem *Howl,* and Burroughs's experimental novel *Naked Lunch.* The world was changing at a frightening rate, lurching toward a future both cloudy and unstable.

In the winter of 1960, shortly after giving a lecture to a group of psychiatrists on the relation between hallucinogenic substances and creativity, Allen Ginsberg answered a knock on his door and met Timothy Leary. At that moment, with John Kennedy on his way to the White House, and with Leary and Ginsberg on the streets of New York, American counterculture eased quietly beyond the point of no return.

Leary's associate at Harvard, Richard Alpert, had just left teaching positions at both Stanford and Berkeley; the network now stretched across the country like a luminous web, capturing Ken Kesey, Hunter Thompson and everybody in the San Francisco Bay area who knew the difference between a waltz and rock and roll.

Sitting among the overflow audience listening to Tim Leary's December 1964 speech at Cooper Union, entitled "You Have to Go Out of Your Mind to Use Your Head," was a twenty-eight-year-old art school graduate in New York on sabbatical from his job writing "Dear Abby" headlines for the *Seattle Times*. It was Tom Robbins, soaking up every nuance of a new world that he feared might never reach the Pacific northwest, and seeing for the first time the man who would become a close friend, and even a character in one of his novels.

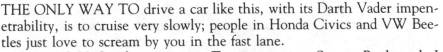

THE OVERSEAS OPERATOR INTERRUPTED the conversation with my editor by sing-songing, "Five dollars more." With an enviable sense of timing, the voice from New York suggested that I call collect next time. Somewhat frazzled, after manically machine-gunning a bare-bones version of how who met whom, and where, I shouted, "Now *there*, is that enough connective tissue?"

Whatever I said must have made sense because here I was, seated in The Perfect Vehicle, headed up the San Diego Freeway toward Timothy Leary's house in the Hollywood Hills.

THE ONLY WAY TO drive a car like this, with its Darth Vader impenetrability, is to cruise very slowly; people in Honda Civics and VW Beetles just love to scream by you in the fast lane.

It was 9:30 Sunday morning. Turning east on Sunset Boulevard, I headed straight into the sun. The twisting street, four lanes wide, begins at Santa Monica beach, then writhes through the opulence of Bel-Aire, before flattening into Hollywood. It is custom-made for a gunpowder-and-midnight machine such as this, where the base of your spine is a half foot from the asphalt. Ferraris are not particularly comfortable cars, especially for anyone over six feet tall, but with five gears, fifteen gauges, and various knobs and buttons, the car began to become fun. After ten miles I learned to shift without looking.

Farther from the beach the houses gradually change. The palm trees become higher, and the lawns get larger and larger, finally disappearing completely behind huge hedges and high stone walls.

Some houses look like Moorish castles. Some houses look like Aztec pueblos, big enough to hold a Mexican border town. Some look like they should be in the English countryside, or the south of France, or the Turkish desert, or antebellum Mississippi. Not one looks like it was made for Sunset Boulevard, and maybe there is consistency in that. On the corner of Sunset and Alpine, where several early-morning joggers were sucking in air they could have cut with a knife, is the estate once owned by a Saudi Arabian prince who painted pubic hair on all the statuary and raised goats in the backyard.

As Sunset Boulevard flattened and straightened, I managed to jam a tape cassette into the player. The opulent houses were gone now, re-placed by eighteen-foot-tall Marlboro Man posters, billboards pushing *Rambo*, and the World-Famous Fat Burger stand. Stopped at a red light, it occured to me that this was the spot where, during the Olympics, there was a camera ad featuring a much-larger-than-life Edwin Moses soaring over a hurdle, seemingly destined to land about three miles down the hill near Farmers Market.

This same intersection, a year later, was where Edwin Moses, by then the Olympic gold medalist in the hurdles, was entrapped by L.A. Vice on a charge (later dropped) of soliciting prostitution. (By then the bill-board had changed.) Now in front of my car walked a disheveled-looking twelve-year-old Mexican kid wearing Levi's cut off two inches below his knees, dirty sneakers, and a brand-new, bright-red Stanford sweatshirt. As I followed this progress, wondering if he was a child prodigy or math genius or had simply stolen the sweatshirt, a sweet female voice hauled me back to reality.

"Hi there. Wanna go party?" The words poured from a painted mouth. The girl's looks were enough to make a strong man go slack-jawed, but I finally regained consciousness, managed to find first gear, and launched myself up Laurel Canyon.

At the left turn on Lookout Mountain Road there was another red light, but this time the only action on the streets, at about 10:00 A.M. on a Sunday, was a steady stream of cars going in both directions. Every-one seemed to be very late for a very important appointment, and you just knew they weren't going to church.

The light turned green, and as I pushed down on the clutch, gear shift still in neutral, the cable snapped like a firecracker. There I was, all dressed up and unable to move. For ten agonizing, embarrassing, and angry minutes I lay sprawled, half in the car and half on the highway, getting my hands covered with grease while assuring myself that this brief gas-guzzling, dollar-eating odyssey was in fact over. On the tape player, Tom Petty was singing, "I was born to rebel," but I was just singing the blues.

The only thing going for me was gravity; I rolled the car back, block-ing all uphill traffic, and tried pushing it into the downhill lane. I couldn't do it. Traffic backed up. My leg muscles ached. Tom Petty sang. Horns honked. Finally, a man driving a VW bug stopped, got out, and helped me push this black Italian albatross into the downhill lane, where I slid ignominiously to a dead-stick landing in the empty parking lot of the Canyon Country Store.

I got out and slammed the door shut as a car pulled in near mine. An attractive blond woman got out and walked past me, smiling, on her way to the store. "Nice," she said, nodding at the black Italian. "Dead," I said, grimacing and holding up my two hands, as black as the car.

What struck me, finally, was that my approach so far had been entirely unpatriotic. Here I was, beginning to write the ultimate American story—the outlaws who rustled up the sixties—and I was trying to start it by driving a Ferrari. It was not right. Something had to be done.

I stuck two greasy fingers in my Levi's and pulled out some change and called Alamo Rental to reserve a Buick. I called Timothy Leary to come down and pick me up.

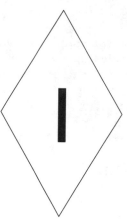

The Fast Track to Yestermorrow: At Web Center

TIM LEARY'S HOME IS just a three-minute drive from the Canyon Country Store. We head first to the kitchen for some coffee, then through the living room, with its 1960s decor—huge pillows on the floor and amputated furniture. On the right side of the stereo set built into an alcove in the wall are vertically stacked albums of Harry James, Duke Ellington, and Benny Goodman. On the left are stacked the Doors, Janis Joplin, Jimi Hendrix, and Jefferson Airplane. On the floor is an album from a New Wave group with Leary's teenage stepson Zack's picture on the cover.

"Web Center," where he now works on legal mind expansion, is a separate structure from the house Leary shares with his wife, Barbara, and Zack. It is purely functional: a desk, a computer, bookshelves, a small bathroom with ivy growing in the window, piles of *Science* and *Scientific American* magazines. The bookshelves are filled with copies of books by Leary, Tom Robbins, Thomas Pynchon, Kesey, and others.

On the corkboard on the wall behind the computer are tacked a crayon sketch by Zack and a five-by-seven-inch photo of William Burroughs. (Leary first met Burroughs in Tangiers in 1961, just after *Naked Lunch* was published in France and before it was published in the United States.)

"Kesey was down here last month," Leary says. "He called up out of the blue one Saturday, said he was in L.A. and wanted to come up. So he appeared here with two Hell's Angels and a hippie girl, and did we have a great time! Talk about rolling back the clock!" Leary and Kesey initially represented East Coast, West Coast versions of the counterculture. (Tom Wolfe once remarked to me that while Leary's approach, using Buddhist writings and Eastern thought, had considerable precedent in American intellectual history, Kesey seemed to get his inspiration "from Captain Marvel comic books.") But the two grew close, as only two old Irish drinking (and drugging) buddies can.

"Kesey and the Angels went through some Alice B. Toklas brownies that the hippie girl brought, then started in on a couple of bottles of tequila," Leary continues animatedly. "Barbara didn't like it too much—just, well, you know—incredibly funny locker-room humor and all, but it sure was great to see him again. It got a little deep at the end, talking about his son—real sad actually—but he is still such an incredible person."

Leary dictates a brief note for me to take to Allen Ginsberg, then asks if I have Hunter Thompson's phone number. Thompson is reportedly working on a book called *Fear and Loathing in Silicon Valley*, and Tim is interested in contacting him. All I could provide was his attorney's number and that of the lodge near his home in the Florida Keys, where he occasionally drops in for a beer. The man himself, like the myth, is a fast-moving target, rarely seen by light of day.

Leary's asking me for Thompson's number is somewhat ironic, because a little over a year earlier I had asked Tim's assistance in calling Hunter, who had been holed up in the Drake Hotel in New York writing an article about the invasion of Grenada. At the very last minute Thompson had refused to be photographed for the cover of *Saturday Review* for an article I had done on him. I had hoped Tim could convince him to change his mind.

When first approached by the magazine, Thompson had said, "Damn! That's great! I'd sit on a barge in the middle of the East River for that!" A day later he had turned churlish, saying, "This article makes it hard for me to hear the word *Saturday*." The magazine wanted to include a few clips of Raoul Duke, Thompson's *Doonesbury* cartoon persona, along with the article. "There's nothing I don't like about the article," Hunter had told me, "just the cartoon-character aspect."

When I pleaded with Tim for intervention, Leary, across twenty-five hundred miles of phone line, had snapped at me, "Welcome aboard! You're now in Uncle Duke Land! You go mucking around with that slime and it'll get ya!"

I'll never know whether it was Tim's call, my call, *Saturday Review*'s editor's call ("This will introduce you to a whole new readership. It'll help sales with *Curse of Lono*," to which Hunter replied, "Well, fuck that! Haven't you seen the *New York Times* Best-seller List? It's already there"), or perhaps the bottle of Wild Turkey that I told the photographer to send to the hotel. But, at any rate, Uncle Duke called the photographer at 3:00 A.M. (he had been sleeping in his clothes for three days), and gave him twenty minutes to shoot pictures before throwing him out.

As the morning progressed, Leary and I discussed my trip north and talked about various people I should contact along the way. My final destination was La Conner, Washington, where I would spend some time with Tom Robbins, so we decided to call him and firm up my arrival date.

It was late morning, but Robbins told us he was lolling around in bed, listening to the radio and reading until he heard the number twenty-three. Only then can he begin his day, it seems. "Some days it takes longer than others, and the music just goes on and on and on," he said, "like the Grateful Dead playing one song for three hours."

I told Robbins I'd see him in a couple of weeks, and then Leary and I fell into a discussion of the cast of players, the starting lineup as it were. Interestingly, he offered no self-appraisal, even though his name was clearly on the roster. Nevertheless, Leary's comments are revealing:

"William Burroughs: Of this list of distinguished minds, William Burroughs is to me the most intelligent, the most far-seeing, the most philosophically receptive and the funniest. I put him up with James Joyce in his complexity and dry wit. I also like the way he created his own role of the underplayed, Buster Keaton writer and the way he managed that role. He is one of the great people of the twentieth century.

"Allen Ginsberg is probably going to be the most famous English-language poet in the twentieth century. Three hundred fifty million people in China are learning English, and Allen Ginsberg, they are told, is the American Shakespeare, the American Homer. I have always seen Allen Ginsberg as a cultural politician. I can't think of any human being that bridges the terrible gulfs of our times with more skill. I don't like his poetry at all, but he brings together straights and gays, Jews and non-Jews, the beatniks and the hippies and the druggies, the straights and the college professors, not to mention the Third World.

"Just as I have raved about William Burroughs's intelligence, I don't consider Allen Ginsberg's opinions worth anything. They are laughable. Whatever the issue at the moment is, he is gung-ho for it, whether it is white bread or toxic waste. There is absolutely no thought there. But he has an incredible heart.

"If you listen to his lectures, it is all babble. He is going, '*Ohm-bom, ohm-bom.*' The chanting is, I think, a symbolic confession that he has nothing to say except the beat of his heart, which keeps energy going. Still, everybody loves him. He and Muhammad Ali clearly are the two Americans who represent America to much of the rest of the world. So he is a gigantic person. Allen Ginsberg is our cultural ambassador to the world. He is the humanist politician par excellence.

"Norman Mailer to me is a clever graduate student. He is a great storyteller. He can write those cute novels and certainly he is usually found on the right side of all the issues. But the question that concerns me about Mailer is what he could have done without being a bully, or selling out all the time. There is no reason to beat him up for that, because he is on our side, the side of evolution, but he is a little shop-keeper, a very lightweight person. I must say, he is almost like a rock star. I have rock-star friends, and at one moment they might come through with a great notion or song, like a Dylan or a Lennon. Mailer did that with the "White Nigger" essay. He understood about drugs and television and many of these issues long before anybody else, but he was always a Jewish American Prince. He saw evolution happening. However, it was always just a means to reflect the Mailer myth. He could never get beyond his own, really rather narrow self-image.

"Hunter Thompson I have no respect for at all. I suppose to many people we are seen as very similar, like troublemaking freaks. But I find running through most of Hunter's books a meanness; he makes fun of everybody. Sure, you can take drugs and get drunk and not show up, or you can get stoned and watch district attorneys, and they are fools and so forth, but there is no warmth, no vision, no humor, and there is a lot of violence. He is like the Grateful Dead. Like the Hell's Angels, who by the way, helped him get started.

"Ken Kesey . . . I am a little embarrassed sitting here like some final judge, you know, laying down these opinions that are just off the cuff, and me a little hung over on a Sunday morning. I am never at my mellowest at this time. I have great love and affection for Ken Kesey. I have a deep sense of brotherhood and companionship with Ken Kesey. I have always seen him as very Protestant and quite moralistic, and quite American in a puritanical way. And basically untrustworthy, since he is always going to end up with a Bible in his hand, sooner or later. But he is a prickly kind of a person. There is a lot of resentment, there is a lot of . . . I think he feels he's been left behind. There is a lot of bitterness in Ken. There is some unhappiness there.

"Tom Robbins is a tremendously lovable, wonderful, intelligent, witty, warm, human, sexy, erotic spirit. I just smile whenever I think of him. There is a strange antitechnological, antiscientific bias in his writings. A lot of love, mush, semen, juice, Jitterbug Perfume.

"It is well known that Tom just can't deal with some of the more real issues of the twentieth century—the information society. Burroughs does. Of all these people, Burroughs understands science, space, information flow, computers, and above all things, immortality, the best. My God, Burroughs's stuff on immortality. . . . Well, these are key issues. Although, to give him credit, Tom's last book took up the issue of immortality, as did Norman Mailer's for that matter. I adore Tom Robbins and his writing."

As I clicked off the tape recorder, Leary cautioned me about my trip and about the people I'd meet along the way, saying, "Do not forget, those opinions are just my own. Don't let them bias you. Be a good, objective clinician, and above all else, enjoy. Since Emerson and Thoreau, Whitman, Hawthorne and Melville, I don't know where you'll ever dig up another collection like this. Now, let's go to the ballgame!"

Timmyball in the U.S.A.

LIFE IN LOS ANGELES is intended to be lived in the fast lane, but this version is absurd. Somewhere near the confluence of freeways for which this corner of the world is so well known, our speeding path from Tim Leary's house in the Hollywood Hills to the Angels' baseball game in Anaheim encounters an impromptu parking lot—hundreds of cars filled with people going nowhere, engines idly spilling pollutants into the mocha-colored air.

This kind of bottleneck is not at all unexpected among the natives, and they come prepared. Convertible tops are dropped for sun soaking; engines are turned off so that the tunes from the stereo cassettes can be heard more clearly; a carload of college students does a very slow Chinese fire drill, strolling around their car, chatting in a neighborly fashion with fellow freeway victims. Two couples in a candy-apple red Cadillac convertible seize the opportunity to open a huge wicker picnic basket complete with a bottle of white wine, designer plastic cups, paper plates, and several Tupperware containers of something probably low-cal and high-fiber. They came fully expecting this immovable feast. This is the western end of Manifest Destiny; U.S. Interstate Route 10 at its Sunday-afternoon finest. The baseball game starts in just under an hour, and Anaheim Stadium is thirty-five miles of four-lane, bumper-to-bumper cars, trucks, and tour buses away.

For most Southern Californians, driving four hours round trip to see a two-hour ball game is something that is accepted with a shrug of the shoulders, a phenomenon that simply comes with the territory. Tim Leary has other ideas.

Never long on conformity (a past record of fifteen state and federal offenses, six years spent in exile and jail) and certainly not keen on sitting in one place for any length of time (in 1970 he escaped from prison in San Luis Obispo by going hand-over-hand across an electric utility line above the compound's fence), Leary's mind quickly sees a way to bypass the petrified traffic and get us to the game in time for batting practice.

Those who know of Leary only from his days as the high priest of 1960s counterculture might question the ability of his once drug-bathed brain to resolve even the most rudimentary problem, let alone something as imposing as a ten-mile-long traffic jam. However, regardless of his sixty-five years, and aside from a past scorched with chemical insult, the brain operating underneath that shock of snow-white hair retains a quickness that can mortify the uninitiated. He accelerates his four-door Mercedes with the crooked hood ornament toward the wall of motionless vehicles, cuts in front of three stunned Sunday drivers, whips across two lanes of traffic, bounces over the gutter and onto the completely empty breakdown lane.

A minute ago, faced with roadblock, he had seemed irritated, brooding, and uncharacteristically nontalkative. Leary's calling card is effervescence. His handshake seems to say, "Welcome to my world." If you don't like his emotional outlook, wait a bit; like the weather of his native New England, it will change. Now, speeding at seventy-five miles an hour past an endless line of brunching, sun-tanning Angelenos, his usual ear-to-ear grin and completely unhousebroken sense of optimism return. He shouts and waves his mason jar of coffee. His Cheech and Chong jacket flaps in the breeze (all the Mercedes' electric windows are jammed in the Down position). He points to the traffic glued to the highway on our left, turns his head like an owl and yells at me over his right shoulder, "God, isn't this great?! Look at us! We're just zipping past those poor bastards. This puts us so fucking far ahead of them it's amazing! It's just like drugs and computers!"

———————— ◇◆◇ ————————

FOR FIFTEEN MINUTES WE speed past enough potential horsepower to launch the space shuttle. His daughter, Susan, and I take turns reading the freeway map, advising him when and where to turn. During our speeding progress toward the stadium, there develops a crossfire of questions and answers about which freeway exit Tim should use after the game. I am carless in Los Angeles—a venial sin—and have to be dumped somewhere near Manhattan Beach. I feel somewhat like excess baggage, but I know the rules of the game with Leary: If you don't sign up for the long haul, get off the bus quick.

His mason jar of legal stimulants now emptied, with both hands on the wheel, Leary turns and looks straight at me, insisting on eye contact. "Just think, Peter. If your Ferrari hadn't blown up, we could be doing a *hundred* and seventy five!" While screaming down the only empty lane of traffic in central Los Angeles, he proceeds to explain my presence to his daughter and to Jeff, a cinema archivist at UCLA and one of Leary's baseball buddies. "Peter is my biographer, but right now he's writing a book on all my old buddies from the 1960s—you know, Burroughs, Ginsberg, Kesey, and even Tom Robbins. He knows more about our family than I do, Susan. He even went to Springfield ten years ago and met Abigail."

He leans over to speak to Susan's third child, Sarah, half Irish and half black ("a great genetic mix," Tim later remarks), and says, "Abigail was your mother's grandmother and *your* great-grandmother." Sarah seems unmoved. Susan seems only mildly interested, as if it were about time a biographer came along to sort things out.

Susan was eight years old when she and Tim found her mother asphyxiated in the family garage in Berkeley; Susan didn't speak for months afterward. Her adolescence had been spent first in a Cambridge hotel, when Tim was at Harvard, then in a house in Newton, another Boston suburb. The more notorious stretch of her late teen years was spent as part of the "liquid family" on the 2,500-acre Millbrook, New York, estate-turned-commune owned by the Hitchcock family, heirs to the Gulf Oil fortune. It was during this time—1963 to 1967—that her life and her father's life became a series of test-case drug busts (thirty years and forty thousand dollars for a half ounce of marijuana in Laredo, Texas, in December 1965), court appearances, and banner headlines in every newspaper in the Western world.

For a period of about seven years—until his imprisonment, escape, and exile in Europe removed him from the public eye—Leary's brazen, smiling, and glibly articulated anti-establishment stance seemed to mirror the thoughts and feelings of a whole generation. What millions talked about, Leary acted out. Demonstrating the very essence of risk was as simple as not showing up to teach his classes at Harvard, or squirming across thirty feet of telephone line to escape from prison; one small gymnastic feat for Tim Leary, one large symbolic step forward for the spirit of a counterculture.

What Susan did not know was that my family had lived in the same hotel in Cambridge, Massachusetts, that winter of 1960; that while I was a student at Berkeley in the midsixties, one of my fraternity brothers rented, and threw hair-raising parties in Leary's house on Queens Road; that I had first met Leary when I picked him up hitchhiking from his Queens Road house to the *Berkeley Barb* office when he was running for governor of California in 1969 ("You can't grow weary if you trip with Leary" was his slogan); that I had corresponded with him in exile in

Switzerland in 1971; that I had visited him when he was in Folsom Prison in 1973 and frequently since his release in 1975, and that in recent months I had been helping him construct his interactive computerized version of psychological testing and feedback. (Because of his past transgressions against humanism, he is barred from the American Psychological Association. I am not.)

Due to a gunnery accident during basic training in 1944, Leary's hearing is less than perfect, and the pregame radio show is turned up so loud as to make conversation nearly impossible. We all therefore learn what a crucial series this is going to be for third-place Oakland and how fired up Reggie Jackson is to be playing against his former team, with just a few victories standing between him and yet another opportunity to be "Mr. October."

Never short on superlatives and always long on baseball, Leary shouts above the deafening interview, "He is just the greatest! Just look at the career he had at Oakland! Look at all the World Series with the Yankees. You know, he's done more for the blacks than just about anybody. I just *love* those niggers. They are so cool!

"Barbara and I were at a party at Hefner's house," he continues, referring to one of the members of the Hollywood set that now makes up Tim and Barbara Leary's social circle. "And this young black actress—I can't think of her name—anyhow she was introduced to me by Reggie Jackson, who was hitting on all the white chicks. And she tells me that her *mother* . . ." Here he pauses, so all listening realize there is some real significance in what is to follow, ". . . that her *mother* told her to make damn sure to meet me; 'You've got to meet him 'cause Timothy Leary's been givin' The Man *fits* for years!'" Leary laughs with a contagious, Blue Valium laugh at this whole anti-establishment vignette.

Regardless of just who "The Man" happens to be ("I'll never go to another L.A. Dodger game again; they are such a tight-assed, cold-hearted, unfeeling organization—just *look* at the way they traded Dusty Baker"), for Timothy Leary the game of baseball and abhorrence of anything that smacks of the Establishment must be understood before his highly energized, tightrope life-style makes any sense at all.

LEARY WAS BORN OCTOBER 22, 1920, in Springfield, Massachusetts. An only child, he was primarily raised by his doting mother and aunt. His father left the family when Leary was fourteen, and his influences were primarily a tight circle of spinster schoolteachers who lived within the even tighter circle of unquestioning Irish Catholic conformity. Among his early passions were his radio, for listening to the Red Sox; and hitchhiking—180 miles round-trip to see the games at Fenway Park.

Part of Leary has always been hermitlike: removed, internal, and very intense. He was the kind of kid who, in studying the American Indian, constructed and lived in a tepee in his parents' backyard. The other part of Leary gives new dimensions to the term *extrovert*. He is not the person you want to invite to a party to liven things up. He *is* the party.

Before leaving for the baseball game, Leary had been running me through the most recent changes in his computer program: "I call myself an episodic academician," he said, as two telephones rang simultaneously in his office and a carload of friends pulled into his driveway, "and right now, I'm going to shift gears." He reached over to pick up the phone with one hand and turned off the IBM-PC with the other. "I'm now an episodic gregarious Irishman! . . . Hello? . . . Helllllloooo, Grace! You know, Gracie darling, I was *just* thinking about you . . . How is my absolute most favorite movie actress?" Leary poured all this out like syrup on a fallen diabetic's pancakes; only the fragile ego of a movie star (Grace Jones, in this case) could possibly find the tidal wave of superlatives comforting.

Over the years people have marveled at Leary's social skills and his delight in the limelight. For casual observers and close friends alike, the question of Leary's style versus his substance has long been a topic of much concern. Some question the true depth of his conviction, that sense of, at best, misguided mission that motivates the man once known as "The Most Dangerous Smile in the World." The voice of social reform is usually expressed in a sober monotone, sprinkled with inflections such as "we *must*," and marked by the occasional shake of a clenched fist. The American public does not expect its martyrs to be seen smiling radiantly while being led in handcuffs to solitary confinement; optimism is one thing, but it's difficult for the general public to feel sorry for someone who seems to be having so much fun.

Whether dealing with the media after the initial public furor over his psychoactive-drug experiments at Harvard in 1962, testifying to Ted Kennedy at a Senate committee on drugs in 1965, running his "Psychedelic Celebration" stage show in 1967, talking to the FBI in an attempt to get a prison release in 1974, or now, on the phone with Grace Jones talking about the "incredible party at Hefner's," Leary has always had the ability to tell his listeners what they want to hear. It's a trait that has been variously described as brilliant, mesmerizing, psychopathic and manipulative. Ken Kesey simply calls it "Blarney, just good old Irish blarney."

For a quarter century Leary's face has grinned at the public from coffee tables, newspaper racks, and post office walls. In the mid-1980s he appears in *Vanity Fair* and *Forbes,* not the kind of publications that usually feature a graduate of the federal penal system, whose FBI files, released under the Freedom of Information Act, are four feet thick and weigh in at twenty-three pounds. The reasons behind his most recent publicity have to do with his "Mind Mirror" interactive software program and his return, full circle, to the cutting edge of consciousness expansion.

"Aha! You bullshitter! Just look at this." Leary is jubilant, nudging me with his elbow, chuckling knowingly and jabbing his finger at the four-color display on his IBM computer. I have just spilled my most private thoughts by answering a long series of complicated, but entertaining, questions about how I would respond when faced with different life situations. Now the true me is displayed in front of my face, as easy to see and as tough to question as life itself. "You tried to con me, didn't you? I *knew* you weren't that mousy, timid guy you claimed to be. Just *look* at this data." Leary goes on the attack, now the hunter, explaining how my reactions have shown "the real me" as more assertive and aggressive than my initial self-description.

"Yeah, you're right, but the 'shy' me really comes out in some situations," I offer as an explanation.

"Of course it does," Leary replies. "Now watch this!" He taps away at the keyboard, hunched over and intense, like Jack Kerouac in the homestretch of typing *On the Road*. Bingo! Up on the screen pop all the situations that elicit my "shy" nature. Tim is exuberant. "You old bullshitter you! I *caught* you! Ha-ha! Ha-ha-ha! Ha-ha!" Suddenly he spots a small typographic error and makes a note to correct the software, with all the attention to detail of the former college professor that he is.

In 1957 his *Interpersonal Diagnosis of Personality* was voted the year's best book on psychotherapy; he recently received a healthy five-figure advance for his "Mind Mirror" software. For someone who has Ping-Ponged between episodic extremes, Leary has woven a lifelong tapestry of achievement.

Watching baseball
sitting in the sun
eating popcorn
reading Ezra Pound

and wishing Juan Marichal
would hit a hole right through
the Anglo-Saxon tradition
in the First Canto
and demolish the barbarian invaders

When the San Francisco Giants take the field
and everybody stands up to the National Anthem
with some Irish tenor's voice
piped over the loudspeakers
with all the players stuck dead in their places
and the white umpires like Irish cops
in their black suits and little black caps

pressed over their hearts
standing straight and still
like at some funeral of a blarney bartender
all facing East
as if expecting Great White Hope
or the Founding Fathers
to appear on the horizon
like 1066 to 1776 or all that . . .

—Lawrence Ferlinghetti
"Baseball Cantos"

Baseball is a game with a rich oral tradition, a virtual blarney of tales and legends. The part of the game that snagged Tim Leary's interest had to do with a simple and logical extension of the rules. If one reads the rule book carefully, the foul lines that define the playing field do not stop at the outfield walls—they can be extended indefinitely. Therefore, a ball hit *behind* home plate was not really a foul ball, it was a home run that simply took the shortest (and smartest) path to the outfield, which now, with our extension of the foul lines, has just snuck up behind us. How very . . . Oriental. How very mystical. How completely unorthodox, how completely un-American, how very . . . scary!

The umpire, appropriately dressed in black clothes and hat, becomes the real antagonist. He is "The Man," the enforcer, the ultimate authority figure, from whom all the declarations of right and wrong—safe or out, ball or strike, fair or foul—are issued. With Tim's new rules of Infinite Baseball, or Timmyball, umpires seemed not merely absurd, they seem downright obstructionistic and perhaps even . . . dare we say it . . . wrong! There! That was it! The men in black who ruled the American Pastime were *wrong!*

Tim's revelation—how "infinite baseball" applies to life and human behavior—came over him gradually. He cannot put a date on when he became aware of the fact that human behavior becomes a series of habits, or games, governed by rules that, with the concept of Timmyball firmly in mind, simply no longer existed. While Eric Berne may have gotten credit for describing the "games people play," Leary has spent a lifetime exploring games that people can *potentially* play. The not-so-subtle difference was that for one decade there were new rules, involving new chemical substances, and the net result was a generation of turbulence, from which many have yet to recover.

———————◇◆◇———————

AT CLASSICAL HIGH IN 1938, when Tim Leary was the senior editor of *The Blue and White,* all students were required by the principal, William C. Hill, to memorize a quotation from Kant: "No one should do that which if everyone did, would destroy society." Leary gave little indication that he believed otherwise; his Irish gregariousness was appreciated by his classmates. He was voted "cutest boy," pictured while dancing with the "best dancer," and involved in some twenty-two activities (Ring and Pin Committee, intramural baseball, golf, Western Massachusetts League of Student Publications . . .).

Leary's grades were not remarkable in spite of his Terman IQ of 127. He consistently got C's and D's in Latin, French, and Math; A's in History and P.E. He graduated 165th in a class of 305, but the competition was tough. Classical High had a tradition of academic excellence, having produced Theodor "Dr. Seuss" Geisel, Larry O'Brien, and historians Crane Brinton and William Manchester, and having for six consecutive years received a plaque awarded by the alumni of Harvard, Yale, and Princeton as the country's top prep school.

One of Leary's closest friends from childhood was Bill Scanlon, who left high school for training to be a Passionist Father. Tim wrote him diligently over a seven-year period spanning high school; two years at Holy Cross in Worcester, Massachusetts; an ill-fated thirteen months at West Point; the University of Alabama; and various stops as an enlisted man, until his marriage to Marianne Busch (with Scanlon as best man), on April 15, 1945—the day President Roosevelt was buried.

Leary's letters to Scanlon reveal some of the hallmarks of his adult behavior: his love of sports and of the limelight.

> We played the best team in the [hockey] league and won again. We play again Saturday. We had warm weather for vacation. Lousy skating. In fact none at all.
>   I was toastmaster at the Camp Norwich banquet. Albert Neale, city auditor, Dr. Sweet, famous surgeon, and others were speakers. Some fun. I am sending you the paper. My picture is on page 4. . . . I am going to West Point, if I get better marks and pass the College Boards.

Leary did not get better marks and ended up at Jesuit-run Holy Cross, probably best known for producing pro basketball player Bob Cousy. He studied Latin composition, Latin literature, and religious history and had to memorize the entire *Hound of Heaven.* If Leary thought that getting out from under the same roof as his mother and aunt was going to usher in an era of newfound freedom, he was dead wrong. His great-uncle, Monsignor Michael Kavanagh, kept close ties with both Holy Cross and Tim's mother and aunt. Any move that Leary made in college was reported to Monsignor Michael and then to Tim's mother. But even if his great-uncle was watching, Leary was no angel. One of his high school friends recalled his "callous disregard for how others saw his behavior." "We were walking back to Tim's dorm room on a Saturday night, just strolling through downtown Worcester and talking. All of a sudden, like out of the blue, Tim grabs a loose brick and smashes in the window of a liquor store we were passing. Scared hell out of me. Then he grabs some bottles of beer and we hightail it up to his room, got his friends together and started drinking. Not a thing was said about smashing that plate-

glass window—as if it either hadn't happened or really didn't matter. I couldn't believe it, but that was Timmy!"

Nearly half a century after Leary's two years at Holy Cross, there are several dusty copies of the 1939 *Purple Patcher,* the college yearbook, on a dimly lit shelf in the library basement. In all but one, the only photo of Leary, standing by a bleacher filled with students and their faculty adviser, Father Hart, has been cut out. The single copy with the picture has the following question handwritten over it: "Holy Cross' most famous alum is in this picture. Hint—it is *not* Father Hart."

Two years with "the Jessys" was ample. Leary took the exams for the army and naval academies, was accepted by both, and went to West Point in July 1940. Tim's stay was over before Pearl Harbor, lasting just a lucky thirteen months, until August 1941, but the experience was the greatest single formative event in his life, drawing out and crystalizing all of his feelings regarding establishments, social traditions, and codes of behavior.

Things went well for the first four months; he actually enjoyed the fraternal life in the plebes' Beast Barracks, the constant hazing by upperclassmen; and somehow he suffered through the shaved-head conformity, saying later that "the appeal was strong. The ancient fraternity of men. A sacred mission backed by the grandeur and panoply that can only be rivaled by the Catholic Church."

So much for positive beginnings. On December 1, 1940, Army's football team was shut out 14–0 by Navy. On the train ride back to West Point some upperclassmen (including a football player) tried to lighten their spirits by drinking in the men's room. Alcohol was no longer an illicit drug, but Leary's first and perhaps most serious "bust" came as a result of liquor.

After the football game, Tim had managed to buy two pint bottles of whiskey that he hid in the doubled cuffs of his greatcoat to take back to his dorm room. The liquor made it to his dorm, but it was inside his body, not in bond. What happened on the train ride was innocent enough: The party in the men's room ran out of fuel; Tim first offered up some of his, then decided to join them. By the time the train pulled into the West Point station, Leary had lost all touch with the Cadet Code of Behavior. He went into his barracks through the front entrance instead of using the plebes' back stairs, and he did so while smoking a cigarette. Morning reveille found him hung over and unable even to stand up. When he recovered enough to face the company commander, Leary admitted having been invited to the party and having consumed alcohol with the first classmen.

Discipline at the academy could take numerous forms: simple "chits," or demerits, handed out freely to plebes and tallied at the month's end; restriction to quarters; tours of walking the area; loss of leave time; or finally, being forced to resign. The upperclassmen involved in his inci-

dent had put in four years' time and would soon take their place among the elite cadre of professionally trained military leaders of a nation at war; Tim was an expendable plebe with only four months' time to his credit.

In addition there was a general feeling on the Honor Committee that this particular plebe simply did not have the makings of a cadet and was probably not earmarked for success as an officer in the United States Army. Leary's class ranking in total demerits received—535th out of 546—clearly indicated that he had more than average difficulty in complying with regulations. For example:

30 September 1940—Not turning in paper as required at written re-
citation in Mathematics—4 demerits.

10 October 1940— Dirty Mirror—2 demerits.

13 October 1940— Violation of 4th Class customs, i.e., late for 1st
call, reveille formation, Oct. 9th; making sev-
eral gross errors in the execution of the "In Bat-
tery Heave," thereby drawing the comment of
officers present at the football rally, dinner formation, Oct. 10th—1 demerit.

The Honor Committee quickly reviewed the situation and formally accused Leary of having lied to the acting company commander by denying that he had brought the liquor onto the train.

Leary responded, "I didn't lie, gentlemen. I didn't deny bringing the booze onto the train. They never *asked* me. It is true that I didn't volunteer this information, and if that's a violation of your code, then I'm guilty."

The committee immediately asked Leary to resign. Tim replied that he would wait and think it over before making a decision. He knew the Honor Committee would be irate if he refused to resign, and he knew that in similar situations others had escaped initial charges only to be later court-martialed, "demerited out," or subjected to psychological pressures such as "silencing," or Coventry.

Leary made the decision to take the tough way out, to fight the system. Shortly thereafter, all involved in the "bathroom party" were given the same "walking the area" discipline. In addition, for the next eight months the Honor Committee unofficially imposed Coventry in an attempt to force his resignation. For the duration of his stay at West Point he was not allowed to speak or be spoken to.

At the mess hall Leary found the seat on either side always vacant. A notepad and pencil were left for him to scribble down what he wanted. Despite his banishment, he remained popular. Leary even took some enjoyment in the notoriety his Coventry brought him. "In one night I became the equal of the First Captain in recognition," he remembers.

The new year of 1941 began a new semester with different classes, but the silencing continued. The predictions of one of Leary's former roommates proved correct, and Tim was ordered to appear at a court-martial trial. The proceedings were brief. The Honor Committee produced witnesses who affirmed Leary's having stated that he denied ownership of the alcohol. This was the sole charge against him.

Leary's testimony was a reiteration of what he had told the Honor Committee months before, that he was never *asked* if the alcohol was his. As Tim recalls, "The court took two minutes to acquit me. They had all been plebes, they had all been drunk after Navy games, and they had all suffered Army hangovers. My lawyer was astonished; the Honor Committee was enraged and frustrated."

The victory soon proved Pyrrhic. Immediately after the acquittal, it was decided that since Leary had refused to resign voluntarily, and because there were no legal means under the Articles of War to warrant his explusion from the academy, Leary's resignation would be forced by demeriting him out. Silencing continued, and harassment reached unprecedented levels. At every examination, he drew inspection officers like moths to a flame. Nothing escaped their microscopic gaze. For a simple shaving cut:

2 February 1941—Injury to Government property—4 demerits.

For having visible hairs in his nostrils:

2 February 1941—Hair improperly cut—4 demerits.

Leary's assigned position in ranks was secretly changed and for lining up in his accustomed place:

5 February 1941—Absent reveille—4 demerits.

He was clearly a marked man, and no move went unnoticed. For eight seemingly interminable months Leary had but two sources of sanctuary, two outlets for communication. The first was the asylum provided by confession. Even though it was almost exclusively a monologue, it provided a vent for his pent-up and nearly uncontrolled hostilities. The second was his writing: letters to his family and friends and papers that he turned in to his English Composition course. An untitled short story, dated February 28, 1941, features the mental ramblings of a young man walking home from work. He feels terribly tired, his legs are "numb sticks of pain," and as he walks again through the rain, he contemplates how he will answer his mother's questions about his day at work.

The young man in the story, who seems "an old, old man of twenty," walks home pondering "the universal reality of man's own wretchedness." When he is finally confronted by his mother, she smiles "softly and tenderly, as though the mysterious power of motherhood reached out and touched the secret in his heart." His story foreshadows the difficulty he was to experience in explaining to Abigail his inability to live up to her high expectations for him at West Point:

> Could he tell her it was all shattered—the ideal, the illusion, the dream: that there was no pity, or kindness, or welcome, just the dirty fight—you against the world—just the merciless system that takes you, clean and fresh and honest and hammers you down into the mold and forces you to fit into the neat pattern of nothingness?

The cry for help went unnoticed by Leary's professor. In grading the theme he commented, "Do you really think this? Rather cynical and disillusioned for one so young. Remember my comment of last week—try to get down to earth . . . check carefully all of your punctuation."

As June approached, the Day of Recognition drew near. This day marked the end of the plebe year and the beginning of life as an upperclassman. It brought with it the promise of change. The summer months, after the arrival of a new plebe class, would be spent in the field, not in the classroom. Any departure from regimen would bring some relief to Leary. There was also in the back of his mind the idea that since the summer field exercises marked formation of a new Honor Committee, there was an outside chance for a reversal of their decision.

General Ulysses S. Grant, near the end of his life, stated that his greatest moment was neither the surrender at Appomattox nor gaining the presidency; it was the Day of Recognition at West Point. The plebes march flawlessly across the parade grounds toward the sally port of Central Barracks until they reach, turn, and face the graduated first classmen. As the band plays jubilantly, the command "At ease" is given and the new second lieutenants and the no-longer plebes shake hands, laugh, embrace, pound each others' backs, and whoop in delight.

For Leary, however, the intoxication of the celebration quickly passed, as he realized that although he had been a participant, he was still an outsider: "As the storm of acceptance swept through ranks I found myself standing alone, invisible, jostled by pumping hands and pushed by bodies straining to embrace. A wave of emotion burst. I hurried out of ranks to the northeast corner of Central Barracks and stood facing the rough granite wall weeping. For a long time."

The newly formed Honor Committee had inherited the task of silencing Leary and was still attempting to "demerit" him out of the academy. Because of Leary's popularity and the growing feeling among many that his silencing was unjust, the committee faced a dilemma. Leary had posed no threat as a silenced plebe, since plebes are not really part of the system. Now, as a cadet, the situation was different. If the Honor Committee reversed their decision, their power base would be seriously eroded; Leary would become the only cadet to buck the system and win.

Pressure to take action was mounting. Abigail Leary believed in her son's innocence. She communicated with Charles Clason, the representative who had secured Tim's appointment, and Massachusetts senator David I. Walsh. Walsh was a close family friend, a classmate at Holy Cross of Monsignor Kavanagh's, and at that time was the chairman of the Senate Naval Affairs Committee. In an ironic play of establishment power versus the establishment, Walsh personally investigated the demeriting. In the official Individual Delinquency Record, the totals for the months of February through May, the period of most intense demeriting, had been gone back over, and the totals were lowered from 93 to 75. It seems that the Honor Committee may have made some attempts to water down the extent of their disciplinary action. In the end, a deal was struck.

Leary demanded that the Honor Committee read a statement of his innocence over the same booming loudspeakers, in the same mess hall, where his original sentencing was announced. He also wanted assurance that no one would again be silenced by a kangaroo court. For this, Leary agreed to resign voluntarily. The message was soon and simply announced: "In the case of Cadet Leary, the Honor Committee agrees to abide by the decision of the court-martial. Not guilty."

The announcement came at lunch and was followed by "stunned shock and scattered bursts of clapping . . . from neighboring tables, waves of congratulations."

The steps toward resolution were taken quickly. Leary tendered his resignation to Lt. Col. Arthur Purvis, stating that he was "ill adapted to a military career." As protocol demanded, he was counseled by a Captain W. W. Stromberg, who stated that in interviewing Leary, "he realizes the opportunity and advantages he enjoys as a cadet."

By August 1, the secretary of war, Henry Stimson, received notice of the proceedings, and Major General Adams notified Leary that "your resignation as a cadet . . . is accepted by the secretary of war." On September 23, 1941, Purvis officially announced Leary's honorable discharge.

He had entered the academy a naive, frivolous teenager with a great deal of creative energy and potential talent. He left the academy in August 1941, older, sobered, yet not a beaten man. His elation at leaving West Point behind and his natural optimism kept him afloat. In an astounding letter to Bill Scanlon, Leary laid out some of his thoughts about the basic nature of human behavior, gestated in the silence of Coventry.

Dear Willie;

. . . The very black moods of pessimism are still with me every time I get to thinking too much. "He who increaseth knowledge increaseth sorrow" was indeed a truism and I can agree with that platitude. Thought without faith is the surest way to pessimism I know.

. . . I have a new idea for a story. A man discovers the "Milk of

Human Kindness" which causes men to forget themselves and act un-
selfishly. He tries it out on different people and the results are apparently
chaotic. Example: clerks cease cheating the public and lying about their
products and their employers go bankrupt, etc. The result of the experiments threaten everything so important in our civilization and it would
seem that civilization would crumble if people were unselfish. Then a
dictator hears about it and steals some of it and injects the opposing
armies and the opposing statesmen. This allows the dictator to conquer
easily. The inventor is held prisoner meanwhile, and in the end, seeing
how utterly preposterous and impossible it is if people were unselfish,
gets back the secret, kills himself and with him dies the "milk of kindness."

The story would be written in a satire similar to Voltaire or Swift
. . . that is the most effective way of . . . showing the faults of man
. . . ruthless satires which pass as simple amusing tales at first glance.

After finding this letter in Bill Scanlon's attic in 1983, I copied it
and sent it to Leary in Los Angeles. It had been more than forty years
since the "Milk of Human Kindness" letter and nearly twenty-five years
after his initial research and experimentation with psychedelic drugs at
Harvard, which had, coincidentally, paralleled the covert research on
the very same drugs being done by the CIA under a program called MK-
Ultra. The intent of the government's work was to find a potent chemical that would disorient and disable the enemy.

The first inkling Leary got that his work at Harvard was something
the government wanted very much to keep in its own domain came from
Frank Barron, a classmate of Tim's in the doctoral program at Berkeley
during the late forties. A visiting professor at Harvard, he shared the
house with Tim, Susan, and Jackie Leary (Tim's son) in Newton, in late
1960 and 1961. Barron, later the chairman of the psychology department
at the University of California at Santa Cruz, was involved with the
operations of the OSS during World War II. After getting his Ph.D.,
Barron worked with another Berkeley professor, Donald McKinnon, on
a government-funded research program investigating creativity at the
University of California's Institute for Personality Assessment and Research. Their research discussed a possible natural chemical basis for
creativity, wherein the body produced chemicals (especially serotonin
and adrenochrome) that were very similar to synthetic psilocybin and
LSD. The research also explored the thin line between genius and
insanity.

At Harvard, by 1961, Leary had begun actively soliciting creative
artists, including Allen Ginsberg, William Burroughs, and Jack Kerouac,
to take the then-legal drugs to see if their creative powers could be further enhanced. The results Leary's team had gotten from "normal" subjects had not been satisfactory. They experienced something profound,
but couldn't seem to articulate it. The new hypothesis was that people
with proven creative talent were experienced in venturing into the unex-

plained areas of their mind and thus might be able to understand and explain what was happening to them. The plan had a double edge; many of the people who were invited to participate (publisher Barney Rosset; poets Robert Lowell and Charles Olson; musicians Alan Eger and Maynard Ferguson; writers Arthur Koestler, Allan Watts, and Aldous Huxley; and psychologist Martin Orne), were public figures. To enlist these people in the cause (all the easier to do when invitations were written on Harvard stationery), was a master stroke. Should anything go wrong, the responsibility would be widely diffused, and if things went right, the message would be carried to thousands by the participating artists. This approach served as a personal safety blanket for Leary and as a clever marketing tool for his concepts.

Barron saw dark clouds on the horizon for any work that had the potential of butting heads with covert government operations. He warned Leary of the dangers, but it fell on deaf ears.

"I never understood it much and I wasn't that interested, I am embarrassed to say," Leary remembers nearly a quarter of a century later. "Frank would get to drinking, we'd both get to drinking at night, and Frank would talk about the CIA research and how they were infiltrating places like Berkeley and Harvard. It was just Frank raving, and after a while it was interwoven with a lot of his Celtic darkness. I was presumably sophisticated, but we were so innocent, it never occurred to us."

It also never occurred to Tim that his role as the 1960s counterculture impresario had been self-prophesied by a callow twenty-year-old. When we got together in Los Angeles a few months after I sent him a copy, I asked his reaction to the "Milk of Human Kindness" letter. We were on the patio of his house in the Hollywood Hills. Leary had his shirt off, his legs propped up on the round patio table. He exhaled a cloud of cigarette smoke from the ubiquitous package of Mores and coughed deeply. Then, slowly, he reached for his cup of coffee and sipped. It was still only 10:30 A.M., and he is decidedly not a morning person. "That was one of the most profoundly shocking events of my life," he finally said. "To read a letter that I had written forty years ago when I was eighteen or so, in which I outlined the hero who discovers the drug that the government is using, for purposes of war, who goes to prison. . . . At that time there was no such thing as the CIA. There was no notion of drugs, the CIA, or imprisoning scientists at all. It was all so prophetic that it just makes a joke of everything I have ever done. Running around unconsciously, blindly, acting out a script that I myself wrote."

He stopped dead, staring into space for a long while, as if he were hoping that more sense could be made out of this visiting ghost from the past. Then he turned toward me, shaking his head in disbelief, and said, slowly, "Scary, isn't it?"

Timmyball in Denmark

IF LEARY HAD FORGOTTEN the prophecy of his "Milk of Human Kindness" letter, he was crystal clear in recalling his first public pronouncement of Timmyball. It came in the form of a paper delivered to the Fourteenth International Congress of Applied Psychology in Copenhagen, on August 19, 1961. The title was simple, like a small chapter heading in an automotive-repair manual: "How to Change Behavior." As rudimentary and plebeian as it appeared, Leary's presentation that evening became the manifesto for the future of societal reorganization and individual consciousness. It became the blueprint for destroying blueprints.

Leary had gone through twenty years of significant personal change between West Point and Copenhagen. He had gotten an appointment as lecturer at Harvard in January 1960. George Litwin, who was finishing his doctorate when Leary's appointment began and who worked with Leary all during the Harvard period, recalls that "Tim was clearly missing something in his life. He talked some about West Point and his wife's suicide, and it was simply obvious that he was deeply bothered by some things and looking for a meaningful experience to fill in some painful times in his past."

Leary had spent a decade finishing his formal education. Despite a temporary suspension for being caught taking a shower in a women's dorm at the University of Alabama, he received a bachelor's degree there in psychology in 1945. "I started to major in philosophy," Leary recalls.

"But it was the longest line on registration day. It turned out all the jocks took those courses. A Dr. Ramsdell—a Harvard Ph.D.—came by and talked me into the very next line. He told me it was 'philosophy with a touch of science.' It was the registration line for psychology."

His master's degree was done under Lee Chronbach at Washington State. Four years later, Leary received his Ph.D. in clinical psychology from the University of California, Berkeley.

He spent the next decade researching the effects of psychotherapy as director of the Kaiser Foundation for Psychology Research in Oakland. He found the results considerably less than impressive. Regardless of the kind of therapy used or the patient's diagnosis, one-third seemed to get better, one-third got worse, and one-third showed no change. The *same* results were seen in patients who were simply put on a waiting list and never got to see a therapist.

Leary left the Kaiser Center a few years after his wife's suicide. With his son and daughter he wandered through Spain, rereading a lot of existential philosophy and working on his own theory of psychotherapy. He ran into David McClelland, the chairman of Harvard's social relations department, at a cocktail party in Florence, Italy. He was offered the Harvard post on his past academic reputation and McClelland's sense that Leary's ideas could prove valuable if researched scientifically in an academic setting.

His first semester at Harvard, Leary presented his ideas in a graduate course entitled "Existential Transactional Behavior Change." George Litwin would attend Leary's lectures in the morning and then spend his afternoons working with psychotherapy patients at Massachusetts General Hospital. In an anthropology course, Litwin had heard about the Navaho Indians' Native American Church and their mystical use of the peyote and mescaline plants. Litwin had also read that Sandoz Laboratories had synthesized a chemical that produced similar hallucinogenic effects— psilocybin. He ordered some (on Harvard stationery) and began using the drug successfully with his patients at Mass General, under the supervision of Dr. Erich Lindemann, who had begun research of this general nature in 1933.

Litwin remembers seeing "an incredible similarity between what Tim would lecture on existentialism and my patients' reports on their psilocybin visions, about the universality of man and the feeling that basically positive things are at the core of human existence. I could not persuade Tim that this was true *or* that my patients were feeling what he was lecturing. Leary firmly believed that drugs were a form of manipulation and that existentialism or total self-control was where it was at."

In the summer of 1960, in Cuernavaca, Mexico, Leary experienced the "magic mushroom." For the fourth consecutive summer, Leary rented a villa near Cuernavaca, where Erich Fromm lived. The cost of living was considerably less than in Berkeley, a perfect, quiet atmosphere for a research psychologist's budget. In 1960 the Casa Los Moros, built by Arabs, was rented with friends from San Francisco, Dick and Ruth Dettering. It was a large, walled-in estate with expansive grounds and a swimming pool.

Leary had met Anne Haas and her twenty-year-old daughter, Emmie. Anne was spending time with Lothar Knout, an East German refugee studying anthropology and the Mayan Nuatl language at the University of Mexico. Leary spent time with Emmie, and a whole social swirl developed around Casa Los Moros.

Knout's research had shown him the extensive religious ceremonial use of hallucinogenic mushrooms by the ancient Indian civilizations and he wanted to do some live field research on the effects. In Leary's absence (he was in Acapulco with another young woman), Lothar, his roommate Ben, the Detterings, Anne Haas, and Jackie Leary drove six hours on unpaved roads to the small town of Tenango, fifteen miles south of Toluca. There, they met a local *curandero*, or indigenous spiritual healer. Juana Sanchez sold the group their first mushrooms, which they took (with differing effects) upon returning to the enclosed Moorish estate.

When Tim finally returned, he joined in; they all sat around the pool in the evening drinking Carta Blanca beer and eating nauseating black fungi while making nervous jokes. Knout soon started to ramble about the geometric forms in the poolside parasols, saying that for the first time he truly understood the Mayan civilization. Dick Dettering heard the stars speak to him silently. Ben played the flute. Leary, Dick Dettering recalled, "was at his best—no longer depressed. He pointed to the closed gates to the grounds and said to us, 'We're all schizophrenics now, you know, and we're in our own institution.' For the first time he understood James Joyce."

A few days later, they trekked back to Tenango; Juana was nowhere to be found.

The first day back for the fall semester at Harvard, Leary found Litwin in the hall of the social relations department, grabbed him by the arm, and asked, "Do you still have that bottle of psilocybin pills??"

Two projects were instigated involving human consumption: one with creative and "normal" subjects and another at Concord Prison, in which prisoners were to be dosed in an attempt to reduce the institution's 80 percent recidivism rate.

"From the very first, as straight as he appeared in his tweed coat and horn-rimmed glasses, Tim was flouting the traditions of Harvard," says Litwin. "He had an exotic Moroccan girlfriend, who decorated his office in an all-Moroccan motif. Thick carpets, white pillows on the floor, no furniture, candles, and brass trays. To say it looked different from everyone else's office is an understatement, but Leary reveled in this kind of individuality. Remember, though, that Harvard was a place that was flexible enough, had enough tolerance for crazies, so that at first it was all right."

When the drug experiments began, with Harvard's approval of a written research proposal, things slowly started to rumble. Leary began to take his research home with him. He would spontaneously phone Litwin, now a chief researcher along with Richard Alpert, and tell him that "a whole bunch of interesting people just came by the house in Newton, and we're all doing psilocybin. Come on over!!"

Litwin was aghast, but not really totally surprised. "You simply do not take that kind of research home with you and do it with your friends. It was against our contract and it was completely unscientific. It was an example of Tim's disregard for the incredible traditions that were Harvard. It was another of his ways of getting at the system."

Regardless, Harvard said little at the time, and some of the initial results of Leary, Alpert, Litwin, and Ralph Metzner's work were so positive that Dr. Lindemann wanted to hire them all away from the social relations department and make Leary the head of drug research at Mass General. After Copenhagen, Lindemann changed his mind.

The conference in Denmark, which lasted from August 13 to 19, drew an audience from around the world. The speakers included Aldous Huxley, Frank Barron, Leary, Alpert, Hans Strupp, Seymour Feshbach, Henry Murray, and Erich Lindemann.

The focus of this congress was to present a blueprint for the future of clinical psychology, a science that was struggling to define itself, and to crawl out from under the oppressive thumb of psychiatry and the "medical model" of mental illness. Psychology was alive and well, and in Copenhagen, intended to announce that it could now stand on its own two feet.

Things started nicely with Aldous Huxley, the respected writer best known to the general public for his book, *Brave New World*. He talked about the "visionary experience," charting its history and citing the Bible, Blake, Milton, and Wordsworth. He discussed the drug-induced visionary experience, aware that everyone listening had read his two books on the subject, *The Doors of Perception* and *Heaven and Hell*. Huxley avoided, however, making any value judgment about the utlimate worth of these experiences. Huxley was always extremely cautious in any public discussion of drugs. His wife, Laura, later emphasized the point, saying, "I don't think that Aldous ever thought that one person should be the leader in this kind of thing, because he wanted it done very privately, very, very discreetly. He was a discreet man, different from Tim entirely. It was really remarkable that Aldous and Tim had met [the previous fall when Huxley was Carnegie Professor in Humanities at MIT] and had a good relationship for a while. Tim became a good friend. Very charming, but Aldous always said he was the typical Irish."

After Frank Barron's presentation, in which he said that psilocybin and LSD (a similar, more powerful chemical) could possibly "restore creative freedom," Leary took the podium:

> It is my plan to talk to you tonight about methods of effecting change—change in man's behavior and change in man's consciousness.
> Behavior and Consciousness. Please note the paired distinction. Behavior and Consciousness. Up until recently I considered myself a behavioral scientist and limited the scope of my work to overt and measurable behavior. In so doing I was quite in the Zeitgeist of modern psychology. Studying . . . Behavior. Routinely following the ground rules they laid down. Scrupulously avoiding that which is most important to the subject—his consciousness. . . . This decision to turn our backs on consciousness is, of course, typically Western and very much in tune with the experimental, objective bent of Western science. . . . Tonight I speak to you from a point midway between the western and eastern hemispheres of the cortex, presenting a theory and method which is Chinese, in that behavior is seen as an intricate social game; Indian in its recognition of consciousness and the need to develop a more cosmic awareness, and finally Western in its concern to do good measurably well.

Leary proceeded to explain Timmyball, wherein human behavior is most accurately seen as a culturally determined game consisting of learned behavior. The game of baseball, Leary said, is far superior to the games of psychiatry and psychology, because it is seen by all as a game, and because baseball is superior in its accurate and detailed analysis of itself. Further, it knows how to change the behavior of its players for the better—through coaching.

> Baseball and basketball have clearly definable roles, rules, rituals, goals, languages, and values. Psychology, religion, politics are games too. Learned, cultural sequences with clearly definable roles, rules, rituals, goals, jargons, values. . . .
> The behavior which psychiatrists label as disease entities can be considered as games too. Dr. Thomas Szasz . . . in his book, *The Myth of Mental Illness,* suggests that "hysteria" is the name we give to a certain doctor-patient game involving deceitful helplessness. The "bluff" in poker is a similar deceitful but perfectly legitimate game device. Psychiatry, according to this model, is a behavior-change game.
> Far from being frivolous, many so-called "play-games" are superior in their behavioral science and in their behavior-change techniques to the "not-called games" such as psychiatry and psychology.
> In terms of epistemology and scientific method employed, the "game" of American baseball is superior to any of the so-called behavioral sciences. Baseball officials have classified and they reliably record molecular

behavior sequences (the strike, the hit, the double-play, etc.). Their compiled records are converted into indices most relevant for summarizing and predicting behavior (RBI, runs batted in; ERA, earned run average, etc.). Baseball employs well-trained raters to judge those rare events which are not obviously and easily coded. Their raters are called umpires.

When we move from behavior science to behavior-change, we see that baseball experts have devised another remarkable set of techniques for bringing about the results which they and their subjects look for. Coaching. Baseball men understand the necessity for sharing time and space with their learners, for setting up role models, for feedback of relevant information to the learner, for endless practice of the desired behavior. And most important of all, baseball scientists understand the basic, cosmic lesson of percentage: that the greatest player gets on the average one hit in three tries, the winning team loses at least one game in three, that no team can lead the league every year, neither Rome, nor Athens, nor London, nor Moscow, nor Washington. Those who wish to measure, summarize, predict, and change human behavior could do worse than model themselves after this so-called "game."

Leary's point revolved around man's basic inability to change his behavior. Cultural stability is maintained, he said, by perpetuating the game nature of behavior. The average man cannot see beyond the rigidity of his cultural game. Such a system increases human helplessness. In a fixed reality, "experts" emerge and evolutionary progress is ossified. In the Western medical paradigm, behavior-change games foster secrecy, control, and manipulation by giving more power to the experts (psychiatrists) and less power to the patient.

Cultural stability is maintained by keeping the members of any cultural group from seeing that the roles, rules, goals, rituals, language, and values are game structures. The family game is treated by most cultures as far more than a game, with its implicit contracts, limited in time and space. The nationality game. It is treason not to play. The racial game. The religious game. And that most treacherous and tragic game of all, the game of individuality. The ego game. The Timothy Leary game. Ridiculous how we confuse this game, overplay it.

The resolution to the problem, according to Leary, was to get beyond the structure of games by having a visionary experience and thereby expanding one's consciousness. This would allow one, with proper coaching, to reprogram all the brain's neurotic and psychotic games. The tools of choice could involve some of the avenues of approach that Huxley had discussed earlier, including sensory deprivation, yoga breathing exercises, or fasting. Leary added a few of his own suggestions:

How do we obtain the visionary state?
There are many methods for expanding consciousness beyond the game limits. Margaret Mead has suggested several cross-cultural methods. Have a psychotic episode. (This is to say, just stop playing the social

game for a while, and they'll call you insane, but you may learn the great lesson.) Or expose yourself to some great trauma that shatters the gamesmanship out of you. Birth by ordeal is a well-documented phenomenon. The concentration-camp experience has done this for some of our wisest men. Physical traumas can do it. Electric shock. Extreme fatigue. Live in a very different culture. Or separate yourself from the game pressure by institutional withdrawal. Live for a while in a monastic cell. Or marry a Russian.

The most efficient way, Leary said, was to use psilocybin or LSD to cut through the game structure of Western life. Essential to this "game" of "seeing the game," was respect for human equality. Leary had developed eleven egalitarian principles in his research that, in essence, destroyed the traditional doctor-patient relationship. Both doctor and subject took LSD together. Subjects were given all information about the chemicals being used, removing the atmosphere of secrecy. Participants were given control of their dosage. A homelike environment was provided; the subject could even bring a friend. In describing these rules for LSD research, Leary was in essence describing the summer of 1967. Once again he was ahead of everyone else.

In summing up his proposed revamping of the way Western man should look at his very existence, Leary added yet another prophetic touch:

> A final word of clarification. Those of us who talk and write about the games of life are invariably misunderstood. We are seen as frivolous, or cynical anarchists tearing down the social structure. This is an unfortunate misapprehension. Actually, only those who see culture as a game, only those who take this evolutionary point of view can appreciate and treasure the exquisitely complex magnificence of what human beings do and have done.
>
> Those of us who play the game of "applied mysticism" respect and support good gamesmanship. . . . You win today's game with humility. You lose tomorrow's game with dignity. Anger and anxiety are irrelevant because you see your small game in the context of the great evolutionary game, which no one can win and no one can lose.

The initial response was overwhelmingly positive, especially from psychologists, who had traditionally played the underdog to anyone with a medical degree. (A residency was not required for a physician to call himself a psychiatrist and practice psychotherapy.)

After the applause ended, however, apprehension set in over precisely who was playing what game, and with which rules. It was an apprehension that was soon to flow over much of the Western world.

That evening, Richard Alpert went to a party attended by a number of Danish journalists. They asked him about LSD. He not only answered, he laced them tighter than the Tivoli merry-go-round. The next morning on the front page of the Copenhagen newspaper was a much-larger-than-life photograph of one of Alpert's eyeballs, and the headline in bold letters, THE FIRST DANE TO DRINK SWAMP POISON. It was taken by the readers as an indication that something was rotten in Denmark and that perhaps the decay was spreading.

Alpert's indiscretion changed the nature of the rest of the congress and caused Dr. Lindemann quickly to retract his offer to set up Leary, Alpert, and Litwin at Mass General. Leary recalls that "the whole conference suddenly changed to an all-drug emphasis. The initial intention was not that at all. I had been at the University of Copenhagen as a visiting lecturer. Gerhart Nielson was an assistant professor who wanted to use my Harvard legitimacy to promote Danish psychology so that they could get more funding, compete with psychiatry, and generally boost their respectability. The next day Alpert gave a talk that was supposed to be more on our research. It turned out to be 'how he found God.' As far as I was concerned, it was 'Adios, Harvard' from that point on."

It took a little longer—until the spring of 1963—and again the real precipitating factor had as much to do with Alpert's chronic "mischievousness" as it did with Timmyball.

Huxley was also beginning to scrutinize the pair, and Leary was singled out in a letter from Huxley to another LSD researcher, Dr. Humphrey Osmond, written in December 1962:

> Yes, what about Tim Leary? I spent an evening with him here a few weeks ago—and he talked such nonsense . . . that I became quite concerned. Not about his sanity—because he is perfectly sane—but about his prospects in the world; for this nonsense-talking is just another device for annoying people in authority, flouting convention, cocking snooks at the academic world; to the headmaster of his school. One of these days the headmaster will lose patience. . . . I am very fond of Tim . . . but why, oh why, does he have to be such an ass?

Leary wasn't the only one "cocking snooks" at the academic world. Alpert had been using psychedelic drugs with undergraduate men, often in return for sexual favors. Specifically he had taken psychedelic drugs with Ronnie Winston, of the jewelry-company family. Winston's roommate was Andrew Weil, then editor of the *Harvard Crimson* and later, after Harvard Medical School and a few years of experimenting with natural herbs in the Amazon, author of *The Natural Mind*. Weil was jealous of the relationship between Winston and Alpert. He disguised himself, and in March 1962, got into a private meeting of the members of Harvard's Center for Research on Personality, where the discussion centered on what to do about Leary, Alpert, and their growing following.

Weil revealed to all—including the Boston newspapers—the seriousness of the problem in a series of articles he wrote for the *Crimson*. Alpert finally admitted to having breached the agreed-upon rules of not giving the drugs to undergraduates. Leary's transgressions were of a more subtle nature.

In the hall outside David McClelland's office was a large bulletin board. On it were sign-up lists for each professor's research project. There is always an intense, unspoken competition for the best and brightest graduate students among professors. It hits at the core of academic survival; good research assistants beget good research. Good research begets grant money and publications. Money and journal articles beget the ultimate academic goal, tenure.

At Harvard, since the days of William James, sign-up sheets were ritualistically hung on the board, then the professors would retreat to the sanctuary of their offices. There they would wait, puffing their pipes, listening to Bach, planning the next phase in their academic careers; in their minds, perhaps they had already attracted a large handful of Phi Beta Kappas to their cause.

In the fall of 1962 a funny thing happened to the lists on the bulletin board outside David McClelland's office. Of that year's thirty-two graduate students, twenty-seven signed up for Leary and Alpert's research. Harvard University made up its collective mind about what to do with the two men. It was merely a matter of finding a rationale. In April 1963, Leary was fired for not teaching classes; in May, Alpert was fired for giving drugs to undergraduates. It was time to move on; the game was going into extra innings.

Changing

AFTER HIS EXPULSION FROM Harvard, Leary, his third wife, Rosemary, and their children moved to the Hitchcock estate (named Castalia after the intellectual commune in Herman Hesse's book *Magister Ludi*), in Millbrook, New York. In the winter of 1965, Leary decided to go to Mexico to do some quiet writing, away from the chaos and evolving carnival atmosphere of the commune. Just an hour's drive from New York City, Castalia was becoming less and less of an "intellectual commune" and more and more of a psychedelic Mardi Gras for curiosity seekers.

Leary and his family, in a nice middle-class wood-paneled station wagon, drove through the U.S. Customs border station at Laredo, Texas. After crossing a half-mile "no-man's-land," they were turned back from entering Mexico proper. Leary had been persona non grata in Mexico since the summer of 1963, when he had taken his Harvard drug experiments to Zijuatenejo and ran into political pressures that forced him to leave the country. Leary was amazed to discover that Jorge Garcia, the same official who had ushered him out of Zijuatenejo, was, curiously enough, waiting at the border to tell him to return to the United States.

Leary acquiesced, turned the car around, and headed back. But then Rosemary remembered two half-smoked joints. She frantically took them out of her silver pillbox and stuffed them into Susan's underwear. A strip search at the U.S. border—not exactly standard operating procedure for the "average middle-class family"—uncovered the pot. Susan and Tim

37

were charged with possession and smuggling narcotics into the United States, even though they had never formally left the country. (The half-mile stretch is now named Tim's Terror.) The original verdict of thirty years and a forty-thousand-dollar fine was, four years later in December 1969, reconfirmed along with a new narcotics charge from Orange County, California. Leary subsequently ended up in prison in San Luis Obispo.

Leary was initially represented by Michael Standard of the New York firm of Standard, Boudin, and Rubinowitz. Standard was the U.S. counsel for Fidel Castro and Salvador Allende, then president of Chile. One of his law partners was the father of Kathy Boudin, a member of the Weathermen. At that time she was on the run from the law after a Greenwich Village townhouse, used for making explosives, had blown up, killing three people.

Standard later turned Leary's case over to a San Francisco attorney, Michael Kennedy, of the firm of Kennedy and Rhine, who had assisted in the trial of the Chicago Seven.

Kennedy, a thirty-two-year-old graduate of the University of California at Berkeley and Hastings Law School, was in contact with the Weathermen and the Brotherhood of Eternal Love. The latter group, which orginated in the mid-1960s in a head shop in Laguna Beach, had grown into a loose network of worldwide LSD and hashish-oil manufacturing and smuggling rings. It was fueled initially by the money and distorted financial visions of Billy Hitchcock, Mellon heir, and part-owner of the Castalia commune. Hitchcock was hoping that LSD would not be declared illegal (it was in 1966) and that he could position himself to be the banker to the world's largest and richest vendors of the substance. He hoped to franchise "chemical insight" to the world and make it a better place. And he tried his damnedest—both legally and illegally.

Timothy Leary's escape from prison was a fascinating "amorality play" set against the bloody and ragged proscenium of the late 1960s and early 1970s. It was an anxious, unpredictable, and often dangerous time. There was the Chicago Seven trial, starring Yippies Tom Hayden, Jerry Rubin, and Abbie Hoffman, and Black Panthers Bobby Seale and Rennie Davis (all accused of a conspiracy to incite riots at the 1968 Democratic convention in Chicago). The trial had barely begun before Panther National Chairman Bobby Seale was imprisoned for contempt of court. Panther leader Fred Hampton was killed in a December 1969 police raid in Chicago. Panther leaders Huey Newton and Eldridge Cleaver split over Cleaver's stance of "revolution now"; Cleaver fled to Cuba and then Algeria.

Late in the summer of 1969, ironically just before the Woodstock concert, actress Sharon Tate and six others were brutally murdered by the Charles Manson family. In April 1970, after promising to end the war in Vietnam, Nixon sent troops into Cambodia. On May 4, four Kent State students were killed by National Guardsmen breaking up an antiwar protest. Ten days later, in a racial incident at Mississippi's Jackson State College, two more students were killed. The Weathermen achieved their first notoriety on August 24, 1970, by blowing up the U.S. Army Mathematics Center at the University of Wisconsin and killing one student.

August 7, 1970, in a dramatic kidnap attempt at California's Marin County Courthouse masterminded by Angela Davis, Judge Harold Haley, shotgun taped to his head, William Christmas, James McClain, and Jonathan Jackson were all killed. A year later in an attempted jailbreak at San Quentin Prison, Jonathan's brother, George Jackson, was killed after reputedly being smuggled a gun by left-wing Berkeley attorney, Stephen Bingham. (After fifteen years underground, Bingham surrendered and was acquitted in the summer of 1986).

Death and riots were not confined to social revolution; at a free Rolling Stones concert at Altamont, California, in November 1969 (an attempted "Woodstock West"), a spectator was stabbed to death—on film, no less. Within months Janis Joplin, Jimi Hendrix, and Jim Morrison of the Doors were all dead. Ken Kesey "left literature behind," said goodbye to the Merry Pranksters and the Bay Area, and returned to a bucolic life in Oregon. In February 1968, Neal Cassady died of drugs and alcohol in Mexico. Jack Kerouac died of alcohol-related hemorrhaging in Florida in October 1969. Many of the visible spokespeople for a generation of change were either in jail, in exile, or dead. Only the mysterious Symbionese Liberation Army and the Weathermen continued to perpetuate the concept of revolution by violent and radical means.

During the times leading up to Leary's escape, the Aquarian Age themes of peace and love had been torn inside out. The Love Generation had turned carnivorous. The counterculture was now gesturing with one finger, not two, and often it was on the trigger of a gun. The level of paranoia in the United States was higher than Tim Leary had ever been. In short, in 1970 the future was dismal for an individual in jail for having made a career out of barnstorming for the positive uses of illegal drugs.

A little more than a month before Leary's Weatherman-aided escape to the supposed security of Black Panther Eldridge Cleaver in Algeria, the FBI issued a document that stated that "the Black Panthers are the most dangerous and violence-prone of extremist groups" and, further, that "the Weathermen are the principal force guiding the country's violence-prone young militants." Leary's escape was an FBI nightmare, a migraine for J. Edgar Hoover. What if Leary's upper-middle-class-white following joined forces with the militant whites, the blacks, and the Hispanic lower and lower-middle class? It was a political coalition that could, theoretically, remold the future of America. At the very least it seemed destined to shatter the old mold.

Michael Kennedy loved the idea, and he persuaded Leary to attempt an escape. But he never specifically told Leary the Weathermen would be his accomplices. Nor did he mention the joining of forces in Algeria with Cleaver as a geographical or philosophical goal. After his escape, Leary was simply supposed to look for a car near the prison with its right blinker going; that was about the extent of his information.

What Leary did know before his escape was that twenty-five thousand dollars from the sale of LSD and hash oil had been funneled through the Brotherhood of Eternal Love to pay for "professional assistance" in getting him out of the country, possibly, he thought, to Cuba.

It was just before Leary's September 1970 escape, then, that the Weathermen claimed responsibility for blowing up the U.S. Government Mathematics Center at the University of Wisconsin, and after assisting in Leary's escape their bombings continued: March 1972, the U.S. Capital; May 1972, the Pentagon; September 1973, the ITT building in New York City; May 1974, the office of the California state attorney general; June 1974, the Gulf Oil building in Pittsburgh. Leary's association with this group was the principal reason for his thirty-two-month detainment by the federal authorities after his extradition from Afghanistan. The U.S. government was seething with frustration at its inability to capture any actual Weathermen. Consequently, they began squeezing Leary for any fragment of information that would provide them with a tangible clue.

In May 1974, nearly four years after his escape and over a year after his return to the United States, the FBI spent months interviewing Leary in a futile attempt to reconstruct his escape. They wanted to find out how it had been possible for Leary to have gotten a passport under the name of William J. McNellis at the Chicago Federal Building with no photograph, no driver's license, and only a Washington State hunting license purchased in a Seattle sporting-goods store as ID. The FBI also wanted to link attorney Kennedy with the Weathermen as a co-conspirator in aiding a fugitive. FBI agents grilled Leary at length about this issue:

> FBI: Were you surprised by his [Kennedy's] attitude . . . did you think he would talk about escape . . . was that . . . in character for him?

> TL: Yes . . . there was no question in my mind that he was a militant person. . . .

> FBI: Okay, did Kennedy . . . ever mention the Weathermen by name during the times prior to your escape? . . . Did he say the Weathermen would work . . . on this thing?

> TL: *No, No, No!* He said it was a group of long-haired hippie political activists! . . . I first found out after the escape.

Despite the hazy nature of Leary's memory, his cooperation with the federal authorities generated a considerable amount of paranoia on the street. In September 1974, Allen Ginsberg, Jerry Rubin, Richard Alpert, and Leary's son, Jackie, held a press conference in San Francisco's Saint Francis Hotel under the acronym PILL, People to Investigate Leary's Lies. "My father has always lied," said Jackie Leary. The FBI wanted Leary to reconstruct his journey from the prison site at San Luis Obispo to Seattle to Chicago to Paris, France, and finally to Algeria. The FBI, in 1974, based their series of interviews with Tim on the supposition that "Leary may well be able to identify the A-frame house and park in northern California where he first met his accomplices. As a permanent residence was evidently being established, it is conceivable that such may still be in use as a Weathermen safe-house." Tim's "reconstruction" of this juncture was as humorous as it was hazy:

FBI: Was it, was it a campgrounds? Do you recall? Was it on the side of the road or did you have to drive awhile to get . . .

TL: Yeah, no, it road . . . the, the . . . there was a road that ran parallel . . . and it was a very small park.

FBI: Maybe it was a road side . . .

TL: Now wait a minute! Wait a minute! Something else! When we got to the park, there were two girls, rather pretty long-haired girls. That's right!! Now I remember! The driver [of the camper] got drunk because he figured his responsibility was over . . . he went into the camper and cooked himself a steak and he had a bottle of whiskey . . .

FBI: Go ahead . . .

TL: Yeah! And the two that met me also stayed in this little park and they had an acid session.

FBI: THEY WHAT!?!

TL: They took acid that night . . .

And so, for months this fruitless game of Timmyball went on at federal prisons all over the country. (Tim later told me that "it was two *guys* anyhow, but those agents were falling asleep—they really needed something to get excited about.") Details were argued over and over— "Did they pay cash or use a credit card for gas driving to Seattle? . . . Where was the bunk in the camper—in the back or over the cab? . . . How many could sit around the table in the camper? . . ."

Leary's correspondence was sent to FBI cryptoanalysis labs. Attempts were made to match fingerprints from the receipt he signed at the Sheraton O'Hare with those on his California driver's license.

The FBI tracked down everyone who had stayed within twenty rooms of Leary at the Sheraton, and four years later, tried to dust off the cobwebby memories of out-of-town salesmen, convention-goers, and airline employees, all with no luck.

Then there was the little matter of Leary's typed and signed statement to the *Los Angeles Times* and *San Francisco Chronicle* in which he identified and thanked the Weathermen for their assistance. He then proclaimed a form of "behavior change" radically different from any of his previous statements. Those who knew him quickly realized it was a con job, a bit of black Irish humor. However, not everyone saw it that way, and many took it at face value—easy to do, given the times.

> I declare that World War III is now being waged by short-haired robots whose deliberate aim is to destroy the complex web of free wild life by the imposition of mechanical order. . . .
>
> Listen Americans. Your government is an instrument of total lethal evil. . . .
>
> Remember the buffalo and the Iroquois!
>
> Resist actively, sabotage, jam the computer . . . hijack planes . . . smash every lethal machine in the land.
>
> Arm yourselves and shoot to live. . . . Life is never violent. To shoot a genocidal robot policeman in the defense of life is a sacred act. . . .
>
> Listen, the hour is late. Total war is upon us. Fight to live or you'll die. Freedom is life. Freedom will live.
>
> > Signed
> > Timothy Leary
>
> *Warning:* I am armed and should be considered dangerous to anyone who threatens my life or my freedom.

With such an update to Leary's résumé, Eldridge Cleaver put out a royal welcome for him. It didn't last long. As Leary remembers it, "all those people who had been surrounding me when I was in prison were having more fun *then* than with me free!"

With Cleaver, Leary made a few tapes to be smuggled back to the United States and played over underground radio stations. He then took off for Switzerland; Cleaver ran too tight a ship for Leary's comfort.

Despite protestations from the international literary association PEN, signed by Allen Ginsberg, Norman Mailer, and Arthur Miller, the Swiss government put Leary in prison for a few months. He ended up regaining his freedom by indirect bribe: He signed over all literary rights and royalties until 1985 to Michel Houchard, a notorious con man (he talked Random House into a $250,000 advance for Leary's escape story, *Confessions of a Hope Fiend,* then went across the street to another publishing house and did the same thing), who then worked the legal system through a Swiss attorney named Mastronardi.

It was a time of dalliance for Leary. Those who visited him then came back with reports of heroin use ("Yes, I tried it for a while") and lavish spending of his modest portion of Random House's advance ("I bought the yellow Porsche convertible only after I had sent five thousand dollars to Susan and to Jackie"). When the manuscript was finally delivered, it was not the manifesto of political, spiritual, cultural, and racial violence in the streets that the Weathermen and attorney Kennedy (and perhaps some people at Random House) had wanted. Kennedy dropped Leary like a hot rock, getting him to sign over his house on Queens Road in the Berkeley Hills in a fast shuffle of papers, Berlitz interpreters, and fee demands. Tim saw about four thousand dollars from the sale. Interestingly enough, nearly fifteen years later I found Leary's old upright piano up in the hills outside Cloverdale, California, in a commune previously owned by Billy Hitchcock through a Panamanian Corporation that the Brotherhood of Eternal Love used to make deals. It is there to this day.

If Tim Leary has an Achilles' heel, it is his seeming inability to function for any length of time without a close relationship with a woman. His tastes have run to the exotic: Moroccan princesses, Chinese secretaries, German baronnesses, and Rosemary, a National Airlines flight attendant and New York fashion model. Then came Joanna. . . .

Leary met her courtesy of Michel Houchard in December 1972, when his relationship with Rosemary was crumbling. Her full name was Joanna Harcourt-Smith d'Amecourt Tambacopoulous Leary. (Although the two were never married, when she later became the sole contact and spokesperson for the jailed Leary, she had a judge change her last name.)

When Leary met her, she was twenty-six years old, an attractive, wealthy, vivacious, thrill-seeking, divorced, multilingual, French-educated, half-Polish British citizen. Some sight for a broke, burned-out fifty-two-year-old former professor on the run. Joanna was born in the Badrutts Palace Hotel in Switzerland, one of a small handful of gathering places around the world for the very rich and famous. At just past 10:00 P.M., after a long dinner, one can find the daily volume leaders of the New York Stock Exchange posted in the lobby of the hotel. They are printed on little yellow sheets and placed in a mahogany wall rack so that you can read them and call your broker before having a nightcap.

But the stuff of easy capitalism was boring for Joanna, and after all, who needed it. The Harcourt in her last name was that of the publishing firm Harcourt Brace Jovanovich. Someone else could call her broker; she was looking for danger, not the Dow Jones, and she saw some in Tim and a little more in Dennis Martino, twin brother of Susan Leary's husband, David.

Shortly after Christmas 1972, Leary, Joanna, and Dennis Martino (who kept resurfacing wherever Tim was) decided that the political climate of Switzerland was becoming hostile. They wanted to go somewhere else but were broke. Tim thought of calling Billy Hitchcock, but Hitchcock and several others (including Leary, whose bail was set at five million dollars), had been named in an indictment handed down against key members of the Brotherhood of Eternal Love. Hitchcock managed to stay out of jail by writing the IRS a check for five hundred thousand dollars for back taxes on undeclared income and by informing on key people in the Brotherhood. He never spent a day in jail himself, but his four "chemists" received combined sentences of nearly forty years. Leary finally contacted George Litwin, borrowed one thousand dollars, stopped in Vienna to make an antiheroin movie, and flew to Kabul, Afghanistan. His every move was observed and conveyed to the CIA in Washington, D.C. At the airport, Afghan and U.S. embassy officials didn't quite know what to do with him other than take his passport and detain him under guard. The charge against Leary was "passport fraud," but he was traveling under a valid passport in his own name. (He had given it to Michael Kennedy before first being jailed, and Kennedy had returned it while visiting Leary in Switzerland.) What happened at airport Customs was quite simple: The Afghan officials asked for Tim and Joanna's passports, took them, and never returned them. They were then arrested for not having passports and were escorted back to Los Angeles.

Joanna and Dennis were not jailed, leading to considerable speculation over who was sleeping with whom and who was spying on whom and why. In the fall of 1974, when Leary was being bounced between prisons and pressured to produce some evidence of "international Communist" backing for the Weathermen (so that the Justice Department could, after the fact, justify FBI break-ins to Weathermen houses), he told Joanna to leave the country. She had been trying to arrange another escape plan for Leary, this time using force, and Leary wanted no part of it. Joanna left the country and was joined in Marbella, Spain, by Dennis Martino, who was soon thereafter mysteriously shot and killed.

Before his death, Dennis and Joanna made quite a couple, another example of how much fun people on the outside could have if Leary was locked up. Joanna raised fifteen thousand dollars by making a midnight call to Allen Ginsberg, telling him of her concern for Tim's life, saying he "had been given the jacket of a snitch, the code name 'Thrush,' and put in a prison where inmates kill prisoners who 'sing.' " Ginsberg cranked up the civil-rights fund-raising machinery, and Joanna took the money . . . and bought Dom Perignon.

In San Francisco, she became the doyenne of the oppressed, the high priestess of the counterculture. She pushed Tim's manuscripts, a movie about the coming of comet Kahoutec (which never came), gave dozens of radio interviews, lined up Melvin Belli's firm to handle legal affairs, raised twenty-five thousand dollars . . . and bought *more* Dom Perignon.

With Dennis's help and his association with the still-viable LSD manufacturing world, the two pulled off an even meatier scam on an underground chemist, exchanging a suitcase supposedly filled with ergotamine tartrate, a critical ingredient in making LSD, for seventy thousand dollars. Only the money was real. *Plenty* Dom Perignon.

Joanna's ultimate aim inevitably involved escape plans for Leary. She once hid a gun in her boot as the two of them were being driven around

San Francisco by two FBI agents in an attempt to identify Weathermen "safe houses." She wanted Leary to use the gun to force the agents into the trunk of the car; the two of them would then flee to Mexico. It was the final straw for Leary.

"She pulled out that gun and put as much pressure as anybody has put on me in my life to shoot those two agents, and she was not kidding. She wanted me to do it. I was supposed to do it and couldn't. She was after the ultimate thrill—to go on the run. Too many "B" movies? I don't know. I can't explain, I'm just giving you the facts."

After thirty-two months in jail, in 1976, when marijuana was slowly evolving to the status of a middle-class recreational drug, Leary was released. His career as a psychologist was beyond recovery. Even though the head of the membership committee for the American Psychological Association was Jeanne Block, a close friend and fellow graduate student of his from Berkeley, his membership was rejected, and he had to take a job as a disc jockey on an Orange County radio station to make ends meet. He received high marks from listeners—the witty, verbal Irishman—until the station owner found out just whom he had hired.

Next came a series of lecture-circuit tours, where he touted his concept, originated in prison, of Terra Two—a space vessel constructed in the shape of a giant sperm that would transport the chosen few into orbit, returning to Earth after the nuclear war had wiped the slate clean. In succeeding years there was the film made with G. Gordon Liddy, whose rise to fame had begun when Liddy, as district attorney for Dutchess County, New York, had arrested Leary at Millbrook. Then came the writing and publication of Leary's autobiography, which he felt would become a smash best-seller and help him "get over my phobic reaction toward money." It was a flop; such a flop that he ended up paying back part of his advance, deciding in the process that "wood-pulp" books were a thing of the past and diving head-over-heels into computers with the same zeal and monomaniacal drive as the twelve-year-old kid in the tepee in Springfield, Massachusetts.

Along the way, his reputation has kept him near the hub of the Hollywood social swirl. In this precarious world, where careers are timed in months and star's names can disappear overnight, notoriety is infinitely more indelible than fame. There is a deep appreciation for Tim Leary—for what he is and for what he has been. The feeling is mutual.

"I should have gone to UCLA, not Berkeley," he said recently, pointing a finger through the smog and in the general direction of the Westwood campus.

"Because you like the excitement of L.A., you mean?" I asked.

"No. Cinema. Film school."

"An actor?"

"Nope—the other end of the camera. A director. I would have been terrific." His eyes seemed a little misty, and his teeth were clenched in dead seriousness.

"What the hell, Tim," I offered in consolation. "You weren't bad at directing the 1960s."

The Beat Begins

*"L.A." I loved the way she said "L.A."; I love the way everybody
says "L.A." on the Coast; it's their one and only golden town when
all is said and done."*

—Jack Kerouac, *On the Road*

SPLITTING THE SAN JOAQUIN VALLEY north of Los Angeles is
Route 5, running for 250 miles of eight-lane emptiness. The heat and
haze obscure the mountains on either side. Few roads are more monoto-
nous, more inviting to speed on, or more heavily patrolled by police.
Your ego and superego debate loudly as the dashed lines in the asphalt
become the pendulum swing of a hypnotist's watch.

The only things to look at are oil wells, slowly pumping up and down.
Many of the ugly devices have been covered by simple wooden cages,
but a few are decorated with the festiveness of a Latin American bus.
Some are painted emergency orange with black polka dots. Some are
striped like zebras or have human figures painted at each end. And then
there is *that* one painted black and red and white, with tail feathers
attached to one end and wings painted on the middle. On top of the
other, rocking end is a bright-red crest set above shiny black eyes and a
long, sharp yellow beak. You can't miss it. It looks like a three-story-
high woodpecker on Quaaludes.

Turning west at Lost Hills onto Route 46, away from the heat and
toward the ocean, I find a wide, well-surfaced two-lane highway that

traverses rolling cattle country as it heads toward the Tremblor Range. For nearly forty miles the road is almost perfectly straight; only two gradual turns break the monotony. In late September the days here are scorching, and the 105-degree temperature creates shimmering mirages.

The only place to stop before Paso Robles is Cholame, which consists of a Chevron station, a small restaurant, eight shade trees, and a myth that captured the world.

Stopping to put in twenty dollars worth of gas, I strike up a conversation with the attendant. He is a punker, with studded neck band and pumpkin-orange hair.

"What's the most common question you get asked by people stopping here," I ask above the endless ringing of the pump.

"Oh, I guess it'd be how hot it is," he replies.

"Other than that?"

"Well," he says, "then it'd have to be 'Why does the gas cost so much?'"

"What about what happened right down there, almost exactly thirty years ago," I say, pointing several hundred yards east of Aggie's Restaurant, to where James Dean was killed in a brutal head-on collision on September 30, 1955.

"Oh that . . . well, not that many ask about it." He shrugs. This latter information turned out to be completely contradicted by the waitress in Aggie's. The restaurant, with its hamburgers so thin they appear to have been sketched on the bun, serves as a virtual James Dean shrine. Perhaps those who know have no need to ask questions of gas station attendants.

A decade before James Dean began acting out the message and the rules of a new generation on the screen, Jack Kerouac, Allen Ginsberg, William Burroughs, and Norman Mailer had begun laying the foundation in their writing.

Jack Kerouac came to Columbia University in the fall of 1940, from the blue-collar mill town of Lowell, Massachusetts, on a football scholarship. By the time Allen Ginsberg entered Columbia in 1943, from Paterson, New Jersey, Kerouac had left formal education far behind. But the campus was a magnet, and after classes, the West End Bar was also. There, in June 1944, began a kind of social ripple effect. The first stone in the pond was Edie Parker, an art student at Columbia and Kerouac's live-in girlfriend. She was the daughter of a wealthy owner of a Grosse Pointe, Michigan, Buick dealership. Kerouac lived in her apartment when not at sea with the Merchant Marine or at home with his mother and terminally ill father.

The ripples quickly grew. Edie introduced Jack to Lucien Carr, who was taking art courses with her. In time, Edie's apartment became a focal point. Lucien brought over his dormmate, Allen Ginsberg, who was interested in Kerouac, having heard that he had already written "over a million words." After an initially rocky beginning, wherein Ginsberg's confused homosexuality sparred with Kerouac's confused heterosexuality, the two discovered they shared a vision of a new world.

Lucien Carr then brought into the circle a good friend of his from Saint Louis, who happened to be living in New York. William Burroughs wanted to find out from Kerouac how to go about getting papers for the Merchant Marine.

The ripples turned to splashes just before Christmas 1946. Justin Brierly, a Columbia grad as well as an attorney and high school counselor in Denver, Colorado, visited the campus in 1945 to see how his protégé, Hal Chase, was doing. He ended up like all the others, at Edie's, which in fact had become the archetype for the "crash pad." Brierly met the whole crowd, but he was most impressed by Kerouac, who was at that time typing the manuscript for his first book (great reviews, no sales), *The Town and the City*. What struck Brierly were the physical characteristics, manic energy level, and intellectual single-mindedness that Kerouac shared with Neal Cassady, a teenager he knew in Denver. Brierly was trying to counsel Cassady through a transition period between reform school (where he had been sent for stealing cars) and a possible formal education at Columbia.

When he returned to Denver, Brierly told Cassady about "the scene" at Columbia, and especially at Edie's apartment. Cassady decided he had to meet these "Ivy League poets, philosophers, and novelists." From Brierly's descriptions, it was Kerouac who intrigued him most; Cassady had a half brother whose part-Indian blood gave him the same coloring as Kerouac. His name was also Jack.

The wave of energy that Cassady injected into Edie's place when he first hit town was undeniable. Perhaps the fact that he was born in the backseat of his parents' car while they were driving through Salt Lake City may help to explain it. He was a high-powered, high-speed human dynamo who churned out schemes and thoughts and grandiose plans and who exuded a contagious sense of adventure, of life on the edge. Around him men's adrenaline pumped faster, young girls' nipples blushed, and married women worried over what ungodly form of trouble Cassady was going to drag their husbands into next. In the simplest of terms he was a benevolent sociopath, "benevolent" in that he was not a violent person, "sociopathic" in his lack of guilt over his compulsive car thefts (reportedly around five hundred—for joy riding) and insatiable sexual drive. He was a bigger-than-life, bicoastal, bisexual bigamist. He became a hero for two generations of counterculture: as Dean Moriarty in Kerouac's *On the Road* and, ten years later, as the manic, pill-popping driver of *Further*, Ken Kesey and the Merry Pranksters' magically painted bus.

Unlike Kerouac, Cassady never seemed to age. Kesey recalled him as "like a noisy, yappy little mutt dog—just always barking away, always underfoot. But lovable and entertaining as hell." Tim Leary's first contact with him was when Cassady made a surprise visit to Harvard after hearing from Allen Ginsberg of Leary's drug experiments. Leary recalls him as "the most horny, manic, chaotic fucker on earth. He would never slow down, let alone stop."

For young Jack Kerouac in the long days between his early vision and the fame that finally consumed him, Cassady served as student, muse, intellectual provocateur, literary stylist, and chauffeur nonpareil.

Cassady had read and loved the twenty-pound manuscript for *The Town and the City* that Kerouac carried around in an old leather bag for anyone to read—or publish. Back in Denver, Cassady would write letters to Kerouac (and later to Kesey), the style and content of which seemed to capture the essence of his manic, speedy view of the world; great, long kaleidoscope sentences that seemed to describe anything in mind or sight. One in particular was known as the "Joan Anderson Letter." It was written on Benzedrine and told a sordid tale of Cassady's life on skid row with a suicidal lover. Twenty-three thousand words of compressed volatility, it helped change Kerouac's writing from an imitative Thomas Wolfe style to the spontaneous, "sketching," jazzlike, write-as-you-see-and-feel prose that mirrored the driven emotionality of his generation. Kerouac felt that America in the 1950s was a vastly different, exponentially more complex place than it was before the war. Neal Cassady showed him that there was a different kind of life west of New York City—and how to record it.

Cassady's affect on Ginsberg was less definable. The two took to each other instantly, talking philosophy and poetry and becoming lovers almost overnight. Cassady's bisexuality made Ginsberg feel somewhat more comfortable with his own homosexuality, but as a creative inspiration, Cassady sometimes played a negative role: When he stood Allen up for a scheduled lovemaking session in Denver, Ginsberg's rejection was worked into the book of poems called *Denver Doldrums*.

To Burroughs, who slowly evolved into a writer, partly out of boredom, partly out of Kerouac's inspiration and Ginsberg's love, and partly as a way of explaining his drug addiction (his first book was *Junkie*), Cassady was a nagging, food-eating, beer-cadging, money-borrowing bother. Burroughs was never long on social facades, despite his blue-blooded heritage and Harvard education. He openly expressed his disdain for Cassady's mad automotive flailings across the country, which inevitably included a stop at wherever Burroughs happened to be. Cassady would descend with no warning, with a carful of people, and proceed to eat Burroughs's food, drink his liquor, smoke his dope, and pop his pills. Burroughs didn't appreciate being a pit stop.

Neal's trips possess a sheer compulsive pointlessness that compares favorably with the mass migrations of the Trojans. To cross a continent for the purpose of transporting Jack to Frisco where he intends to remain for three days before starting back to New York . . . obviously the 'purpose' of this trip is carefully selected to symbolize the basic fact of purposelessness. Neal is, of course, the very soul of the voyage into pure, abstract, meaningless motion. He is the mover, compulsive, dedicated, ready to sacrifice family, friend, even the very car itself to the meaning of moving from one place to another.

—William Burroughs to Allen Ginsberg, 1949

The second big splash in the forming wave of counterculture came in the form of John Clellon Holmes, whose involvement with the Columbia crowd brought with it a singularly powerful force: media attention. The meeting of Holmes with Ginsberg, Burroughs, and Kerouac took place at a memorable three-day party, on the long July Fourth weekend of 1948.

Holmes and Kerouac had a mutual friend in Alan Harrington. He knew that both were involved with their first novels. Kerouac's manuscript was finished and actually in attendance at the Fourth of July party, nestled comfortably in its battered leather carrying case. Holmes was in the middle of his first novel, about which he now says, "It was never published. It was awful." The initial attraction between the two had little to do with their respective manuscripts: Both were New Englanders with some war involvement and a literary bent. It was later that the two got down to comparing literary notes.

Holmes grew close to the whole scene at Edie's place, finding Kerouac the most kindred soul. Ginsberg was fascinating but mystic and manic; blowing up flowerpots with firecrackers in the middle of parties, standing on couches reading his poetry to a heedless crowd. Burroughs was in his late thirties and "that seemed like an absolute greyed image" to Holmes.

Kerouac's novel was published first, and he was completing *On the Road* as Holmes was working on his second novel. But it was Holmes's second novel *Go*, an eloquent diary of his life amid the Columbia and New York City crowd between August 1949 and September 1951, that got the media ball rolling.

Holmes's book suffered a fate similar to Kerouac's, selling twenty-five hundred copies, then quickly disappearing until being reissued in the 1957 post–*On the Road*, Beat Generation mania that swept the nation. But a reviewer at the *New York Times*, Gilbert Millstein (who would later review *On the Road*), saw something significant in *Go* and asked Holmes to write an article for the Sunday, November 16, 1952, *New York Times Magazine*. The article created a scene.

Go contains a good amount of sex, drugs, jazz, and a handful of wildly eccentric characters, but Holmes's point, as articulated in the article "This Is the Beat Generation," was that the manic excesses of the characters were simply symptomatic of a generation "moved by a desperate craving for affirmative belief."

> Their own lust for freedom and their ability to live at a pace that kills, to which war has adjusted them, led to the blackmarket, sexual promiscuity, narcotics and Jean Paul Sartre. The beatness set in later . . . the cohesion of things had disappeared. . . . Today's Wild Boys are not lost . . . drugs are a curiosity, not a disillusionment. They live with the future in jeopardy. . . . The hot rod driver steering with his feet is not fed up with life—he's affirming life the only way he knows how—at the extreme. They are the stirrings of a quest.

Holmes's article stirred more than four hundred letters. Teenagers wrote. Old people wrote. Taylor Caldwell (whose two sons were somewhat overage for Holmes's demographics, at twenty-eight and thirty-six) wrote, saying that Holmes must be from New York City, since the kids she saw were "healthy, courageous and ambitious."

The argument went on, week after week. A Harvard professor wrote saying that yes, the problem with life is essentially a spiritual one. Others wrote in, chalking off the whole problem to nuclear bombs. Regardless, the article galvanized the public, the media, and the people at the core of it all. The movement now had a single label—Beat—like it or not. Soon the media would provide it with a uniform (sandals, Kafka-black turtleneck sweaters, blue jeans) and other signs of membership, such as goatees, bongos, bare light bulbs, empty beer cans, cheap furniture, and an aversion to soap and water and social conformity. "Pad," which originally and literally meant a mattress on the floor, ended up implying a communal apartment where who-knows-what went on.

Television offered shows such as *Dobie Gillis* and *Route 66*; jazz, then rock and roll gained popularity; Smirnoff vodka advertised a drink called the Mule, which made "swingers go! go! go! and get their kicks." However, one point of confusion in the growth of the Beat Generation from a small handful of college students into a nationwide business was the meaning behind the word *Beat*. *Beat* was sort of like the Swiss Army knife of social terminology. It could mean: "tired," "raw," "beatific," "with-it," "out-of-it," "lost," "disoriented," "worn down," "cranked up," "cool," "hot," "used," "alive." Or maybe it had something to do with music, especially jazz, but very soon the *beat* of rock and roll. Some related to one of Kerouac's many definitions: "We were just a bunch of guys out trying to get laid." In the end the meaning of *beat* or *hip* (later turned into *hippie* as a derogatory term for imitators) was a multiple-choice test whose answer was probably "all of the above."

————————◇◆◇————————

James Dean had the beat, and so did Norman Mailer. The two played influential roles in the maturing counterculture, if different in nature and in timing. Dean popularized it; Mailer legitimized it.

From left: Peter Orlovsky, William Burroughs, Norman Mailer, Allen Ginsberg, Anne Waldman, and Reed Bye at the Naropa Institute, Boulder, Colorado, 1984. Mailer and Burroughs both gave readings from their respective "Egyptian" books. *(Naropa Institute)*

From left: William Burroughs at home in Lawrence, Kansas, 1984. Norman Mailer leaving courtroom during the Jack Henry Abbott trial in January 1982. *(UPI/Bettmann Newsphotos)* Allen Ginsberg at home in New York demonstrating body language, as taught to him by photographer friend Robert Frank.

Timothy Leary charting research data on psychotherapy as Director of the Kaiser Foundation for
Psychology Research. Oakland, California, 1957.

Artist's reproduction of William Burroughs at the
moment he was told of his wife's death in the
"William Tell" shooting incident. Mexico City,
September 1951.   *(Original photo by U.S. Berkeley Library;*
artist retouch by Paul Smith)

Hunter S. Thompson (*right*) and author after the tornado at the Sugar Loaf Key Bat Tower, Florida, 1984.

Allen Ginsberg and Lucien Carr reading a review of Robert Frank's photography exhibit, July 1985.

Timothy Leary listening to Allen Ginsberg read poetry at the Naropa Institute's 25th anniversary celebration of the publication of *On the Road*.
(*Naropa Institute*)

Hunter S. Thompson   *(Eric Liebowitz)*

Left: Sather Gate, University of California, Berkeley. *Right*: Mario Savio exhorting a Free Speech Movement crowd, as painted in the FSM mural at Berkeley.

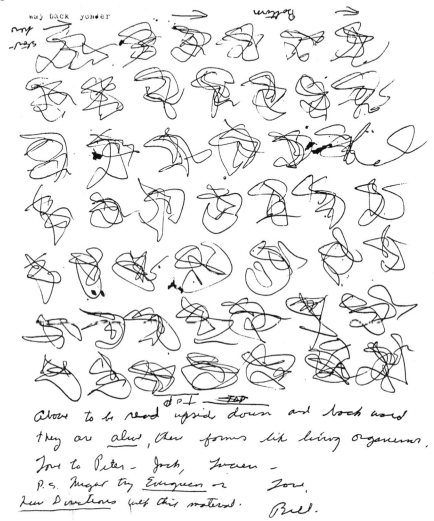

The visual analogue to *Naked Lunch*: Burroughs's calligraphic art, with viewing instructions, sent in a letter to Allen Ginsberg, with regards to Peter Orlovsky, Jack Kerouac, and Lucien Carr.   *(Columbia University Libraries)*

Detail of Free Speech Movement mural depicting the fatal shooting of James Rector by Alameda County sheriffs (nicknamed the Blue Meanies).

Another detail of FSM mural showing a street scene on Telegraph Avenue during the Summer of Love of 1967.

Millbrook, New York: Counterculture East. The Mellon-Hitchcock estate, home to Leary's Castalia Foundation after his leaving Harvard.

LaHonda, California: Counterculture West. Home to Ken Kesey and the Merry Pranksters from 1963-1968. Kesey finished writing *Sometimes a Great Notion* here.

Parnassus Street, San Francisco: Hunter Thompson wrote his first book, *Hell's Angels*, in an apartment on this street, while rooming with Tiny, a 280-pound biker.

Ken Kesey with William
Burroughs *(left, partially
obscured)*, 1982.
(Naropa Institute)

Tom Robbins and Ken Kesey at *Esquire*
magazine's 50th anniversary party,
1983. *(© 1987 Jill Krementz; courtesy of the
photographer)*

Bhagwan Shree Rajneesh at
morning discourse, Rajneesh
puram, Oregon, August, 1985.

It took Norman Mailer only five years after graduating from Harvard (1943) to explode onto the literary scene with his war-and-manhood best-seller *The Naked and the Dead*. (The publisher Little, Brown offered a three hundred dollar advance, but only if he would clean up the language. Mailer went elsewhere.) He was lionized before he was twenty-six. He'd never had a job, yet he was a literary hero of the returning GIs with a book that sold over two hundred thousand copies.

His second book, *Barbary Shore*, was different in every respect. Political with clear overtones of Marxism, it met with poor reviews, and the timing couldn't have been worse; just a few months before its release, the Communist Chinese had entered into the Korean War. Things did not get better with his third book, *Deer Park*, published to consistently bad reviews. Mailer became involved with drugs—especially alcohol, sleeping pills, and marijuana. In 1955, he and three others started a little antiestablishment newspaper in Greenwich Village called the *Village Voice*. The *Voice*, of course, developed into a model for underground and countercultural newspapers. It carried the news (and strange want ads) for readers who wanted the news the *New York Times* felt was unfit to print, a sizable and growing population.

Mailer's second contribution to the burgeoning counterculture was his essay, "The White Negro," published by City Lights Books. The essay, which was later published in Mailer's fourth book, *Advertisements for Myself*, caused more controversy than Holmes's "Beat" article in the *New York Times*.

Mailer wrote that since the war the world had turned apocalyptic. Its future was so bleak and its culture so totalitarian that violence was the only remaining form of self-expression. The "hipster" (a term first seen in print in a 1948 *Partisan Review* article) was simply responding appropriately to his environment; his behavior was not unlike that of a psychopath or an angry black. He was simply turning his feelings of helplessness into violent actions. He was trying to beat the world at its own game. The new generation was heroic, not criminal.

By his own admission, Mailer's research was first person in nature.

> All I felt then was that I was an outlaw, a psychic outlaw, and I liked it. I liked it . . . better than trying to be a gentleman, and with a set of emotions accelerating one on the other. I mined down deep into the murderous message of marijuana, the smoke of the assassins, and for the first time in my life I knew what it was to make your kicks.
> —Norman Mailer
> *Advertisements for Myself*

Soon after Mailer's essay was published, Ginsberg—who already knew Mailer—and Kerouac made a number of visits to Mailer's Perry Street apartment. *On the Road* had been published the same year, and the two men were only months apart in age, but Mailer was much more naturally extroverted than the shy-when-sober Kerouac. Kerouac was appreciative of Mailer's early success, and he had also dated Mailer's wife, Adele Morales. Ginsberg recollects their meetings as congenial, gentlemanly, even scholarly. By 1958 Ginsberg was less impressed with Mailer's essay:

> I don't mean to be presumptuous, but I thought the essay was very square . . . the whole point of *On the Road* . . . as well as all of Burroughs's writings, all of mine, and everything else going on with the Beat thing had to do with American tenderheartedness. Norman's notion of the hipster as being cool and psychopathic and cutting his way through society with jujitsu was a kind of macho folly that we giggled at. We giggled because it's silly and misses the point. In '45 and '46 Burroughs was experimenting with what it was like to be a thief, rolling drunks.
>
> So Norman grasped the apocalyptic nature of mind literature in the late fifties and later in the sixties . . . our basic take was the same, and so "The White Negro" was something positive. It was the most intelligent statement I'd seen by any literary-critical person . . . there was such a poverty of intelligence at that point.

6

The Electronic Mailer

INSIDE THE SMALL CONTROL room the only light comes from a crack under the door to the hallway and a red clock rigged so that its hands turn counterclockwise, counting backward to zero. A shadowy figure next to me begins a countdown. "Ten . . . nine . . . eight . . ." I have waited, written, bribed, and pleaded for four years to get where I am. "Three . . . two . . . one . . ."

Bam! Lights!! *Showtime!!!* Across the front of the room are nineteen black-and-white television monitors. Seventeen are displaying various angles of Norman Mailer's head. It rarely moves. *Not* so, his mouth. He cranks out words in a runaway stream of run-on sentences. Ralph Hefner, the narrator for *Open Mind* on New York's WPIX, tries halfheartedly to interject a point. Mailer says, without moving his head and barely breaking his verbal stride, "Wait a minute . . . I haven't finished *this* point yet," and rachets up a half gear to drive home an argument. He can talk like Neal Cassady drove.

As my eyes adjust, it becomes clear that this is not really an "interview" in the classic sense. The narrator is using one basic quotation—his favorite, he gushes—from Mailer's book *Of a Fire on the Moon* to provoke Mailer's thoughts regarding the explosion of the space shuttle. Over and over again, until the five of us in the control room have it memorized, comes the either-or question: Now, in the afterglow of the national fireball that killed seven astronauts, Mailer is being asked to retrace his steps two decades and decide if the exploration of space is, as

55

he put it then "the noblest expression of mankind or the quintessential expression of our insanity."

Hefner keeps repeating the quote, and Mailer keeps refusing to answer a philosophical question with a yes or no. On the nineteen TV monitors, there are seventeen Norman Mailers, one dead screen and, in the far reaches of the upper-righthand corner, a very wet man playing golf. It looks like Pebble Beach in a rain storm.

"NASA people are the ones who are suffering most . . . they take failure very personally . . . like a monk takes sinning." Mailer motors on, with a faint hint of a Texas twang to his voice. New Jersey born and Brooklyn raised, he supposedly picked up the accent during the war in the Philippines with the 112th Cavalry from San Antonio. "NASA is a predominantly WASP organization," he concludes. It is a curious non sequitur and has the effect of making everyone pause, while Mailer catches his breath for the next charge. One of the technicians quips, "W, A, S, P. Wouldn't those make great call letters for a new station!" Quietly and out of the dark, another voice responds, "Wait a minute. If you're an 'A, S, P' doesn't that mean you're *already* 'W'?"

On the screens, Mailer is saying *"Ronald Reagan* may be the quintessential expression of our insanity. . . . He knows how to charm us all a lot better than I do." His *I* comes out as a chili-twangy *Ahh*, his eyes twinkle, and he grins a bit in antiestablishment impishness. The cameras zoom back, showing the clenching masseter muscles of Ralph Hefner's face.

Over the next twenty minutes Mailer, in a virtual monologue, throws verbal jabs and hooks at an impressive array of cultural establishments: "Ahh study the Bahhble in church all the tahhm; but ahh go to church like a tourist, only without a passport."

The monitor in the upper right has switched to a basketball game as Mailer double-clutches, shifts into a higher gear, and starts talking about some of the serious writers in America. He mentions his long-time pseudo-enemy, Gore Vidal. A voice in the control room mutters, "I wondered when he'd get around to that." At about that time, a long-held theory of mine suddenly seemed validated. Norman Mailer's life has been read about more than his books have been read.

The question arises: Which came first—Norman Mailer or television? The answer is on page 819 of my *World Almanac:* "Invention: television. Date: 1923. Inventor: Zworykin. Nation: U.S.A." The evidence is irrefutable. Television was invented the same year Norman Mailer was born. It is as though the former was created to provide mass-media coverage of the latter.

He was a golden boy, this good-looking, curly-haired Jewish kid whose first book stayed on the *New York Times* Best-Seller List for eleven weeks. But after the next two books, *Barbary Shore* and *Deer Park*, were trashed by critics, the media needed a new image for Mailer. The one he provided was perfect for the times: a bad boy—a well-educated, grown-up, articulate juvenile delinquent. In was an unlikely role for a Brooklyn kid who, as his eighth-grade principal once publicly announced, had "Public School 161's highest-ever IQ—165"; a kid who attended Harvard with such interesting characters as Caspar Weinberger and George Goethals, the grandson of the engineer who built the Panama Canal; a kid who majored in aeronautical engineering, yet won a nationwide short-story contest as a sophomore.

But in the late 1950s, after starting the *Village Voice* and publishing *Advertisements for Myself,* he began giving the media just what it needed. They couldn't get enough. He stabbed his wife in 1960 and was committed to Bellevue, then released as perfectly sane. In 1967, he marched on the Pentagon to protest the Vietnam War. There was a brush with respectability when he received a Pulitzer Prize for the book *The Armies of the Night* in 1969, the same year he ran unsuccessfully for mayor of New York. But there was always a new, hot flash to tantalize the public: He was either getting arrested for fighting a policeman in Provincetown or coldcocking some guy at Birdland over a bar tab, or charging admission to his own fiftieth birthday party at the Four Seasons (fifty dollars, of course). He seemed to drink a lot, and it appeared that he was always getting divorced or married or fathering another child. And every once in a while, one of his ex-wives would surface, making a public plea for more alimony.

There were photos of him arm wrestling with Muhammad Ali; he was seen boxing on *The Dick Cavett Show* with Jose Torres. Then along came a *second* brush with respectability, in 1980, with another Pulitzer Prize for *The Executioner's Song.* But right on the heels of that second Pulitzer Prize came the hottest hot flash of all: Mailer saw literary talent in an imprisoned killer, Jack Abbott, and got his book published.

After Mailer helped to get him out of jail and into a job, Abbott stabbed and killed a man over a petty disagreement. In the resulting ruckus, Mailer claimed, "Culture's worth a little risk," and the furor continued. But then, with his marriage to Norris Church, Mailer seemed to slip into the comforts of home cooking and out of prime-time coverage, with the single exception of his "Egyptian" novel, *Ancient Evenings,* a book eleven years in the making.

Here and now, in his—and television's—sixty-third year, his voice twangs out, "Ahh can argue both sides to *any* argument, with the single exception of why we people get taxed but cannot vote. If you can tell me how to vote yes on Star Wars, tell me—I don't know!"

Then something happened that briefly shook my image of the Media Man: One of the shadowy figures in the small control room, surrounded by Ampex tape boxes, dials, and levers, started quietly humming the theme song from "Mickey Mouse." As the show was ending and the credits were running, somebody switched camera angles and came straight at Mailer from the front. His ears stuck out like satellite dishes.

The director of the show, Jan Weldman, turned on the lights and said, "I'll take you in to see Mr. Mailer." She led me through the door into the studio. This was it! Was there a real Norman Mailer? I almost expected to find an out-of-work, off-Broadway actor, madly gasping for air while struggling to pull off a rubber Norman Mailer mask. "I don't care if I don't get steady work," he'd say. "This goddamn mask is so goddamned sweaty . . . I can't take it anymore! And just how do you expect me to talk like a Texan when I'm from the Bronx? How the hell can I talk about all those topics so fast if you use such tiny little cue cards. This is an absolutely impossible job!" Throwing his curly, white-haired rubber image down in a heap, he'd storm out the door, never to be seen again.

What I found was an elegantly dressed, impeccably mannered, thoroughly cooperative, open, and friendly gentleman. He was seated on a dais at the round interview table, dutifully autographing a pile of books for the WPIX personnel. Finished, he buttoned his double-breasted blazer, stepped down from the dais, and shook hands politely; he was not only real, but a lot taller than I had expected.

> *"Boredom slays more existence than war."*
> —Norman Mailer

> *"Norman thinks playing it safe is the worst violation in life."*
> —Montgomery Clift

In the clear light that comes thirty years after its writing, "The White Negro" seems disturbingly precise in its prophecy, its description of human behavior. Constantly faced with the fear of death, a generation looked inward, finding the courage to be unconventional and consciously deciding that rebellion is not merely justified but necessary. The hipster, the White Negro, the psychic outlaw, were the seeds of generations to come. From the 1960s "be here now," "do your own thing," through to the Me Decade, and the cult of narcissism, this was the fount.

Mailer felt it in himself and saw it as a growing force in society in general. He felt the early surges of psychic revolution, and through a curious sequence of events, he got his message across. To understand Mailer's message, as articulated in his essay, is to come closer to understanding him. Further, it allows a clearer view as to how many of the pieces of the puzzle that was the 1960s fit together.

Mailer and I had, over four years of haggling, come to an agreement that we could talk, *only* if our conversation was limited to "The White Negro." "He does not talk about topics on which he may decide to write in the future," I had been told repeatedly by his secretary, Judith McNally. Given his past writings, from combat in the Philippines, to Marilyn Monroe, to life in ancient Egypt, that seemed to exclude a considerable amount of conversation. However, once we found a quiet corner in a midtown Manhattan bar, and after the Oriental waiter had successfully wrestled his way through "any bourbon *but* Jack Daniels, water on the side," Mailer's four years of hesitancy seemed to evaporate. He suggested that I put a pad under my tape recorder, "a good idea, because I have found from experience that noise levels are tough on it when you are trying to transcribe." Mailer seemed more instinctive than calculating, and I felt him relax. Many people fear a tape recorder; he saw it as a necessary tool of the trade.

"The White Negro" began with the simple suggestion that Mailer write a comment on school desegregation for a monthly magazine. The journal was *The Independent,* run by Mailer's friend, Lyle Stuart, whose later pursuits included a high-stakes professional gambling magazine and *The Sensuous Woman,* by "J." At the time, Mailer was married to his second wife, Adele, and they had just returned from Paris, where he had given up barbiturates and Benzedrine. The writing was painful and arduous: Mailer believed no newspaper would touch it. Stuart published Mailer's brief first draft and sent copies to a number of influential people. He got back some responses that stirred Mailer's competitive nature. Eleanor Roosevelt wrote, "I think Mr. Mailer's statement is horrible and unnecessary." Mailer laughed it off, saying it was probably the first time Mrs. Roosevelt ever used the word *horrible.*

However, when William Faulkner responded, it convinced Mailer he had to "do better—a good deal better."

Faulkner had won the Nobel Prize in literature six years before and had just won the Pulitzer Prize in fiction for *The Fable.* He wrote of Mailer's essay: "I have heard this idea expressed . . . though not before by a man. The others were ladies . . . around forty or forty-five."

Challenged (did Faulkner mean he was less than a man?), Mailer replied that "Mr. Faulkner is a timid man who has had a sheltered life. So I would not be surprised if he has had his best and most intense conversations with sensitive middle-aged ladies." He then took up his pen, with a sense of mounting dread that his entire literary future depended on what he wrote in the "The White Negro." "I was hurt and irritated," Mailer says now of Faulkner's cavalier dismissal. "I revered him, so it was a little bit like the coach saying, 'Kid, you don't belong on the team.' It was just bad news coming from him."

Regardless, Mailer had an inner conviction that he was ahead of his time. "In 1957, it felt as if Eisenhower had been in forever. There was a terrible paranoia about the Russians. The military establishment was dominating everything. We really felt like Fascism was gonna come and we were going to be exterminated. I think that was the prevailing attitude. So these were gestures of dissidents. We were dissidents against America because of the way we felt. So when the 1960s started and things opened up and suddenly we were in the vanguard, it was an incredibly heady and exciting time."

Before he holed up in the Connecticut countryside to write the essay, there were some predisposing factors that fed into the work to be done. Mailer's whole life has been constructed around seeking out experiences, partly out of curiosity, partly from a conscious effort to immerse himself in situations that might provide the grounding for future writing. This self-motivated search for novel experiences, in his years at Harvard, led to his riding on the Boston MTA, fascinated with the Irish, and rushing home to type up notes from his field research. He later took a job at Mattapan State Hospital in Boston, and quit after one week over inhuman treatment of the mental patients. After the Coconut Grove fire of November 1942, he spent hours in the Boston morgue in order to capture in his mind, precisely, what dead, charred bodies looked like. Even during the war he left the safety of his army cook's job and volunteered for jungle reconnaissance patrol to get closer to the core of human experience.

Mailer's maid, his discovery of marijuana, a close relationship with a clinical psychologist, and a nonstop week in Mexico—all were essential ingredients in the writing of "The White Negro." "I discovered pot about that time," he recalls, "and I felt about pot the way Freud felt about cocaine when he discovered it. I thought it was a wonder drug. A panacea for the universe. What it did was to bring me in touch with my own unconscious. As a result, I had this free, but arduous, self-analysis that went on for about five years with pot.

"I discovered jazz through pot. I had always had a tin ear for jazz, and suddenly on pot one night I was hearing some on a car radio, and it hit me. These guys were talking about their lives—it was as simple at that. What do you call it," he asks me, "when you discover something whole, without any intermediary steps?"

"The *aha!* experience," I tell him, and he laughs at the complex academic terminology.

"Well," he continues, "I had an *aha!* experience with jazz. I was connected with jazz for the next five years. While I smoked pot, I listened to jazz all the time."

Mailer describes his self-discovery as a psychedelic experience, one that gave him tremendous insight and self-knowledge. Why didn't he elaborate on drug use as a tool for exploring the psyche when he wrote "The White Negro"? "I was saving it for a novel I was going to do, which I never did; and to this day, I am still waiting to write about that drug experience. You have to understand," Mailer explains, "in those days I thought *everybody* could be enlightened. I was very much like Allen Ginsberg was in those days. We each, quite separately, felt 'Here is the new religion!' It should be carried out. Pass it on to people, and if you did, then that was wonderful!"

Some of the field research for the article was done by immersing himself in the world of Harlem blacks; his introduction came from his maid. "She was a black woman who had been a whore. She used to give rent parties up in Harlem. To raise money for rent, she would sell drinks in her house cheaper than in a bar. We were great friends. We would go to these rent parties, and I met a lot of working-class blacks and nonworking blacks.

"She would have twenty or thirty people there. We were celebrities because we were Whitey from uptown, and they were delighted to have us." Mailer hints at his lack of sophistication at that time, saying, "I would get into conversations with those guys, who would love to hear me: 'Here's Whitey . . . he's discovered pot . . . and he's coming here to bring us the old religion!' "

Mailer has had a lifelong interest in unconventional behavior, and when he received a letter in 1953 from a clinical psychologist whose professional specialty was psychopaths, it led to a relationship that helped Mailer to refine his thoughts on the topic. Robert Lindner, a Cornell Ph.D., had spent several years diagnosing, treating, and writing about his psychopathic patients, first at Lewiston Federal Penitentiary in Pennsylvania, then in private practice in Baltimore. His books were written for a general audience, and he wrote Mailer for advice on writing style. What developed was an ongoing intellectual argument that formed the basic structure of "The White Negro." In simple terms, Lindner told Mailer that the psychologists' psychopath, or Norman's "hipster," was the analyst's nightmare: slippery to diagnose, virtually beyond treatment, intractable to any form of behavior modification, and a brutal danger to society. Mailer agreed with parts of Lindner's argument, but differed with him on the place of the psychopath in society. He felt that to be unconventional took guts, to act in a way counter to society's values was not only inevitable but healthy. It was cathartic and cleansing and purifying for the individual and, on a more abstract level, it put society closer to the life force, releasing creativity that would counterbalance any destructiveness.

Mailer remembers his first meeting with Lindner and the resulting relationship, one that lasted until February 1956, when Lindner died at forty-one. "I forget which book it was, maybe *Rebel Without a Cause*. He sent it to me; he wanted me to react to it, and I did. I wrote him back a mean letter, telling him everything that was wrong with the book. He wrote back and said, "O.K. . . . I was mad when I read your letter; I thought about it and let's talk.' "

"His letter was so essentially congenial that I said, 'Fine, let's get together.' And we got together like brothers. I rarely have had a friend that I was as happy with as Lindner. We just got along. He was a marvelous guy. He was a charming man, but I never thought he was that good a writer.

"He had a lot to do with 'The White Negro,' because his notions of psychopathy turned me on. I took off on his notions of psychopathy. But my thesis that psychopathy is one's cure, he *hated*. We used to argue over that a lot, the cathartic nature. He said, 'It's just acting out. You'll get into a lot of trouble. You don't realize how serious this is.' And of course he was right," Mailer admits, in reference to the stabbing of his wife and the Jack Abbott experience. "Eventually I *did* get into a lot of trouble." When Lindner died suddenly, Mailer was shocked and felt doubly bad since the two had recently argued to the point of fighting. "At any rate," Mailer concludes, "he was one of my closest friends during that period."

In "The White Negro," Mailer used James Dean, who had starred in the movie version of Lindner's *Rebel Without a Cause*, as an example of the kind of behavior he was talking about. "I met Dean once at a party Bill Styron was giving, but I never really had a conversation with him. I was just taken with the quality he had that was a lot like what Lindner and I had discussed. Also, I was looking for examples people could understand. My socialist friends on *Dissent* [the magazine that first published the final version of "The White Negro"], I had to give them some image that they could picture."

Mailer was nearly ready to write his essay; he had delved into his subconscious, he had probed the world of the black, and he had fine-tuned his thoughts on behavior with a professional. One final experience remained between him and a long, difficult session with the typewriter: a week in Mexico. "The week in Mexico had a lot to do with it. I was traveling so scared and crazy, and drinking tequila, getting by with about three hours of sleep a night. I would take tequila and keep going—raw stuff—really tasted like fuel oil.

"I think an awful lot of 'The White Negro' came out of that week in Mexico, in the sense that at every moment I could experience life. All the insulation was scraped off. The only insulation I had was the tequila. There was not that much going on, going to a few whorehouses and getting in and out of a few scrapes. Nothing really gung-ho, but I was so tired, so drawn out. At that point, life seemed very, very dangerous, the way it does when you are remaking your personality. I went through the equivalent, without putting a name to it, of self-analysis. What happened was that a lot of anxiety had broken loose, and I was living with it, acting it out. Acting out a lot of themes in my life."

He reveals the core of his essay, that violence can be therapeutic as well as contagious, in one lesson learned in Mexico. "One of the things I discovered about Mexico was that the man with the most authority always carries the day. So if you were the most potentially violent person in that place, everyone would fall in place for you. If you were the *least* violent person, you were made violent by the number of insults and rebuffs you got. Those sorts of sketchy elements went into it. I was scared when I wrote it, in a lot of ways I almost could not name. I had a feeling I was saying too much, that it was dangerous stuff I was revealing. It was going to excite violence in the world, and maybe violence toward *me*. The simple concept of Kierkegaard's *Fear and Trembling*. If *ever* I wrote a piece that way, it was 'The White Negro.' I just wrote on a huge head of anxiety, and probably wrote no more than a couple of pages a day."

He had no preconceived feel for what the public response would be, just his intuition that he had a message that had to be communicated. "I thought it was terribly important, enormously important, then I'd say, 'If it doesn't have any effect, I am going to feel totally walled in.' "

Its acceptance was of essential importance to Mailer's development as a writer. "I think, in a way, after it came out, it opened up a great deal for me. Because, when no terrible retribution came, I realized that the paranoia I had about saying these things was exaggerated. One could write *more* than one thought, and the world would not come and smash your door in."

In due time, Mailer connected with others who made the same discovery: Allen Ginsberg, William Burroughs, Jack Kerouac, Hunter Thompson, and Tom Robbins. Even Neal Cassady, by proxy, made an entrée into the world of Norman Mailer.

"I was married to a woman who had had an affair with Kerouac before I ever met her, and she knew Neal Cassady. So I always had the funniest relationship with Neal Cassady. Adele was always terribly, well, she was not exactly caustic, but she would put everybody down. So what I heard about was 'the nut that Kerouac used to go around with, Neal Cassady, who is off the wall,' and I didn't take Neal Cassady seriously. Then, of course, in later years I began to realize that once again she'd missed the boat in her evaluation of somebody. He was much, much more important than she had ever given him credit for."

With Kerouac, "it was a funny situation, because *I* knew she had had an affair with him, but he didn't know that I knew. It was a California situation; everybody saying hello in a slightly different way."

Kesey, in Mailer's eyes, has stayed close to his vision. "When we meet each other, we are cordial and respectful of one another. I respect Kesey. We were never drawn close because we were never together. I think if we were thrown together, we would have ended up great friends or not at all. It's hard to say which. We are a little uneasy with each other because we are so different culturally. I mean, Kesey has stayed close to his roots and was probably absolutely right to do it."

Mailer first met Hunter Thompson in a Denver television studio, where each was promoting his new book. For Mailer it was his eighth, for Thompson his first—*Hell's Angels*, and his intentions were loud and clear. "He was a guy on the make. He said things like, 'I am here to promote on this goddamned show. This book has got to sell. I wanna get a little back.' Later, of course, he just amazed me, because *Fear and Loathing in*

Las Vegas was one hell of a book. Hunter continues to amaze me. I have never seen anyone who can take so much crap into his system at so great a rate and not die from it. If I lived my life one day the way that Hunter does, I would be in the hospital. If I did it for three days, I would be dead. And he does it over and over. He comes out of something that has yet to be measured. Of all the writers we talk about, I probably understand Hunter the least, because of the prodigious capacity he has. The man is a legend in successful self-abuse."

The initial connections with Burroughs and Ginsberg are cloudy. "The meetings were not great occasions. We had other people around. We were all politically sympathetic of one another before we were at all close, so we got to know one another gradually." Mailer saw a good deal of Burroughs at the 1962 Edinburgh Writer's Conference, where *Naked Lunch* "was *the* book everyone was talking about. I thought *Naked Lunch* was absolutely extraordinary, still do. And I did defend him. I think Mary McCarthy had even more to do with defending him than I did. She was vastly more respected than I was, and her imprimatur really knocked everyone out. 'Mary McCarthy defending *Naked Lunch!* My God! I've got to look at this book!' You see, if I was saying it, the reaction would have been, 'Well, there is that madman, and of course he is defending it.' Burroughs is not a demonstrative man; I never knew if I had any effect on him. Those days, he spoke to his friends exactly the same way he spoke to his enemies, which was somewhat remotely."

The two were recently on a panel at Naropa Institute in Colorado, and Mailer still sees him as "probably the shyest man in the world, and that could be a big part of him. He is fierce. He is a very odd man. He is one man I would never insult for too little; incredible pride and reserve. But we had the damnedest time out in Colorado. There was Bill and myself, and Allen was the moderator. Being on with William Burroughs is like being with W. C. Fields. He is one of the funniest men alive. He can say, 'It is eighty degrees today in Kansas,' and the audience is just wiped out. I still believe in *Naked Lunch.* I simply think that the number of things it did in American literature are still to be measured. One of the great seminal works of the sixties."

Mailer's greatest accolade is held for Ginsberg: "Allen Ginsberg and the Beats started down at their end. I thought I was the only person in the world in possession of these insights and materials, living in Connecticut and writing 'The White Negro.' Then he read *Howl.*

"Ginsberg and I met in a strange way. Like scientists who are each working on the same problem—far apart in every other way. So we sort of looked each other over, and we were dubious about each other in the extreme. Only very slowly have we gotten to be friends.

"Now, I honor Allen. I have a lot of respect for him. He is truly one of the few honorable men I have known in the literary world over all these years, in that he has really kept to what he believed, in as simple a fashion as possible."

THERE IS A TIMELESS quality to "The White Negro," regardless of Mailer's comment that he only gets a few letters a year from readers on it or that its language is antiquated, that it is tough to read, and that its initial impact was felt in intellectual circles only. Its warning still rings clear: that new times demand new behavior, the likes of which might be somewhat frightening at first. But as he says, "Culture's worth a little risk."

Come Back, Jimmy Dean

THROUGH THE SWIRL OF the 1950s, James Dean studied as com-pulsively as Kerouac wrote and began getting small, local TV parts and theater roles. Dean, destined to become a hero to decades of misunder-stood youths, never really knew how much of the groundwork for his audience impact had already been put down on paper by Kerouac, Ginsberg, Burroughs, and Mailer.

By the summer of Dean's death, Kerouac had written nine books. Ginsberg had completed three volumes of poetry and, less than two weeks after Dean's death, would reorient the world of poetry by his reading of *Howl* at the Six Gallery in San Francisco. Burroughs had written *Junkie, Queer,* and the bulk of *Naked Lunch.* Mailer's output was prodigious.

Whether or not Dean felt himself to be an integral, or even periph-eral, part of the Beat Generation is immaterial. In the first months of 1955, photographer Dennis Stock traveled with Dean, meeting him in New York and later going to visit his relatives in Indiana. A photo al-bum, long since a collector's item, stolen from most libraries, resulted. Dean was photographed in every conceivable pose that would warm the hearts of the new generation—and those to follow. There he was, listen-ing to jazz in his cramped West Sixty-eighth Street apartment, existen-tial philosophy books lining the walls; or walking, lonely, alienated, through a raw and rainy dawn in Times Square (his insomnia was so bad that *Life* refused to photograph him for the cover because of the dark bags under his eyes); in Strasberg's Method Acting class with black girlfriend, Eartha Kitt; taking conga drum lessons. Yes, James Dean had the beat. And James Dean carried it with him, into three motion pictures that seem destined to live forever in American mythology. Dean's talent and self-discipline landed him a role in the Broadway production of *The Immortalist.* His performance was stellar; he received the 1954 Donaldson and Perry Award and, more significantly, caught the eye of movie director Elia Kazan, who was casting for a movie based on John Steinbeck's novel *East of Eden.*

For all practical purposes, James Dean was unknown and untested. Yet, in the first nine months of 1955, Dean, aged twenty-four, made three movies. They were the only movies he would make; he completed the last, *Giant,* the day before his fatal accident.

It was for his performance in *East of Eden,* John Steinbeck's modern-day version of Cain and Abel, that Dean was awarded the Most Promising Young Cinemactor of 1955. Kazan recalled the astonishing audience response to the preview of *East of Eden.* "There had been no publicity, and the audience didn't know who Dean was. But there was some kind of immediate recognition . . . the audience was screaming over Dean, and when the preview was over, the balcony cascaded with applause, like a waterfall."

While this movie gave Dean instant stardom, and a five-year, six-movie contract with Warner Bros., it was the "in-between" movie, *Rebel Without a Cause,* that really tapped the collective psyche of post–World War II America. Based on a case study, Robert Lindner's book had been printed by an obscure medical publishing house, but it became the script for a generation.

Mailer quoted Lindner's book in "The White Negro" and included as a preface another writer's comment that "The late James Dean, for one, was a hipster hero." But, the true Mailer-type "hipster" was more the celluloid Dean. The real Dean's greatest act of defiance was wearing T-shirts and blue jeans for press conferences, something that has since become standard practice. The real Dean was more like Ginsberg's "tenderhearted" Beat. *Rebel Without a Cause* features Dean in both roles. Straight out of Mailer was the "chicken scene," where each man races his stolen car toward the edge of a cliff, the last to jump winning. And then there is the touching scene just before the movie's end that gave young viewers hope that they might develop their own vision for a new world. Dean and Natalie Wood, and the childlike Sal Mineo, break into an abandoned Hollywood mansion. The garden is overgrown; the swimming pool empty and filled with rubble. For a brief, Brigadoon moment, Sal Mineo sleeps peacefully and Dean and Natalie Wood lounge innocently on a bed talking out fantasies about the future. We knew it could never last; they were vagabonds, fugitives on earth. It's the kind of moment that enabled Dean's movies to transcend faddishness, to become a timeless celluloid record of the turmoils of adolescence.

———————◇◆◇———————

ROUTE 46 BETWEEN BAKERSFIELD and Cholame is a concrete deception, a trick played on the senses, rising nearly two thousand feet almost imperceptibly. The straight, well-paved highway is a clear invitation to excess. In this country, normal sensory awareness can easily be eroded by the heat, the monotony, and the tricks of Mother Nature. Thirty years ago, James Dean was driving this road with Rolf Wuethering, his German mechanic. The sun had just set. Adding to the difficulty of driving through twilight was Dean's chronic nearsightedness. Regardless, given the emptiness of this vast land, one hundred miles an hour is not only possible, it almost seems appropriate.

Dean was a skilled driver, having just won an amateur race in Palm Springs. His car, which he had named Little Bastard, was a new Porsche Spyder especially built for racing. At 1,350 pounds, with no windshield, it still had its racing number—130—painted on the side and across the hood. Wuethering, a Porsche employee, had installed one safety belt—on the driver's side—the day before and was along to tune the car before Dean entered it in a race at Laguna Seca, near Monterey.

From the top of Tremblor Range pass, the gas station and Aggie's restaurant are clearly visible as the main road crosses Route 41 in a long, slow sweep to the left. According to reports, including that of Wuethering, who survived by being thrown clear of the car, Dean was slowing down somewhat as two cars in the opposite lane, still a mile away, were waiting to turn left across his lane onto Route 41. Behind Dean was a driver towing an empty trailer in which his Porsche was to have been carried; behind that vehicle was Lance Reventlow, Barbara Hutton's son, who was to have had dinner in Paso Robles with Dean before entering his own car in the Laguna Seca race.

As the Spyder screamed downhill at eighty-five miles per hour, the second car waiting to turn left pulled around the first and crossed into Dean's path. He shouted to Wuethering, "Oh, my God, he's not going to . . ."

The tiny Porsche was so thoroughly demolished that the steering wheel was pushed to the wrong side of the car; Wuethering spent months recovering, and Dean died of a broken neck. Donald Turnipseed, the driver of the other vehicle, a 1949 Ford, went to work the next day with a slight bump on his head.

Twenty-five miles down the road, in the *Paso Robles Press* newsroom, owner and editor Ben Reddick tells me, "Dean was no hero. He was a hophead kid who was out there endangering other people's lives by driving ninety miles an hour. And people come in here to the newspaper and they cut out our front-page copies and steal our photographs. I tell you, I've had it. Two hundred letters a month. These girls come in here with big tears, and the damned Japanese—why they can't even *spell* James Dean!"

Inside Aggie's Restaurant is a four-foot-high colored cardboard advertisement for the hottest item in Tokyo: James Dean designer jeans. His name is embroidered in English on the back; a photo of him from *Giant*, snarling back over his right shoulder, sticks up out of the pocket.

Just outside the restaurant is a monument to Dean. Erected in 1977 by Japanese film producer Seita Ohnishi, it is striking for its simplicity and directness, like Dean's life itself. The metal memorial partly surrounds a small live-oak tree, a tree that sinks its roots down hundreds of feet to find water in a parched land. Live oaks are amazingly resilient to fire and often live for hundreds of years.

And indeed, Dean's posthumous influence was powerful and shows little indication of slowing down. When Elvis Presley first met director Nick Ray, he recited all of Dean's lines from *Rebel Without a Cause*. Rock groups still sing about him. Charlton Heston remarked that within one year of Dean's death, people knew more about his life than Christ's. Nearly three thousand people came to his funeral in Fairmont, Indiana. The French Film Academy awarded him the Best Foreign Actor award more than a year after his death.

The timing of Dean's death—before the release of his last two movies—coupled with the supermarket-tabloid mentality of those seeking to cash in on the wave of national hysteria, nurtured a complex myth. There are true believers who claim he was not killed in the accident, but so terribly disfigured that he lives in a sanatorium. There is also "evidence" of a supposed evil spell on all those involved with Dean.

While his wrecked car was actually cut up into tiny pieces and sold to rabid fans, the still-intact transmission was purchased by a physician, who put it in his race car and was subsequently killed. Reventlow was later killed in a plane crash. Actor Nick Adams, head of the James Dean Memorial Foundation, died of a drug overdose in 1968. Sal Mineo was stabbed to death in 1976. Rolf Wuethering was killed in 1981 in Germany while driving a Porsche. Natalie Wood drowned off Catalina Island in 1982.

To this day, the faithful stream to Dean's gravesite. It is a difficult pilgrimage, an off-the-beaten-path trek to a small town in central Indiana, yet the tombstone must repeatedly be replaced, because the visitors chip away the granite until Dean's name becomes as fuzzy and obscured as the truth itself.

The Thinking Man's Lourdes

ESALEN INSTITUTE HAS, SINCE 1961, been doing its evolutionary best to bring solutions to the world. The concept of a place where minds could meet in free-form, where synergy could be given free rein, and where the boundaries of the human frontier could be restaked was the idea of two thirty-year-old Stanford graduates, each with a degree in psychology.

Michael Murphy, whose grandparents owned the land where Esalen was built, left the area in 1967. He lives north of San Francisco but continues his involvement with programs of the institute. Esalen's co-founder was Richard Price, who, at the time of my visit, still lived with his wife and daughter on the property. He is intimately involved with every detail of Esalen, including setting up a preschool for children of the forty-some residents, organizing workshops, making sure the acres of gardens are producing food for the primarily vegetarian dining hall, and acting as host to the curious—like me.

At seven o'clock in the evening the parking spaces in front of the forty connected cabins are nearly all filled. While searching the map for cabin 10, I ponder the fact that the world's best-known center for removing inhibitions and unshackling the intellect is, in the urgent 1980s, quite seasonal. Seekers from the world over must organize their precious few hours of "off time" months in advance, so that a long week-end at Esalen can be jammed into their tight schedules like a rushed business lunch.

But here they are, in cabins named after the people whose visions, intellect, and personality have steered this place through three decades: the Abraham Maslow house, after the Brandeis University professor who was one of the founders of humanistic psychology; the Fritz Perls house, where he lived from 1963 to 1969 while practicing, preaching, and popularizing Gestalt psychology; the Ida Rolf house, named after the woman who put into practice many of Wilhelm Reich's "bodywork" theories; and the Aldous Huxley Lodge, named after the writer who personally helped guide the early thinking of Price and Murphy and who coined the phrase *Human Potential Movement.* As I venture down to the lodge to meet Price, my attention is drawn to the base of the cliffs and the casual nudity displayed at the famous healing sulfur hotsprings. Esalen is a living refutation of the mind-body dichotomy. If the aim of psychotherapy—Rolfing, massage, tub soaking, meditation, t'ai chi, Gestalt workshops, or orthodox psychoanalysis—is to bring together loose and forgotten psychic parts into an integrated functioning whole, this seems the absolute best place that nature could provide in which to do it.

The view to the west from the floor-to-ceiling windows of the dining area runs to the infinity of the horizon. In Spanish, *Big Sur* means "big southwind," and it is only that breeze that brings clear days. The sea is rumpled gray, flecked with orange from the setting sun. The raw surf, which erodes three feet off the cliffs each year, has subsided to a mere frosting of waves. The fog, which rolls in like clockwork each night, delivers a sense of edgelessness and seems to encourage introspection. What more could one ask from an environment for exploring the soft frontiers of the human mind?

People are milling about, talking, eating, taking their cafeteria trays to or from the serving area in a contented kind of loud hush. No one seems to move or talk with any sense of urgency.

If a cornerstone of psychology is the appreciation of individual differences, this is fertile country. An elderly professor emeritus from Berkeley with white hair and thick glasses shuffles by. A college student from New York City joins me at the dining table, saying excitedly, "I got massaged today by six people at once. What an incredible sensation. They chanted, the sea gulls cried, and the surf was pounding fifteen feet away. I'll never forget it. Can you imagine it? That's twelve hands!" Another man, in his late forties, sits next to the animated undergraduate. He will not talk. "Where are you from?" brings a vacant, almost angry stare. He then picks up his near-empty bowl of yogurt and leaves. This large room, filled with people of all ages, sexes, and description, looks like the main terminal for a Ph.D. bus line.

Given the kaleidoscope of milling people, most of whom seem to be smiling, I do not feel conspicuous or out of place standing alone in the middle of the room, taking everything in, yet it takes Dick Price less than a minute to pick me out of the crowd and welcome me to Esalen.

He is in his early fifties and his face has the tanned look of well-worn leather. He, like cofounder Michael Murphy, smiles a lot. It is not a false smile, but rather a smile that comes from knowing that the hardest work of your life is behind you and the most interesting work lies ahead.

Esalen has been through several crises and much turbulence, but has landed in the 1980s with its feet planted solidly on the ground. It has finally stepped beyond its early image as a cult center where the narcissistic, wealthy, and educated went to get a $400 massage, or a $750, three-day grease job for their gray cells (a "lube job for the personality," Tom Wolfe termed it). Esalen now features a standard offering of workshops, taught by a wide range of people from legitimate academic and professional positions in the outside world. Emphasized are Gestalt therapy, bodywork (the physical dimension to human behavior), and a third area, "personal process," that involves individual or small group therapy. Other offerings touch on a variety of issues, including diet, exercise, meditation, women's issues, and wilderness programs. For those interested in the spiritual side of competitive running, there is the Annual Big Sur River Run, which includes T-shirt, picnic, massage, and the 1980s answer to the team photograph, a video rerun of the race.

As Dick Price and I talk, he over coffee, me trying to see if it is possible to eat spaghetti with chopsticks, the hushed tones of the dining area are shattered by raucous laughter, group cheers, and the pop of champagne corks. The revelers are seated behind us, and one is Chris Price, Dick's young wife. They are members of the Esalen women's softball team. The Karma Krazies is boldly emblazoned across their braless chests, and they sound as though they have just won the all-commune World Series. Dick went over to ask what the score was. Their answer, shouted in unison and with much toasting of champagne, was an egalitarian "three." At Esalen, it's *really* how you play the game that counts.

Walking with Price through the grounds and across the stream that separates the three older houses from the newer cabins and lodge, we see the ravages of a forest fire that recently blazed to within one hundred yards of the buildings. The peak, which burned straight up and across Route 1, looks ominous as the fog rolls in, like the shaved head of a brooding giant. "We had two hundred and fifty people mobilized and organized—and the fire just stopped on the far side of the road. Incredibly lucky," Price says, with a half smile that seems to hint that maybe the giant was more beneficent than brooding.

On the path to Price's house a woman on the trail sees Dick through the pines and rushes toward him. She clasps his hand in both of hers, stands stock-still, eyes locked into Price's . . . and simply glows. She is one of the many returning clients. Price listens to her and talks with her briefly as I politely busy myself inspecting a grove of immense sunflowers. From the sheer radiance of her face it is obvious that any introductions would fall on deaf ears. Price says good-bye several times, but each time he starts to walk away, he nearly has his arm jerked out of his shoulder socket. It brings to mind the fact that Richard Price is not only the cofounder-in-residence, but for many of the seekers he possesses superstar status, whether he wants it or not. Esalen owes as much of its existence to its dominating personalities (from Fritz Perls and Maslow to Ida Rolfe, Virginia Satir, and Will Schutz), as it does to the sensuousness of Big Sur.

———————◇◆◇———————

THE LAND ON WHICH Esalen rests has been in the Murphy family since 1910. Even the hot sulfur springs were tamed years ago, when Michael Murphy's grandfather rented a fishing boat from Monterey, brought in two huge, lion-pawed ceramic bathtubs and hooked them up to the natural waters: the first California hot tub, perhaps. In 1943, seven years after Route 1 was completed, cutting through this previously inaccessible wilderness, Henry Miller moved to Big Sur and set up living in a wooden cabin originally built to house the convict road crew. He was the author of *Tropic of Cancer* and *Tropic of Capricorn;* could the media be far behind him? "The new cult of sex and anarchy" was how *Harper's* trumpeted Big Sur to the world in 1947, and the world could not resist finding out for themselves.

Murphy and Price both graduated from Stanford with degrees in psychology in 1952, but that was pure coincidence; they didn't meet until 1960, and it was a year later before they set up shop above the hot springs, compelled by a vision of providing a smorgasbord of intellectual offerings. Kennedy had pointed to the New Frontier, and Murphy and Price were determined to provide it with a New Consciousness.

Murphy's view of what Esalen should be reflected interests gained during sixteen months living at the Sri Aurobindo ashram in Pondicherry, India. He had gone there with the encouragement of his (and, coincidentally, Price's) professor of Asian studies and Oriental religion, Frederic Spiegelberg, who had just returned from a sabbatical spent at the ashram, and felt deeply that the time was ripe for transferring Eastern beliefs to Western culture.

In India, Murphy wrestled with the synthesizing of psychological growth, evolution, mysticism and the philosophy that the key to bringing about political change was to first change man's spirit. In San Francisco, Spiegelberg was busy founding the American Academy of Asian Studies, in order to spread the word of this new philosophical brew. The Academy was a place to live as well as to study, and it became a magnet for a fast-growing circle of scholars, students and the curious. Alan Watts came to lecture on Zen Buddhism, Fritz Perls to lecture on Gestalt therapy. The core of the west coast and east coast Beat movement came: Jack Kerouac, Allen Ginsberg, Lawrence Ferlinghetti, Philip Whalen, Lew Welch, and Gary Snyder. The academy and its unofficial boarding house, the East-West House, near Post and Buchanan in Japan Town, became the center of the cyclone for an aggregate of young artists, writers, and philosophers referred to as the San Francisco renaissance; they were the seedlings of the Bay Area counterculture. What Murphy and Price ultimately did was to move the show south 170 miles. Undistracted, now they could really concentrate on their vision. Price's view on the New Consciousness reflected his own path during the 1950s. After beginning as a graduate student under Talcott Parsons in clinical psychology at Harvard, and working on government-funded LSD research under Dr. Hyde at Boston Psychopathic Hospital, he ultimately experienced a psychotic break. After a series of sixty insulin-shock treatments at the Institute For Living in Hartford, Connecticut, he pulled himself together and headed back to the west coast.

When he and Murphy met and discussed their respective visions, Murphy stressed the blending of Eastern and Western philosophies into a spiritual, searching model; Price's approach was from a more therapeutic and clinical perspective. Having just experienced an environment that was not conducive to the growth of consciousness, he had a clear idea on an appropriate alternative setting.

—————— ◇◆◇ ——————

PRICE IS AT HOME in Big Sur, weathered like the huge trees around the Little House and as easygoing as the fog. Part of the continuing success of Esalen reflects his warm and human style. He is a Gestalt therapist, personally trained by Fritz Perls, and appropriately, he uses a metaphor for the function of Esalen that relates to food. In Gestalt work, eating is seen as a universal process where individual and environment interact.

"The people that are here use the place almost as a buffet. In other words, Esalen is a place for experimentation in self-selection of therapies, theories, and ideas. You don't necessarily take as much as you can of everything, but you select from the range of offerings. Out of that you develop your own practice and get something for yourself that you can take *out* of Esalen. Something that is not just a very special experience that only happens at this special place and this special weekend. This is not a place for experiences that have no relation to the participant's outside life."

A trio of people come through the screen door of the Little House, their greetings no more disturbing than the sound of ceramic wind chimes outside. We all talk for a while, again without introductions, as if to reinforce the message that at Esalen you are accepted simply *because* you are, regardless of *who* you are. Young Jennifer Price races through the living room and out the same screen door, intent on catching Oreo, a cat I never see. The phone rings, someone answers it. Christine and Jennifer prepare to go somewhere and disappear with no good-byes. As an outsider, I am moved by the effortless mutuality of thought, the word-less conspiracy of action. Life is less formal here, and people just blow like a warm Big Sur from one part of Esalen to another. The phrase "do your own thing" was coined here, and clearly it lives on, in spirit and action.

"In 1960, the basic model Michael had, after his year at the Aurobindo ashram, was something more spiritual and searching, while my interests are what I call therapeutic and clinical. I was more interested in prob-lems that result from psychosis and human development. It may have been a bit more prosaic in some ways, but the two ideas there were a good match: a spiritual model coupled with a place to help people at various levels of emotional difficulties. It was not well defined beyond that, to begin with."

"This place here just presented itself to us," Price says. "It was then owned by Bunny, Michael's grandmother—very run down—just the baths, really. And it was as if, given the time frame of the early sixties, a void was waiting to be filled."

Murphy and Price consulted people they knew at Stanford and wrote invitations to give workshops to a lot of people they did not really know. The response was surprising; seldom had such expertise come so far for so little payment. It was a shared risk; the heads of workshops were paid based on the number of participants who showed up. But then, even if no one came, the baths were always refreshing.

"One beautiful thing about Michael," Price reflects, "is that he would write anyone, without much fear. Some would answer, some wouldn't. Aldous Huxley did, and he and Gerald Heard, who had started his own alternative education at Trabuco Canyon south of L.A., both came here. That shocked us! We started with people we had known at Stanford and in San Francisco, people who had their own following. Gregory Bateson [an anthropologist once married to Margaret Mead, who developed the nonmedical "double bind" theory of schizophrenia] was very helpful. He connected me with a psychiatrist in the Bay Area, a Dr. Schoen, who had also been Allen Ginsberg's therapist. Both Michael and I knew Alan Watts from the Asian Academy, and he was an immense help in the early days, saying 'try so and so, try so and so.' "

The concept gained momentum with such speed that Murphy and Price quickly had to pack their gear and head to the then-seedy Slater's Hot Springs to start the necessary repairs. They were not the first to head out of urban congestion for the area's sheltering woods and rejuvenating waters. Jack Kerouac was there late in the summer of 1960, just before Murphy and Price went down to rejuvenate the rejuvenating baths.

Kerouac wrote about the place in his 1962 book *Big Sur*. In typical Kerouac style, just the names were changed to protect the guilty. He described a weekend stay at the Bixby Canyon cabin owned by Lawrence Ferlinghetti (Lorenzo Monsanto), with poets Lew Welch (Dave Wain),

Philip Whalen (Ben Fagan), Michael McClure (Patrick McLear), and Neal Cassady (Cody Pomeray). Even Michael Murphy's younger brother, Dennis (Kevin Cudahy), whom Kerouac knew in New York City, is mentioned.

Dennis Murphy's book *The Sergeant* had been released by Viking in the spring of 1958. It was climbing the best-seller list and was in the process of being sold by Murphy's editor, Malcolm Cowley, as a movie. This news was music to Dennis's ears, who had seen virtually all of his book royalties disappear into the hands of blackjack dealers in Reno, Nevada. To help negotiate the film rights, Murphy flew to New York and was introduced to Kerouac by another editor at Viking.

The two not only hit it off from the start, they painted the town various shades of red. "Kerouac would act as my public relations man." Dennis Murphy remembers vividly the good, loud fun they had rambling between the Cedar bar and San Remo and Googies in the Village. "We would roll in to the bar, have a few drinks, then Kerouac would pull out my latest reviews. He kept them stuffed in the inside pocket of his coat, and he'd begin reading them aloud to the entire bar. *Real* loud!" When Kerouac drank moderately, he was contagiously gregarious, and for a brief time he and Murphy were the best of buddies.

Kerouac had taken the train from New York to San Francisco, wondering all the way what readers of *On the Road* and *Dharma Bums* would think could they see him traveling in such style and comfort. His intent on this trip was to isolate himself from his North Beach San Francisco friends by staying in Ferlinghetti's cabin and working on a book of poetry to be published by City Lights, called *The Book of Dreams*.

At this point, Kerouac's alcoholism was killing him, and he knew it. The trip to Bixby Canyon, which he aptly called Raton or "Rat" Canyon, was a benchmark in his life. He never hitchhiked again, perhaps because his physical appearance was so haggard that no one dared pick him up. In Big Sur, Kerouac went through delirium tremens, the alcoholic's nightmare. The King of the Beats was in the process of abdicating his throne. Mornings were always the clearest time of day for Kerouac, as he compulsively took notes of the preceding day's happenings. Then by noon, he would try to shake the previous night's hangover and then start the vicious, downward cycle all over again.

> But the new Big Sur Autumn was now all winey sparkling blue which made the terribleness and giantness of the coast all the more clear to me in all its gruesome splendor, miles and miles of it snaking away south, our three jeeps twisting and turning the increasing curves, sheer drops at our sides—The boys reassure me the hot springs bath will do me good (they see I'm gloomy now hungover for good) but when we arrive my heart sinks again as McLear points out to sea from the balcony of the outdoor pools: "Look out there floating in the sea weeds, a dead otter!"

As it turned out, Kerouac's trip to Slater's Hot Springs didn't exactly cheer him up, as this passage from *Big Sur* makes clear:

> The hot water pools are steaming, Fagan and Monsanto and the others are all sitting peacefully up to their necks, they're all naked, but there's a gang of fairies also there naked all standing around in various bath house postures that make me hesitant to take my clothes off just on general principals . . . With horror I realize there's spermatozoa floating in the hot water—I look and I see the other men (the fairies) all taking good long looks at Ron Baker who stands there facing the sea with his bare arse for all to behold, not to mention McLear and Dave Wain too— But it's very typical of me and Cody that we won't undress in this situation (we were both raised Catholics?)—Supposedly the big sex heroes of our generation, in fact—You might think—But the combination of the strange silent watching fairy-men, and the dead otter out there, and the spermatozoa in the pool makes me sick, not to mention that when someone informs me this bath house is owned by the young writer Kevin Cudahy whom I knew very well in New York and I ask one of the younger strangers where's Kevin Cudahy and he doesn't even deign to reply . . .

Kerouac didn't know it, but "Kevin Cudahy" and a whole new generation was getting ready to take up residence that summer of 1960. One man in particular had come to Big Sur, like Kerouac, looking for Dennis Murphy, and a quiet place to write a novel, based on experiences he had had as the South American reporter for the *National Observer* and the *New York Herald Tribune*. His name was Hunter Thompson.

As Michael Murphy recalls, "Hunter Thompson was in New York in the late 1950s. Both he and John Clancy—his friend, who later became our lawyer for Esalen—had admired my brother's book, *The Sergeant*, very much. Dennis and Hunter and Richard Price became quite close. So that is one reason Hunter went to Esalen, before it was 'Esalen.' He got a job with my grandmother, who owned the place. And Clancy was at Fort Ord in Monterey."

In those early days, Dennis Murphy and his wife lived in the "small house," while Hunter and his wife Sandy lived in "the Big House," where Hunter was caretaker. Dennis Murphy's initial impression of Thompson was of a good guy to have on *his* team during the impromptu touch football games they'd have on the lawn.

There was another side of Hunter that he never knew about, yet Sandy was repeatedly telling the best-selling author, Dennis, that "my husband is going to be a great writer." Dennis didn't even know he could spell; it just was not part of their relationship. One day when the ragtag collection of Big Sur gypsies were up the hill helping to construct a communal trimaran for sailing around the world (no one could quite figure out how to launch it without getting it crushed in the rock and surf), Dennis sneaked into Thompson's room. What he found amazed him: a thoroughly annotated copy of *The Sergeant* and the beginnings of *Rum Diary*. "Hunter had studied my book like a Bible, and I didn't even know he had a copy," Murphy recalls with lingering amazement. "He had taken it apart sentence by sentence, underlining, marking in the margins with questions and comments like 'notice how this character is introduced' and 'this is a good idea to fit these pieces together.' He had studied it and never said *anything* to me! And as for *Rum Diary*, when I saw some of the vivid scenery from his times in Latin America, I *knew* that he had the makings of a writer."

Thompson made beer (with too much head, so the bottles kept exploding) and worked on the still-unfinished novel, *Rum Diary*, during the day in a room off a wing of the Big House. At night he was a security guard, hired to keep people from sneaking into the house and to keep the gays away from the baths. (Had he worked the baths during the day, perhaps Kerouac's experience would have been more comfortable.)

Richard Price recalls that it was not just Hunter Thompson that they "inherited" when he and Murphy went down to refurbish the birthplace of the Human Potential Movement. "Hunter was the caretaker of the Big House, and Joan Baez was living there too. When we got down in April 1961—Bay of Pigs day—I can't forget that, Lew Welch was living there with Lenore Kandel. Some were friends of ours from the East-West House and would eventually help us paint buildings and fix the place up."

Thompson's job, however, was a bit more active than wielding a paintbrush. The baths had been wide open for a long time, and the people using them did not want any change in policy.

"We were not trying to pass judgment on anyone," Price remembers, "but we couldn't have *that* going on and do what we were planning to do, so we would try and close down the baths at ten in the evening. It wasn't just the gay groups, it was locals, too, the "Big Sur Heavies," or mountain men, who lived back up in the forest and grew lots of marijuana. Not a group to mess with."

The natural hot tubs that were to put Esalen on the map were a shambles, filled with litter, clothing, and broken beer bottles. Price and Murphy did two things to enforce the rules of the new leaseholders: They gave Hunter a baseball bat and put up a barbed-wire gate.

"Hunter had a lot of aggression and a lot of severe homophobia," Price recalls. "He would go down there and actually try and pick fights. I remember one time they literally tried to throw him off the cliff." After coming back from Fort Ord one night with some hitchhiking soldiers, Thompson decided it would be safe to use the baths with his military reinforcements. On the way down the hill over what was then a narrow path through the scrub (later widened and paved so that Fritz Perls could, with his bad heart, drive down in his tiny Fiat), Thompson and his companions were jumped by some of the locals he had crossed. His friends in uniform, perhaps fearing the wrath of their commanding officer if he were to find out where they had been, deserted. Hunter got badly beaten up, struggled back to his room in the Big House, and spent the rest of the night repeatedly firing his rifle out the closed window.

————————◇◆◇————————

ONE OF THE COFOUNDERS of the school of New Journalism, which in many ways seemed a nonfiction version of Kerouac's new prose, Thompson had not yet written his first book. *The Hell's Angels* would come along in six years. He did some writing for *Rogue* magazine. His July 1961 article, "Big Sur: The Tropic of Henry Miller," showed the signs of things to come; he described the people at Big Sur as "expatriates, ranchers, out-and-out bastards, and genuine deviates." After reading the article, Bunny Murphy, then in her eighties, summarily fired him.

A quarter of a century later, after the publication of his *Fear and Loathing* books, *The Great Shark Hunt* and *The Curse of Lono,* and after Gary Trudeau's Doonesbury cartoon persona, Uncle Raoul Duke, had firmly established him as a larger-than-life character, I had set out to meet the real Hunter Thompson. Following his directions, I had flown to Miami, rented a car, and traded urban blight for the eerie isolation of a tiny key off the southern Florida coast.

Hunter S. Thompson #1: Rest in Peace

Walk softly through the desert sand, careful where you tread.
Underfoot are visions lost, sleeping; not yet dead.
Hang On! Wind's starting to howl . . .
Hang On!! The beast is on the prowl . . .
Hang On!!! Can you hear the strange cry: Winds of Change are going by.

—The Jefferson Starship, 1983
"Winds of Change"

I HAVE BEEN HERMETICALLY sealed inside a motel room in the Florida Keys, waiting for Hunter Thompson for nearly two days. It's the shortest night of 1982.

My air conditioner coughs, wheezes, and shifts into a higher gear. The noise is a reminder of the oppressively hot, wet world lurking just outside my door. June weather in the Keys hangs heavy and ominous.

I switch on Monday-night baseball and the TV speaker nearly explodes with the home-crowd noise. The Expos are taking advantage of an off-night by Phillies pitcher Steve Carlton. Tim Raines has stolen second base after a pitch-out had him virtually picked off first. The crowd goes berserk.

The crowd noise crescendoes to a level that jars me out of my chair. I realize that not even twenty thousand beer-crazed French Canadians can make that much commotion. The TV suddenly goes morgue-dead as do the lights and the air-conditioning unit. The noise continues, building into a chilling, rushing roar. Outside, there are rasping sounds, snaps, clangs, pops, bangs, and a huge wet crunch, like the world's largest boot stomping the world's largest cockroach.

I twist the doorknob ever so gently. The door is immediately blasted out of my hand by a wind of immeasurable force. I grip the doorjamb and pull myself outdoors. Two hundred yards to my right, across U.S. Route 1, is a violent flash-dance of lights and sparks from exploding gas lines, electrical wires, and power boxes, all being whirled and blown about with brutal force. The lights from the blue-and-white explosions are reflected off a jumbled kaleidoscope of what had been, one minute before, several three-bedroom houses.

I see camper tops and aluminum boats wrapped around concrete poles like knots around your fingers so you won't forget. Trees have been jerked out by their roots and are lying on their sides.

The tornado has passed. The spark-fest and crunching sounds subside. The silence is deafening. The auxiliary diesel generator begins *thump*, *thumpa*, *thump*ing, and soon everything electric starts up again, except the television. The TV just sits there glowing, as if covered by a blue rhinestone paste.

A few moments later, Hunter Thompson walks in. "What the fuck was that?" he snaps. He is tall and lean and tanned, wearing tennis shoes and an aloha shirt; he looks like an off-duty split end for the Miami Dolphins. He strides over to the television, slopping a little beer from his Heineken bottle, and stands staring at the phosphorescent set, as if its lobotomized blue eye could possibly help make order out of chaos.

"Tornado," I say.

"Yeah. Shit, the lights were out all the way down here. Let's get some dinner." He turns and heads out the door toward the restaurant, with all the arrogance of a guy who has just caught the winning touchdown pass against his former teammates.

———◇◆◇———

HUNTER S. THOMPSON'S CAREER could serve as an instruction manual for living life on the brink. His self-documented antics of excess became an increasingly visible part of the American scene in the late 1960s and mid-1970s, but his alcohol- and drug-filled wanderings began long before that.

After graduating from high school in Louisville, Kentucky, he got an early release from the air force in 1957 (for behavior "not guided by policy or personal advice, for poor judgment and for controversial written material") and became a "nonstudent," auditing courses at Columbia University while living in a twelve-dollar-a-week tenement "full of jazz musicians, shoplifters, mainliners, screaming poets, and sex addicts." He then spent a few years around Big Sur and San Francisco before spending three years in the Caribbean and South America as a journalist for the *New York Herald Tribune* and the *National Observer*.

When Thompson graduated from high school, he knew three things: He liked excitement, he liked to write, and there was a whole lot of the world he had never seen. "Journalism has always seemed a good way to get someone else to pay to get me where the action really is," he says.

He liked snooping around and writing about it so much that while struggling with the constraints of the air force, he took on pen names to write for local small-town papers. Articles by "Sebastian Owl" and "Thorne Stockton" bear testimony to his early zeal to explore and report.

As an impressionable teenager, Thompson read Nelson Algren's *A Walk on the Wild Side* and was never quite the same again. He saw a lot of himself in the hero, Dove Linkhorn, a marijuana-smoking country boy out on the road for sheer adventure. When Thompson read the passage where Rhino Gross counsels Dove Linkhorn, he saw a mirror to his soul, a reflection of his own volcanic personality:

> "Son, you look to me like a man of two great weaknesses, either one of which may ruin you. Women and whiskey, in that order. Take my advice . . . If you drink, lock the doors and drink by yourself. Conviviality leads to fist-fighting, fist-fighting leads to rage. Look out for rage, son. People never forget a man they have seen in a rage."

Thompson added "women and whiskey" to the "Five W's" of journalism, and the raging search for real-life characters to match Algren's literary ones was on. He says, "I admired Algren and still do. I thought at the time that no living American had written any two books better than *The Man with the Golden Arm* and *A Walk on the Wild Side*."

Armed with only his discharge from the air force and a Dow Jones line of credit as a reporter for the *National Observer*, he headed to the Caribbean and South America. It took a few years, a few beatings, several brushes with penniless vagrancy and a near nervous breakdown before Thompson was drawn back to the United States.

As Thompson recalls it, "Rio was the end of the foreign correspondent's tour. I was twenty-five years old, wearing a white suit and rolling dice at the Domino Club, the foreign correspondent's club. And I thought, 'Jesus Christ, what am I gonna do now?' Then, I would roll dice more and more and write less and less, and worry about it until I'd have a nervous breakdown. So, I just came back here, in a sort of frenzy of patriotism—Kennedy, Peace Corps."

Writing for the *National Observer* and *Scanlon's*, both in Latin America and back home in the United States, Thompson more often than not chose to champion the underdog. A close look at some of his "prefame" work is fascinating. It shows heart and curiosity and more insight than one would expect from a writer who later seemed to trade his reportorial skills for hype.

In one piece he describes the maître d' at the Hotel Cuzco in Cuzco, Peru, pulling down the blinds so that the wealthy tourists eating a six-course dinner will not be offended by the impoverished Incan Indians who come each evening to squat and silently watch them eat. He portrays a portly Englishman, driving golf balls off the roof of his penthouse in Colombia, into the God-knows-where and who-the-hell-cares low-rent district. The bitter message seems to be that gringo is gringo, peasant is peasant, and even if they are only a five-iron shot apart, never the twain shall meet.

The resultant portrait of the gonzo journalist as a young man is that of a very capable writer with a Balzacian eye for detail. He was on top of things, and his writing showed it.

In his first book, *Hell's Angels, The Strange and Terrible Saga of the Outlaw Motorcycle Gang*, Thompson once more dove into the world of the underdog. Almost totally overlooked amidst his descriptions of the Angels' vulgar brutality is Thompson's prophetic shot at the U.S. auto industry. Commenting on the market share of American motorcycles (specifically Harley-Davidson, the only machine an Angel would ride) evaporating to the Japanese, he wrote, "there is surely some powerful lesson in the failure of Harley-Davidson to keep pace with a market they once controlled entirely. . . . What if Ford, for instance, had been the only American manufacturer of autos at the end of World War II? Could they have lost more than 90% of the market by 1965?" Thompson was ten years ahead of his time, but gonzo journalism was not read much in Detroit.

In 1965 Thompson moved to Parnassus Street, near Twin Peaks in San Francisco's Noe Valley. Times were tough, his spirits were low, and money was nonexistent. If you were a wino, you could get day jobs doing gardening for wealthy suburbanites. You lined up just off Market Street, and people in Mercedes came and looked you over to decide whether to buy you for the day, a true rent-a-slave operation. They seldom picked Thompson. Perhaps it was because the glint of hunger in his eye made people think he would eat his way through their garden, instead of weeding it; perhaps, because when he introduced himself as Hunter, they thought it was his profession, not his name. There was something feral about him; his name seemed to fit a little too well. At any rate, the residents of San Mateo and Hillsborough inevitably passed him by in favor of some skinny, toothless, sterno-demented vegetable they *knew* their Dobermans could handle.

Thompson's apartment at 318 Parnassus Stret, where he lived with a 280-pound Hell's Angel named Tiny, is still there. The apartment's backyard was a real plus for Thompson. Not only did it offer a nearly unobstructed view of the San Francisco 49ers' games in Kezar Stadium, it was also large enough for him to practice his lifelong habit of "big bang psychotherapy"—firing rifles out his window. As he recalled in *Fear and Loathing in Las Vegas:*

> I did, after all, have weapons. And I liked to shoot them—especially at night, when the great blue flame would leap out, along with all that noise . . . and, yes, the bullets, too. We couldn't ignore that. Big balls of lead/alloy flying around the valley at speeds up to 3700 feet per second. . . .
> But I always fired into the nearest hill or, failing that, into blackness. I meant no harm; I just liked the explosions. And I was careful never to kill more than I could eat.

Times were tough for an unemployed journalist trying to write his first book, but Thompson was always creative when he felt the need to vent a little steam. Another middle-of-the-night boredom breaker involved one of the trolley cars that regularly came down the hill in front of the apartment.

"It was one of those situations—maybe with Kesey—when I was cranked up to do something interesting," he recalls. "One of those buses came over the hill, and I said, 'This'll be fun,' and threw a garbage can underneath it. Goddamned thing got caught, dragged the whole way. And of course, the driver couldn't stop going downhill. A hideous screeching, ungodly sound. I still remember it. Like ripping a blackboard apart. It was a violent thing, yet it didn't hurt anybody."

The winos were getting the day jobs, and Thompson had been released by the *National Observer* when an offer came from *The Nation* magazine to do an article on the Hell's Angels, recently the focus of considerable attention from the California attorney general. The article paid one hundred dollars. Thompson took the money and wrote.

By the time the article appeared in May 1965, the one hundred dollars was long gone. His phone was disconnected, his rent was overdue, and it looked as if the time was ripe for another downhill slide, but fortunately, incoming mail is free. Thompson's mailbox was soon jammed with offers to do an entire book on the Hell's Angels. One publishing house offered him fifteen hundred dollars if he would simply sign a statement of intent. "Christ!" he recalls. "For fifteen hundred dollars I'd have done the definitive text on hammerhead sharks and stayed in the water with them for three months!"

Thompson got an agent and fired him. "He wouldn't send in my outline for the book. It was sold as a quick paperback. Then, when I sent a few chapters in, they decided that it was a serious book and they'd better sell it as a hardcover. So they put it up for auction. I had Grove, Random House, and Viking to choose from. All I had to do was give them the outline. . . . The agent I had thought that this was so childish and silly, he wouldn't send it. I said, 'Fuck you, you're fired!' and sent my carbon copy to the publisher.

"It was a ten-page piece of craziness. I don't think I ever went back to it at all. Outlines are only political documents, things that people give to their bosses and say, 'This is what I just bought.' You can't give them something scratched on a paper bag.

"In a sense, that agent could have completely changed my life. It's hard enough to get an agent as a writer, without firing him right away on your first book and sending something in to the publisher that the agent says is going to ruin your future. But that's my tendency to take risks. That might also be a characteristic difference between the time of the 1960s and now."

If firing an agent was risky, Thompson's involvement with the Hell's Angels was an invitation to death, RSVP. Doing the book brought him face-to-face with some insights that changed the direction of his career, or perhaps better put, provided him with a career.

In little more than a year, Thompson went from being an unemployed journalist to being the author of a fast-selling book. Along the way he was nearly killed by the Angels, who thought that anyone who wrote a book became an instant millionaire. They turned on him for not sharing his riches. He met Ken Kesey, introduced Kesey to Tom Wolfe (then writing part-time for the *New York Herald Tribune*), and introduced the Hell's Angels to Ken Kesey. Throw in the Merry Pranksters, the Grateful Dead, Timothy Leary, Allen Ginsberg, the Berkeley nonstudent left, the Fillmore West, Day-Glo orange VW bugs, ten hits of LSD, eye of newt, toe of frog, and you have the bubbling witch's brew that was the San Francisco Bay Area in the mid-1960s.

Thompson had known of Tom Wolfe from his *New York Herald Tribune* days, so when Wolfe wanted to do an article for the *Tribune* on Kesey and the Merry Pranksters, Hunter was the catalyst. The original article, filled with photos of the great, painted bus with the astrolabe bubble on top, later became the book *The Electric Kool-Aid Acid Test*.

When the two finally met, after publication of *The Electric Kool-Aid Acid Test*, Wolfe took Thompson to lunch at New York's Brasilian Tea Room, as a way of thanking him for providing several descriptive long-distance phone calls and tape recordings of the party at Ken Kesey's with the Hell's Angels. At the height of lunch hour, Thompson set off a marine distress signal, igniting chaos; it was just his way of loosening things up. "He stopped the place in its tracks," recalls Wolfe.

Thompson had met Kesey in August 1965. "It actually came together in a TV studio, where I introduced Kesey to the 'Frisco Angel people. We later went out to their garage and got ripped up, torn apart, crazed. And Kesey ended up bringing the whole thing down to his house!

"After Nelson Algren, I was impressed with Kesey. No writer around at that time had written two books that good—a real achievement. I liked him a lot—still do—a class act. Maybe he is as crazy as four goats. Maybe I am too. I was impressed with the 'shock of recognition.' I recognized [in Kesey] that high white stone. . . . He was very kind to me. He helped me sort out my thoughts on *Hell's Angels.*"

Thompson then dove into the deep end of the pool to find out what it looked like from the bottom up, a trademark of his work to come and the essence of New Journalism. At one point he was no longer sure if he was "doing research on the Hell's Angels or being slowly absorbed by them."

He soon came to realize the power of the media. The Hell's Angels had been a microscopic spot of decay until the press discovered them. After making the cover of *Saturday Evening Post* and appearing in *True* and *Nation* magazines, they started charging money for interviews and photos. They quickly became the superstars of scum.

Thompson didn't need a college education to realize that if he wanted to write articles and books that appealed to the masses, then it wasn't necessarily a bad idea to drink excessively, drug indulgently, shout abusively, *and* write. Three out of four came to him naturally. "Birds fly, fish swim, I drink," he says. "I've a lot in common with the Hell's Angels, the main difference is that I've got a gimmick—I can write."

———————— ◇◆◇ ————————

THE FIRST SENTENCE OF *Fear and Loathing in Las Vegas* begins, "We were somewhere around Barstow on the edge of the desert when the drugs began to take hold." It therefore seems incredible that Hunter Thompson *ever* had a fear of anything chemical. Surprisingly, he was reluctant to take LSD for years.

"I first ran into acid down in Big Sur in 1959 or '60, through a psychiatrist at Stanford named Joe Adams, who had flipped out on it. And Mike Murphy at Esalen. They counseled me that I was far too violent to take it. I had good reason to believe I was a violent person. At least, I was a little more comfortable with violence than some people. I have been beat up so often that it doesn't worry me to get beat up. That's an attitude that allows you to take risks. It seemed to me at that time that I should not take acid, because of the stories I had heard from psychiatrists who said I couldn't handle it."

Thompson had plenty of opportunities to expand his consciousness in the early swirl of San Francisco's heyday, but did not accept the offers— at first. Instead he immersed himself in the Hell's Angels and found some larger-than-Algren characters. There was Smackey Jack, the Western world's most unorthodox orthodontist, who practiced ad-lib tooth extractions (others' or his own), with a rusty pair of pliers he kept stuck in his belt. Bartenders would stand in a clammy sweat as Jack jerked out a bloody incisor and plopped it on the counter. Anyone not giving him a free drink just to get rid of him was crazier still.

Thompson met Preetam Bobo, a motorcycle outlaw who was also a karate expert and writer, and Sonny Barger, the Hell's Angels president, whose definition of love was "the feelin' you get when you like something as much as your motorcycle." (Despite this display of emotional sensitivity, he ended up in Folsom Prison for killing an Oakland cop.)

Absorbed by the Angels, caught up in the "scene" of San Francisco, Thompson says that "it was inevitable that one day I would pass through the gates at Kesey's. Even though I was keeping my 'left-hippie' life separate from my 'Hell's Angels-Oakland-violence' life, they came together at Kesey's." It was there that Thompson tried LSD for the first time.

After surveying the scene at Kesey's Hell's Angels party, he remembers thinking, " 'The odds are that not too much worse can happen to me than this. So, I'll eat the acid.' By the time I decided to do it, I really had lost my fear of it. And when weird things happened to me, like a tree turning into a snake—I wasn't afraid. It was wonderful! I never had any trouble with acid. What I like about it is that it cleans out the pipes."

Once anointed, Thompson proceeded to establish a literary style—and a life-style—firmly based on the principle of "cleaning out the pipes." After the success of *Hell's Angels*, he kept on firing. *Fear and Loathing in Las Vegas* was followed by *Fear and Loathing on the Campaign Trail* and the anthology *The Great Shark Hunt*. One decade, four books.

His writing is commonly lumped into the growing pile labeled New Journalism. In Tom Wolfe's 1973 book of the same title, two of Thompson's exemplary pieces are included. (For this, Wolfe gave him the honorary "Brass Stud Award.") Most noteworthy is his 1970 story for *Scanlon's*, entitled "The Kentucky Derby Is Decadent and Depraved." Unable to meet his deadline, Thompson simply submitted his raw, unedited notes. The jagged realism of the writing struck a nerve that was directly connected to the increasing fragmentation of American culture.

And when it came to politics, Thompson was there, not just telling it like he saw it, but also squirting a little lime juice in the politicians' eyes, just to see if they were real. He even dedicated *Shark Hunt* "To Richard Milhaus Nixon, who never let me down."

"Politics is like watching big weights moving around. I think it has to do with controlling our environment, which is one of the main reasons we are here," Thompson says. He once ran for sheriff of Pitkin County, Colorado, on an antidevelopment platform aimed against the condominium and ski industries. He was narrowly defeated, but wryly admits, "I didn't want to *be* the sheriff, I just wanted to *own* the sheriff."

His documentation of Nixon's 1972 election campaign in *Fear and*

Loathing on the Campaign Trail showed his ability to get to where the action was, not only to touch the untouchable but also occasionally to grab them about the throat. He spent an hour with Nixon, then stumping in New Hampshire. Thinking that Nixon's reputed interest in professional football was something his staff had suggested to make him appear real, Thompson was flabbergasted to find Nixon remembered not only the anonymous wide receiver (Bill Miller) who caught the previous year's winning Super Bowl touchdown pass but where he had gone to college (University of Miami).

A warning signal was set off in Thompson's brain. He found it exceedingly strange that the most powerful man in the world had a Lombardi-like obsession with a bunch of twenty-five-year-olds playing football on Sunday afternoon. Thompson's "exposé" of Nixon's monomaniacal concern with winning was a prime example of the idiosyncratic kind of half-mad, retrograde patriotism that made him the darling of *Rolling Stone*.

With his demented mischief (in real life and in *Doonesbury*), Hunter Thompson provided America with a kind of Mad Murphy Doll. Wind him up tight, lace him with illicit substances, point him toward any social event requiring some pretense of decorum and protocol, and watch the whole thing collapse. It is a form of demolition derby, using people instead of old Chryslers. Thompson always ends up running amok, a literary bull in the china shop of Western civilization. His forte is the quick punch, the whipsaw attack line. Indeed, when asked what his own favorite book is, he says, "I tend to think more in terms of paragraphs than a whole book. I remember one I wrote when I had just come back from a screaming ride on my motorcycle. I could barely see the typewriter, but I was so cranked on adrenaline and everything else that when I came in, I felt like I should make a few notes. It was one of those things that pops out every once in a while in the middle of the night."

> History is hard to know, because of all the hired bullshit, but even without being sure of "history" it seems entirely reasonable to think that every now and then the energy of a whole generation comes to a head in a long fine flash, for reasons that nobody really understands at the time—and which never explain, in retrospect, what actually happened.
>
> My central memory of that time seems to hang on one or five or maybe forty nights—or very early mornings—when I left the Fillmore half-crazy and, instead of going home, aimed the big 650 Lightning across the Bay Bridge at a hundred miles an hour wearing L. L. Bean shorts and a Butte sheepherder's jacket . . . booming through the Treasure Island tunnel at the lights of Oakland and Berkeley and Richmond, not quite sure which turn-off to take when I got to the other end (always stalling at the toll-gate, too twisted to find neutral while I fumbled for change) . . . but being absolutely certain that no matter which way I went I would come to a place where people were just as high and wild as I was: No doubt at all about that. . . .

There was madness in any direction, at any hour. If not across the Bay, then up the Golden Gate or down 101 to Los Altos or La Honda. . . . You could strike sparks anywhere. There was a fantastic universal sense that whatever we were doing was right, that we were winning. . . .

And that, I think, was the handle—that sense of inevitable victory over the forces of Old and Evil. Not in any mean or military sense; we didn't need that. Our energy would simply prevail. There was no point in fighting—on our side or theirs. We had all the momentum; we were riding the crest of a high and beautiful wave. . . .

So now, less than five years later, you can go up on a steep hill in Las Vegas and look West, and with the right kind of eyes you can almost see the high-water mark—that place where the wave finally broke and rolled back.

—Hunter S. Thompson
The Great Shark Hunt

Hunter S. Thompson #2:
Prowling the Bat Tower

HISTORY IS HARD to know, perhaps because that "high and beautiful wave" broke so precipitously. And yet Hunter Thompson has survived, and even prospered. He and I sit eating dinner at midnight in a restaurant on a tornado-scarred key, closer to Havana than Miami. He is just waking up.

As we talk, he drinks and slowly comes to life. After the original six-pack of Heinekens come two more bottles. As the evening progresses, he leaves me in his suds. He orders and consumes two Bloody Marys, each with a side of black coffee. Chemically, this does not make sense, but the waitress knows him, and much of the drink ordering is nonverbal. As the night passes, he sucks down four tall Chivas Regals.

Thompson is a tough guy to get to open up. It is nighttime, and he is not wearing his trademark mirrored sunglasses. He seems quite uncomfortable. His eye contact is like the flippers on a pinball machine: *Ping-a-ping.* He gives me fleeting glances and then goes back to talking while staring at his untouched side order of tomatoes and onions. Perhaps he ordered it as a still life.

As he consumes more, he loosens up, but still retains a trace of shyness. As he talks, he alternates between rocking to his left like an autistic child and reaching straight overhead with both arms, stretching. The one thing that never changes is his voice. Muffled, monotone, staccato bursts are delivered with the ultimate stiff upper lip and punctuated by noisy silences.

I ask what has drawn him to this part of the world. I ask him how he has changed since the 1960s.

"I have created a new persona named Gene Skinner," he says. "I have given up Raoul Duke—he's funny. Skinner is not so funny. That's why I chose this place, with its cruel, savage, fucking people. It is decidedly not Key West, this strip of fishheads and conches."

The Keys is a chain of mangrove swamps that hooks back to the west off the southeastern tip of limp, penile Florida. It is a place that is not too tough to get to, yet it has a totally foreign atmosphere. The hundreds of nooks and crannies provide the perfect place to hide out until the feds forget about you, or until your wife decides you are gone for good. Wintertime is vacation time, and in the summer you sit and you sweat; or you move and you dehydrate. You exist in a glistening world of perpetual perspiration, as if covered with a Vaseline glove. It affects the way you think.

"Around here there is a strange sense of cruelty" Thompson says. "The people have the kind of brainless predatory nature that comes from being pirates for ten generations. This whole place has thrived for hundreds of years on that kind of trade—a whole lot longer than other parts of the country—and is still going strong.

"The ocean interests me. If I had a choice between writing or learning more about the ocean, I would prefer learning about the ocean. Unfortunately, as always, the writing just finances my education. I've always looked at publishers as people paying for my continuing education. By the age of twenty-seven I had gone through about six or seven lives. I never thought I'd live this long. It's puzzling when you live beyond a time when you figured it would be all over. It's like budgeting one million dollars to spend by Christmas, thinking you'll be someplace else after Christmas. When you find you're still around, the budget is all screwed up and you have to reschedule."

Thompson is writing a novel based in part on his experiences as a foreign correspondent, in part on contemporary pirating. (The working title is *Rum Diary*.) He is certainly in the right place for it. The keys near here are covered with striking new waterfront homes, yachts alongside. They are inhabited by young people driving Ferraris and Jaguars—some both. It is a new form of the American Dream, a high-stakes game in which the winner takes all and the loser lies dead on the floor in a pool of blood.

The Florida Keys and Hunter Thompson, "America's Quintessential Outlaw Journalist": The fit is like tequila and lime.

———————◇◆◇———————

COCAINE AND MARIJUANA ARE the smugglers' current drugs of choice, but a milestone in psychedelic history took place just twenty miles from here in 1959.

That summer Cary Grant was shooting the movie *Operation Petticoat* at the Key West Naval Base. The normally reclusive Grant opened up in an interview with two journalists, one British, the other Joe Hyams from the *New York Herald Tribune*. The world's most popular movie star related a personal saga that he later tried to squash, but couldn't. He told of his LSD psychotherapy—more than sixty sessions since 1957— under the supervision of two Hollywood psychiatrists, Mortimer Hartman and Arthur Chandler. Relaxed and tanned, sitting on the deck of the pink-painted submarine from the movie, Cary Grant, then age fifty-five, said,

> I have been born again. I have been through a psychiatric experience which has completely changed me. It was horrendous. I had to face things about myself which I never admitted, which I didn't know were there. Now I know I hurt every woman I loved. I was an utter fake, a self-opinionated bore, a know-all who knew very little. . . .
>
> The moment your conscious meets your unconscious is a hell of a wrench. With me there came a day when I saw the light. . . . Before this I was in a fog. . . . I have been married three times, but never had a child. Now I am fit for children. I hope I will beget some. . . . I am no longer lonely. I am a happy man.

Thompson says his own psychedelic experiences helped him learn to trust his intuitions, but he has little good to say about LSD's high priest, Timothy Leary.

"I distrust Leary's credentials as an outlaw. He is far too eager to join whatever mainstream there is around him. Not just as a gadfly. I think he likes that, being a part of the process and I don't really. I have never figured out how to sign autographs. An outlaw is not some *thing*. I don't think it is spelled with a capital O. But I think if there was an outlaw club on top of a fantastic building in L.A., that Leary would join it."

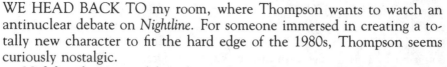

WE HEAD BACK TO my room, where Thompson wants to watch an antinuclear debate on *Nightline*. For someone immersed in creating a totally new character to fit the hard edge of the 1980s, Thompson seems curiously nostalgic.

Nightline features a debate between a spokesperson for Berkeley's Los Alamos Research Lab and Dr. Benjamin Spock, who looks like a moth-eaten Santa. He sounds, sadly, as if he had left his best thinking behind with his last baby book. As we watched, they debated the Nuclear Freeze Movement.

Thompson gets excited. "Hot damn! Now listen, I think we've really got something going here," he says, squeezing his glass of Wild Turkey in one hand, a smoking joint in the other, and leaning toward the TV.

He is involved, and his strange, cryptic economy of emotion is finally beginning to erode—after ingesting amounts of armor-loosening juices and smoke that would have put a normal man on his back for days. He clearly wants to be a part of the action, especially when the screen shows the police in Los Alamos hauling away passive resisters who had tried to block the entrance to a nuclear arms repository.

Nostalgia, they say, is an exercise in grammar where in you find the present tense and the past perfect. I had seen the same thing in Tim Leary, in Ken Kesey, and now again in Hunter Thompson. It was clear that his mind, triggered by the sit-in scenes in Los Alamos, was fluttering its way back through a time warp to Sproul Hall, to the Vietnam Day Protest, to People's Park, to the Golden Gate Park Be-in, to all the nameless and forgotten causes and demonstrations he'd witnessed. There never has been and never will be another time quite like that, he thinks.

"In the sixties it got contagious. Then, it turned into a brushfire. It got to be fun. You looked foward to the next demonstration. Nobody does now; it's like looking forward to your next beating. Jack Kennedy gave people the sense that if you could get over the fence and across the White House lawn without being caught, the president would talk to you. He would be, if not amused, at least civil. He wouldn't chop your hands off. I think what has evolved is a sense of sort of a plastic blanket filled with broken glass around the White House. You can't get through to the White House anymore."

Nightline goes off, not surprisingly without resolving the nuclear-freeze question, but Thompson rolls on. "The rebellion of the 1960s carried with it a kind of naive sense that since we were right, then 'right' would prevail, and we would stop the war and find better ways to live.

"I think that what we have now is a loss of that sense, and people are wondering why there is no rebellion. I think there is no rebellion, not because kids are stupid or slothful, or whatever, but because the dark side of America is now in charge. That's a political statement."

I tell him I'm not really clear what he means by "dark"—that it sounds more mystical than political, less an explanation than a description.

He ponders an answer, looking away and out the sliding glass doors just as he had stared at his uneaten tomatoes and onions. He can see a jumble of headlights from what appears to be heavy construction equipment. He suddenly comes to action, saying, "Look! Look! Bulldozers! Over by the airstrip! Damn, I wonder if the tornado cut across there, it might have ripped up the Bat Tower!" He is up on his feet now, pacing and agitated. I offer to drive out and look things over and he says, "Yeah, yeah. Boy, it would be a damn shame if we lost that Bat Tower." And we pile into my rented Chevette and head down the debris-strewn road toward the Sugar Loaf Key Bat Tower.

I had wandered out here earlier in the day. Even after reading about the thing, I couldn't really believe it existed. But I had found it and I had taken a picture. So, if it was now scattered across the Everglades, at least I had the memory captured on Kodak.

The Bat Tower is an architectural piece of craziness that somehow never made it into the art history books. If the Arawak Indians had developed a man-in-space program, this is what their launch vehicle would have looked like. It is wooden, about sixty feet high, rectangular in cross-section, pointed on the top, and sits eight feet off the ground on four pylons.

It was built in the early 1900s by a visionary Englishman, who imported thousands of bats to roost in it. His idea was basically sound: The bats would leave the tower each sunset, eat ten times their weight in mosquitoes, return to roost at dawn, and make guano to be collected underneath for fertilizer. A sort of vertical cave. Mosquitoes in the Keys can be vicious, and there was no such thing as metal screening until 1911. The theory was that bats would beget little bats, and another tower would be built. The only problem would be if they ran out of mosquitoes.

Unfortunately, they ran out of bats long before they ever ran out of mosquitoes. The very first night, the old Englishman pulled the rope on the trapdoor to begin the world After Bats. (A.B. was how time would be told in the Keys from this point forward.) The bats took off, as bats will do, and kept *on* going. One flew east, one flew west, one flew over . . .

We reach the unscathed tower, and Thompson is ecstatic and relieved, as if his best friend had just walked away from a flaming ten-car pileup. Now we are off to see the real carnage, where several houses have been carried away, leaving very clean and very bare lots.

As we pull up, the blue flashing lights of the sheriffs' cars light up the roped-off access road. Thompson urges me to pull over to where a policeman in a blue jumpsuit seems to be in charge.

I pull up next to him and Dr. Gonzo leans over me and starts shouting at the sheriff over the din of a couple of auxiliary generators nearby. "What the hell happened? My God, do you mean to tell me those were houses over there? Holy shit! What a terror job." He points out the window to the spotless concrete slabs. The sheriff makes an attempt to respond, adding something about ". . . not only three houses, but a sailboat, a camper, and . . . ," but Thompson is not really looking for answers.

Somehow, amid his senseless prattle and mad flailing, pointing at different points of the wreckage, his full glass of Wild Turkey has passed under my nose and slopped on the pantleg of the policeman's jumpsuit. The whiff of 101-proof whiskey gets his attention.

I turn and look at the cop; he sticks his face in the car window, six inches from mine. In spite of the heat and humidity his gaze is frosty. I try to hide my own cheap motel glass of whiskey by shoving it into my crotch and casually putting my right hand over it. We go eyeball to eyeball for about five seconds, then he looks at Thompson, turns, and leaves. Maybe they know Hunter Thompson, maybe they don't want to. Maybe drinking and driving is a distant second to cleaning up after a tornado.

We head back to the motel room; it is getting late—or early, depending on how you look at it.

After countless Heinekens, two Bloody Marys, two black coffees, four Chivas, a half bottle of Wild Turkey, and a skinny joint, Thompson is in a strange mood. I turn off the tape recorder, and all of a sudden that pinhole to his persona I had been trying so desperately to peer through opens up wide.

He chortles about the carnage around us and conjures up an ultimate destruction scene, a creation of truly Thompsonian dimensions.

"After a tornado anything weird might happen. Find a human head on the seat of your car. Get in your car in the morning—find something in your way—push it over—wondering what the hell it is—something heavy. You come out of the motel to get on the road and you are late. Move this—what the shit is this?—start the car and look over and see this human head. Down here it is something that could happen."

He leans back and laughs his first true, let it all out, cathartic laugh, and he opens up so wide you can see that none of his top front teeth are his own. The Hell's Angels probably have the original set.

This macabre scene he draws, make-believe as it may be, makes him laugh endlessly. His laughing is not peaceful. It is surprisingly disturbing, perhaps because it is a 180-degree turn from his tight-muscled, terse behavior of a few hours before. It sounds like something left over from Halloween. I don't know whether to launch myself at the nearest exit or to play it cool, put a supercilious smile on my face, and hope for the best. I opt for the latter, as a manic vision of *Mr. Rogers' Neighborhood* runs across my mind. Mr. Rogers slowly hangs up his alpaca sweater, straightens his one-inch-wide tie, puts on the same supercilious smile, and says, "Now, boys and girls, can you say 'Raving Lunatic?'"

As the laughter fades, I ask Hunter Thompson what about himself puzzles him the most. His response is lightning-quick. "My inability to be massively rich. I should be rich, and it all makes perfect sense. It all makes an extreme kind of mechanical, high-tension sense. I am like a weird engine that runs in a lot of different ways. And you think, 'It can't be sane. Nobody would put something like that together.' But it all makes some kind of terrible sense. I am not at all puzzled. I have all the engines harnessed, it's all working, except it's just a weird machine. There is not a piece of mystery to any of this stuff."

In the deep reaches of Hunter S. Thompson, there is a figure that looms tall, *behind* those longed-for "massive riches." It is the key to understanding the fundamental person. Dressed in a three-piece white linen suit, holding a mint julep in a frosted silver glass, a Kentucky Gentleman sits on the front porch of his vast estate. He is serene, intensely proud of his heritage and accomplishments, and looks out over his gathered family with a truly compassionate heart.

That need for the respectability of the white-suited landholder is what lurks behind Thompson's self-proclaimed *Doctor* Hunter S. Thompson, a title he always uses when arriving at a hotel or making dinner reservations at places where his name alone does not bring instant recognition.

The same longing for respectability shows up in his eye for money and his respectability-by-association with lawyers (even if Acosta, the huge Samoan in *Las Vegas,* was shot and killed in a cocaine deal in the Florida Keys). He regularly phones his son like a dutiful father, to "check in," and can act in an awkward, embarrassed way when he has a girl-friend with him among his friends. The ultimate slap in his "respectable" face came when Garry Trudeau made him a cartoon character. Thompson remains livid about it, even after writing long, scathing letters to Trudeau.

"Writing is a hard, fucking dollar," he says of his chosen profession. "I am a lazy bastard. I am a hillbilly. I don't see much sense in working hard all your life and being successful if you can't rest for a minute. This mania of having to work hard all the time; I would much rather be on my boat. I would like to be a fisherman. I would like to be able to con these people into letting me take them fishing. Gonzo Tours. I have been missing something all this time; I should have been down here running a fifty-foot yacht, doing nothing at all."

So saying, he signs my copy of *Shark Hunt* with "To Pete, with many thanks for the heroin—HST."

Then he starts his car, and heads across the parking lot, slaloming between a land crab big enough to rip open a tire and a pile of tornado-strewn coconuts. He turns left onto U.S. 1 and heads into the rosy glow to the east that marks the end of the shortest night of the year.

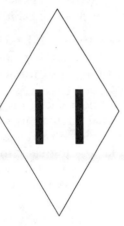

December 1985—and Back Again

DENNIS MURPHY, MICHAEL'S YOUNGER brother, was on the phone, talking about Hunter Thompson. Dennis, like Thompson, is no stranger to violence. In 1963 at Esalen, he got into a knife fight in the main Lodge and was badly cut up. "One puncture wound just missed his jugular vein by this much," Price had said, holding thumb and forefinger a half-inch apart. "Michael was worried to death. Rushed him unconscious to the hospital in Monterey. The next day he went back and found Dennis sitting up in bed, puffing on a cigar, and trying to blow smoke rings through his wounds."

Dennis does not seem to have tranquilized his life style much in the intervening twenty-some years, and he bellows into the phone like a madman shouting above a thunderstorm. "Hunter learned everything *from me*. He learned *fear* from me. I dealt with him. He was *at my knees*. Did you hear that? I taught Hunter Thompson *fear!!*" After learning I had gotten his phone number from Michael Murphy, he bellowed again, "My brother is a *wimp!*" and he summarily hung up.

A half-hour later the phone rang. It was Dennis Murphy again, with a message that shook me to the center. "Dick Price was killed just six days before Thanksgiving. A *huge* boulder. Eleven tons. It just crashed down when he was out walking *in my canyon!!* They charted its path. It hit a grove of redwoods and one piece crucified him. That country is *cursed.* I knew it. Kerouac knew it. Hunter knew it." Most clearly Dennis Murphy knew it. After Thompson had been fired by the Murphys's grandmother, author Clifford Irving and his wife moved in. One day Dennis's and Irvings's wives were driving north to buy groceries when their car went off the cliff, killing both women and leaving Dennis with two young daughters to raise.

The voice continues to thunder out of my phone. "Richard Price was brought down by the *most occult* circumstances. No one knows what will happen." And again, in the middle of the night he hung up. My ears were ringing and my mind kept going back to Price pointing up Dennis Murphy's canyon, showing me the fire damage on the night-filled mountain that looked so much like a brooding giant.

LEAVING ESALEN, THE NOSE of the Buick points to the north like the needle of a huge compass, as though magnetic powers were drawing me up the coast. After an hour the knot-tight curves ease, gradually becoming graceful arcs of concrete. Around Carmel, the West Coast's response to Newport, Rhode Island (no Frisbee throwing or dogs in the park, no more ice-cream parlors), the hills this time of year are sculpted gold and dotted with random clusters of live oak.

North of Santa Cruz, at Pescadero State Beach in the slanted sun of late afternoon, school is out for the day. Amid some early fog and the salt spray of an onshore breeze, are three dozen windsurfers, each perched athletically atop a twenty-five-hundred-dollar board, each with a color-splashed sail brighter than the next.

They circle like technicolor sharks, feeding off the incoming surf, then coming about. Catching the stiff wind, they circle back out to sea, vaulting over the crest of the incoming wave, suspended for a second completely out of the water; then they turn and begin the perpetual cycle again.

As I push on, the red-, blue-, and purple-striped triangles of the sails are muted by the mist in my rearview mirror. The rental-car map of the entire Bay Area is guiding me, propped up on the dashboard. From my quick, repeated glances at the map, the landmass surrounding the San Francisco Bay suddenly seems like a metaphor for what this part of the world was all about during the 1960s: a large head with screaming mouth where Berkeley is, connected to a well-muscled arm, its flexed bicep bulging out of the hills behind Stanford. San Francisco is the defiant, white-knuckled, clenched fist, shaking angrily at a world that does not understand.

The hulking bicep actually exists, on the south side of Route 84 as it hooks and slides over the ridge between the Pacific and the Bay. Ken Kesey lived here, in remarkable style, in a log house near La Honda. The place is still there, I am told, and I have directions provided by Vik Lovell, to whom Kesey dedicated his modern-day classic, *One Flew Over the Cuckoo's Nest.*

As if Kesey and La Honda, together with Hunter Thompson and Esalen, are the glue that holds together the two decades of the fifties and the sixties, the continuity from Beat to hippies can also be found, in perfect alphabetical order on the shelf of any large bookstore: Kesey comes immediately after Kerouac, and *One Flew Over . . .* sits right next to *On the Road.* It is as if the alphabet knew how to tell time and separate generations. Ken Kesey, the log house in the La Honda woods, the Merry Pranksters and their bus, *Further,* are forever etched into American cultural mythology. They created perhaps the most colorful, bizarrely tribal, consistently unpredictable attempt at an "alternative life-style" ever to fall to earth. La Honda is Spanish for "slingshot," which is precisely how this nugget of counterculture hit the world around it: Primitive, speeding and totally unexpected. From July 1963 through early summer of 1967, when Kesey began serving jail time for two marijuana busts, life at the homestead in La Honda was lived in the ultimate "here and now." In the final analysis, two decades after Kesey and the Merry Pranksters disbanded, after his jail time, after he drove his family back to Oregon in *Further,* all that happened here in the woods alongside snakelike Route 84 seems a perfect allegory for the 1960s. Populated by intellectuals as well as street people, idealistic yet without any blueprint for the future, peace-loving yet constantly harangued by the San Mateo County sheriffs, they were the beat from which the West Coast's syncopated rhythms emanated. Kesey, the Pranksters, and *Further* have disappeared—vanished like magic in a wisp of sulfurous smoke. And yet the log house is still here, a sturdy residue of times past.

It looks much as it did when Kesey bought it in the summer of 1963, after the stint in Stanford's creative-writing program that produced *Cuckoo's Nest.* In turn, the novel produced the capital to buy the house and support the growing collection of people. The circle included, among many others, Jerry Garcia, Larry McMurtry, Vik Lovell (Alpert's first therapy patient), as well as Freewheeling Frank, Black Maria, the Hermit, and Gretchin Fetchin the Slime Queen. All were drawn to Kesey's charisma and the lab of life in La Honda. Whatever they did around the log house was, until 1965, entirely their own business; the few neighbors in the area were more than a gunshot away. Then two things happened that brought enough publicity and media attention to the spot that it became known all around the Bay Area simply as Kesey's.

The first event was Kesey's marijuana bust in April. That brush with the law (Best-Selling Novelist Arrested for Drugs, the papers shouted) paved the way for event number two: Kesey's introduction to the Hell's Angels. Hunter Thompson brought them together, and Kesey invited them down to La Honda in August for a two-day orgy of beer, drugs, and sex, the likes of which the San Mateo County sheriffs could never have imagined if they hadn't been watching through binoculars from across the road.

The Angels couldn't imagine it either; few of them had ever been on *anyone's* guest list, and certainly not all forty of them at once. Their approach on unmuffled, Harley-Davidson 74's, resounded through the canyon like theme music for the end of life on earth. Many thought that would be the net result. The Angels and the Pranksters were mutual cults of anarchy; beyond living life at the extremes, the two groups seemed to have very little in common. And yet there were some similarities, such as the way each group found new members. It was that old shock again: Neither group *picked* members; they *recognized* them.

At the end of the well-chronicled fest, the Angels' industrial-lathe philosophy of "when in doubt, bore it out" had melded peacefully with the Pranksters' dictum of "go with the flow." As one Angel put it, "It was all *ha-ha.* No *thump-thump."* The two-day cross-cultural experiment brought such an avalanche of publicity that Kesey's became a sort of intellectual tourist site, the way Haight-Ashbury would become in the summer of 1967.

———————⟨◆⟩———————

"IT IS ON THE south side, past the Boots and Saddle Inn by a couple miles," Vik Lovell had told me. "I don't know what's left, but I'm sure it has changed a bit." There is a little footbridge over La Honda Creek that connects Route 84 with the front yard of Kesey's.

The bridge now has a partially closed gate, the top of which is covered with nails, sharpened points hammered skyward to pierce an unsuspecting hand. No Trespassing and Keep Out signs and an empty yard have replaced the No Left Turn Unstoned sign and the painted bus that so vividly marked the entrance in 1965.

Twenty years ago, walking across this footbridge, one left the roadmap of the civilized world behind and entered a Magic Mountain of the mind. Christmas lights flashed like fireflies, burning day and night, hanging from the lower branches of the surrounding trees. The huge ponderosa pines are as old as the Magna Carta, twenty-five feet in girth, and over a hundred feet tall. All of these lumbering giants were painted Day-Glo yellows, reds, and blues as high as a ladder could reach. So, too, were people's faces. When seen in the long rays of sunset or caught by headlights through the fog, the impact was unforgettable. Strangers passing by either got the hell away or else they stayed for months. There seemed to be no middle ground. As Kesey used to say, "You're either *on* the bus or *off* the bus."

Between two of the trees, close to the shack where Kesey wrote the final part of *Sometimes a Great Notion,* had been a giant mechanical "thunderbird," strung up by wires. One could sit in it and flap its wings and make noises over a carefully rigged speaker system.

Off to the side of the front yard, there had been a metal construction of a *Kama Sutra* love position, to which a garden hose had been tied and left turned on, so that it appeared that the man was in a perpetual state of orgasm. The electronic system installed here and on the bus truly brought the woods "alive" with the sound of music. And the sound of the sound of music. And the sound of the sound of the sound. It was more than huge loudspeakers playing Bob Dylan, accompanied by Neal Cassady's jabbering commentary over imaginary radio station KLSD. Every person, place, and thing was wired to send and receive; it wasn't so much a log homestead as an electronic force field. Pickups hidden in the woods across the road captured and replayed, with a one-second delay, every word spoken by the staked-out sheriffs, who found found it all very disconcerting disconcerting but could do absolutely nothing nothing nothing about it. Microphones were stuffed down *Further's* (carburetors; they were nailed up next to squirrel's nests, dangled over burbling waters, hidden in the bathroom and in the "Screw Shack," or taped to pranksters' stomachs at dinner hour. Musical, mechanical, natural, and biological, it was all just joyful noise on man's march toward the Great Wherever.

Standing just on the cabin side of the footbridge, I size up the current boring and barren state of affairs through the lens of my Pentax. Four or five people spot me as I spot them. They all sprint in different directions into the woods. I stand stock-still. Two people suddenly materialize on the front steps, screaming expletives, gesturing maniacally, and coming straight at me across the open area under the huge pines. In front is a middle-aged mountain mama, her long ponytail grayed, her secondhand-store clothes frayed. A step behind her is a tall man aiming the large-bore barrel of what looks like an elephant gun directly at my lens.

"You filthy motherfucker, can't you read those signs? Get your ass outa outa here before my old man turns your head into red pulp!" I take the hint.

Crossing the footbridge, backward, my eyes on the glint of gunmetal, it is painfully obvious that things have changed here. In the 1980s the magic has gone; now it's all *thump-thump*. No *ha-ha*.

———————◇◆◇———————

TWO HOURS PAST LA HONDA, on a crest of the freeway entering San Francisco, the city and Berkeley are visible simultaneously. The home of the University of California and the city of San Francisco seem to stare at each other across the bay, like two men dueling over the interpretation of a fine point of ethics. They are separate worlds, self-contained, each with its own history and traditions.

Berkeley represents the intellect, the tradition that is academia. San Francisco celebrates, dancing pagan rites around night fires, heating caldrons of unscientific magic and laughter. But for a short period of time—about three years—the barriers were dropped. This was before the "Tuning Fork" appeared on Twin Peaks, or the TransAmerica Pyramid dominated the skyline, during the mid-1960s. The two areas virtually merged to form one immense, synergistic city-campus whose sole purpose seemed to be to redefine the limits of human consciousness and social tolerance. Berkeley and San Francisco were not cities so much as they were magnets of experience.

Each side of the bay had its own showcase of life *in extremis*. The campus at Berkeley was the East Bay's; the Haight-Ashbury was San Francisco's. Haight-Ashbury's evolution was typical of urban America; old, wooden, single-family houses became low-rent student and black tenements. The influx of displaced farm labor and the post–World War II growth in the student population at San Francisco State College were also factors. During the blaze of light that was the early summer of 1967, when everyone old enough to escape parental control migrated to San Francisco, Haight-Ashbury was the Electric Tibet. If you didn't have money to rent or friends to crash with, Golden Gate Park offered ninety-one thousand acres of bush-and-tree-covered acres on which to pitch a tent, park a VW camper, or simply unroll a blanket. The Diggers provided free food, the Grateful Dead the music, and nature the weather that allowed it all to happen.

By the end of that summer, however, peace and plenty were replaced by poison and profit. By October 1967, when the "Death of the Hippies" funeral was held, making and selling illegal drugs was a way of life for thousands. Street dealers were killed; poisonous chemicals turned health clinics into drug-induced psychosis wards at an epidemic rate. The Summer of Love soured quickly on Haight Street.

Today, Haight-Ashbury has continued its urban evolution. It has been gentrified. Between 1970 and 1980 many tenements returned to individual family dwellings; home values have increased by 430 percent—the median home value here is $250,000—and occupancy is 99 percent.

A gentrification of consciousness pervades the shops and their prices. An avocado, sprouts, and tuna sandwich at All You Knead costs nearly five dollars, and they have a long-term lease, which "keeps their overhead down." At 1553 Haight, where the Psychedelic Shop once sold almost anything for the creation of altered states, Zula's sells Osh-Kosh toddler clothing to upwardly mobile Yupsters. There is no tie-dye or paisley for sale here. Down the street, the Drogstore, once the favorite all-night gathering place for human flotsam and jetsam, is now a Tex-Mex burrito barn.

Walking east on Haight, I see a black punker playing a guitar. He stops strumming as I approach, and I prepare myself to be hit on. Panhandling evolved into an art form here during the sixties ("just a quarter, man—it's for my mother's chemotherapy"), and I mentally rehearse my standard rebuff, "There is no such thing as spare change."

He puts down his guitar and looks straight into my eyes. "Hey, man, can you tell me what *time* it is?" Clearly, everyone has appointments to keep these days, and the young man puts away his guitar and hurries off into the fog.

There's No Place Like Home

ON THE STREETS OF the Haight-Ashbury in the 1980s, it is popular for punk-rock teenagers to dress up for Halloween as William Burroughs, in a gray fedora and long trenchcoat. Why does someone sporting an orange-and-red spiked Mohawk, a small, rusty kitchen utensil dangling from his ear, ever need to wear a costume? Who knows? An even more perplexing question is why the punkers have developed a taste for America's landmark experimental novelist. And yet they have, descending on City Lights Bookstore like droves of war-crazed Iroquois to purchase anything and everything in stock with Burroughs's name on it. Paul Yamazaki, a long-time City Lights employee, says, "We cannot keep up with the punkers' demands for Burroughs. As soon as it is on the shelf, it's gone—and with any luck it's even paid for."

If the adage that all fiction is autobiographical holds truth, then one can proceed on the premise that William Burroughs's entire life has been experimental. In his midseventies, he continues to mix together novels with bizarre characters, perverse sex, violence, Egyptology, and sado-masochism. His writing burns with a lifelong sense of psychic anger that seems to rage, "What am I here on earth, and why am I trapped in this body?"

Burroughs's work, from *Junkie* and *Naked Lunch* to the recent *Place of Dead Roads* and *Western Lands*, is as complex, multilayered, and bizarrely unpredictable as he is. In 1949, while visiting Burroughs, his wife Joan Vollmer, and their son and daughter in Algiers, Louisiana, Jack Kerouac wrote the following description of Burroughs, then thirty-five, in what ultimately became *On the Road*. These three sentences may be the most accurate biography anyone will ever write:

> He has a set of chains in his room that he said he used with his psychoanalyst; they were experimenting with narcoanalysis and found that Old Bull had seven separate personalities, each growing worse and worse on the way down, til finally he was a raving idiot and had to be restrained by chains. The top personality was an English Lord, the bottom, the idiot. Halfway he was an old Negro who stood in line, waiting with everybody else and said, "Some's bastards, some's aint, that's the score."

In May 1984 I had gone to find the score for myself.

————————◇◆◇————————

AT HIS FOUR-ROOM wood-framed house in Lawrence, Kansas, William Burroughs appears anything but mythical. With his bony, shuffling gait and his nasal tones, he neither looks nor sounds bigger than life. As he gets up from the sturdy oak table in the living room, carefully lifts his feet over the cord of my tape recorder, and shuffles to pull down the shades, closing out the first rays of sunlight after a week of midwestern rain, he seems a furtive, nocturnal animal. The fact is, when he does venture out from hiding, when others do catch a fleeting glimpse, he comes across tight and controlled, yet there is an odor of sulfur about his aura. Kerouac saw him as "a Kansas Minister with exotic, phenomenal fires and mysteries." The artist Brion Gysin, who introduced Burroughs to the cut-up, fold-in writing technique, said, "An odd blue light often flashed around under the brim of his hat."

I ask him, "Where does one go to see the real William Burroughs?"

Instantly he is animated in an irritated, aggressive way, as if I were accusing him of something. "No, No, No!" He is nearly shouting in his strained, nasal whine, like a propjet on takeoff. "That's what Kerouac said in *Vanity of Duluoz*. There is no Kerouac, that there is *no me!* There is no real William Burroughs." His eyes come alive, and I find for the first time they have color. Blue, I think. He sounds like William F. Buckley after a long, hard night. There is a clear and cultured way of pronouncing words, an ever-so-careful articulation of sentences, and a craftsmanlike sculpting of responses to avoid any error of commission. He is a master at answering questions with another question. He did, after all, graduate from Harvard. And his voice has the patrician ring of a silver dollar dropped on a cold marble table.

One of the many myths hovering around Burroughs has to do with money, specifically, his possible association with Burroughs Corporation, now a five-billion-dollar-a-year concern. A popular street legend has him the heir to the Burroughs Welcome Drug Company. According to this line of thought, he became addicted because of easy access to his family's company's products.

There is something oddly appealing about this myth; someone who has riches, birthright, breeding, and a Harvard education and who chucks it all for a syringe of morphine and a life in bug-infested wino dives. The money myth is just one of many that surround Burroughs and that have helped garner him larger-than-life status. A second unswayed myth is the drug myth. The myth here is that Burroughs received a miraculous cure in 1957 at the hands of Dr. John Dent—the apomorphine cure—and has been clean ever since. His first book, *Junkie*, written during his addiction and under a pseudonym to protect his family, was written in the flat narrative style he called factualism. This style had logic, syntax, cohesiveness, and maybe even a message:

> My first experience with junk was during the War about 1944 or 1945. I had made the acquaintance of a man named Norton who was working in a shipyard at the time. . . . Norton was a hard-working thief, and he did not feel right unless he stole something every day from the shipyard where he worked.

Burroughs also wrote *Naked Lunch* as an addict, but there was nothing flat to its narrative. It is so different from *Junkie* that it seems written by a different person:

> The date palms have died of meet lack, the well filled with dried shit and mosaic of a thousand newspapers: "Russia denies . . . The Home Secretary views with pathic alarm . . . The trap was sprung at 12:02. At 12:30 the doctor went out to eat oysters, returned at 2:00 to clap the hanged man jovially on the back. 'What! Aren't you dead yet? Guess I'll have to pull your leg. Haw Haw! Can't let you choke at this rate—I'd get a warning from the President. And what a disgrace if the dead wagon cart you out alive. My balls would drop off with the shame of it and I apprenticed myself to an experienced ox. One two three pull."

Everything he wrote after his cure was even more abstract, in both style and content. These homosexual, sadomasochistic, disease-riddled, science fiction travelogues "extend the boundaries of the novel toward the public lavatory," according to the *New York Times*. Burroughs's homosexuality, although he is not as outspoken an advocate as Ginsberg, is confusing to those who discover that he has been married twice and had a son, William Seward Burroughs III, who was also a writer. And the pariah's life-style—settling down in Lawrence, Kansas—puzzled many. How could someone settle for such flat, rectilinear monotony after the rich crush of excitement that comes from living in places such as the French Quarter of New Orleans; the Amazon jungle before the Trans Amazon Highway; Tangiers, when it was still a wide-open international zone; Paris before Pompidou and London with the Beatles and Rolling Stones?

Burroughs, the myth: What manner of creature is this? What kind of man cuts off his left little finger with a pair of hedge shears in a pique of adolescent love; or plays William Tell with his wife, misses the apple, and shoots her through the head? This is indeed a beast of mythical proportions.

Historically, the myth begins with Allen Ginsberg. He was responsible for getting *Junkie* published in 1953 after meeting Carl Solomon (to whom *Howl* is dedicated), nephew of the owner of Act Books. Both were inpatients at Columbia Psychiatric Institute in 1949. Ginsberg had played the role of literary agent for Kerouac as well, and Burroughs appeared, in various personae, in six of Kerouac's novels. In Paris in 1959, Ginsberg persuaded Olympia Press president, Maurice Girodias, to put a three-foot-high stack of typed pages into book form and publish it as *Naked Lunch*.

In spite of Burroughs's animated contention that even in his books, "There is no me," all his writings are densely packed with true-to-life childhood phobias; dark, disturbing adolescent memories; and tormented adult experiences that are purely autobiographical.

Burroughs seems to be trying to find a way out of the trap of human existence on earth. He has both eyes fixed on a distant point in time, far beyond our lifetimes. "One of my preoccupations," he says, "is to consider that the next evolutionary step will involve drastic changes or perhaps getting out of the body altogether. The body is almost an escape-proof jail. Almost. As soon as you call something a jail, it becomes escape-liable."

Burroughs makes his escape daily, from his body into the ongoing, fifteen-book-long typewritten cosmic vision. Here, addiction to "junk" is perfectly analogous to the universal spiritual bondage in which most people are unwittingly trapped. Those who "survive" do so in different forms than we presently know. Suddenly, as if all of his past nightmares have appeared at once, crowding his room, he quickly stands up, flailing in a mad, slow way while shuffling in a big circle toward his kitchen. "Practically everything puzzles me," he whines, arms outstretched, head and eyes rolling toward the ceiling as if possessed. His favorite Russian-blue cat, Roosky, darts out the door. "The fact that we are confined in a very awkward contrivance, the body, and that so much of our thinking is of a compulsive verbal nature puzzles the *hell* out of me. But, as the Buddhists say, life is unsatisfactory. Actually they say it is less than satisfactory. Well, that is putting it mildly. *It's fucking terrible!!!*" This last phrase comes out with all the deadpan seriousness of Kerouac's Kansas minister.

———————◇◆◇———————

There was Burroughs with his great idea, greater than any of us could appreciate, and with his meager capital of $300. But as his resources dwindled, his courage rose. I used to leave him at his bench in the

evening and find him still there in the morning. . . . It was his way of drafting plans for what he knew must be minutely accurate.
—Joseph Boyer
Unisys Corporation Archives

Genius often skips a generation. The description of the monomaniacal creator working through the night with total disregard for time was of William Burroughs's namesake, his grandfather, William Seward Burroughs. It was an observation made in the 1880s, as he pushed himself toward an early death trying to invent, perfect, and sell a practical automated adding and listing machine. In the process he patented ten inventions and set in motion what is now Burroughs Corporation.

Burroughs's grandfather was born in 1856, in Auburn, New York, a small town seventy-five miles west of Syracuse. The original William Seward Burroughs worked as a bank clerk in the counting room of the Cayuga County National Bank. It was a time when the Industrial Revolution was spawning corporations with urgent needs for extensive and immediate record keeping. Stress took a toll on Burroughs, and when he was twenty-four, his physicians diagnosed tuberculosis, advising a warmer climate. Burroughs moved to Saint Louis, Missouri, with a self-inflicted mandate to produce an accurately functioning adding machine. The climate was not much better, and his work pace did not decrease. In 1893 severe health problems forced him to leave the company he founded— American Arithmometer Company and move to Citronelle, Alabama, a dot-on-the-map town thirty-five miles northwest of Mobile, best known as the place where the mosquito repellent citronella was made. Even in ill health and semiretirement he pursued his life's work. He set up his own study in a house adjoining the residence where he lived with his wife, Nina, and their four children, Jenny, Horace, Helen, and Mortimer, William Burroughs's father.

Still compulsively in pursuit of new and better ideas, he wrote to one of his colleagues in 1895 that "I am feeling so well lately that my old-time energy has returned and I take a very deep interest in my work. And I tell you this is the place to work, I have a cottage away from the Hotel, and it is as still as death. I can sit and study over my work for hours without interruption."

While not the first to produce a device for calculating, at age twenty-eight he held the patent for the first machine capable of printing a list of figures and automatically adding them. The initial machines were demonstrated and sold in 1889, with Burroughs taking personal control of all the details. The machines were large and cumbersome. To show the world their capabilities, he would load one into a wheelbarrow and haul it from saloon to saloon, betting drinks on his machine's accuracy in doing the books. Often he lost, because the handle had to be operated with finesse and precision. Always the perfectionist, Burroughs locked himself in his shop and devised a cylinder filled with oil that regulated the machine—the "dash pot." He emerged victorious, went directly to the company storeroom, and singlehandedly threw all fifty of the old machines out the window.

Burroughs the elder had projected that the entire United States market would bear only 7,800 calculating machines, yet that many were sold in 1905 alone, when the company name was changed to Burroughs Adding Machine and its assets were valued at five million dollars. By then the elder Burroughs was dead.

He died in Citronelle on September 14, 1898, three months after his last will and testament was handwritten (an anachronism for the holder of the original patent on the automatic ribbon reverse used in typewriters). He was only forty-one years old and—other than two houses in Citronelle and one on West Belle Place, Saint Louis—he had few possessions. These included $828.83 in cash, one gold watch, one pair of cuff buttons, one spring cart, one diamond finger ring, and ninety-seven shares of American Arithmometer Company, soon to be bought back by Burroughs Company. Its current value would be around $60 million.

——————◇◆◇——————

THE FIRST PAINTING PURCHASED by the Museum of Modern Art, in 1929, is of a simple white wooden house sitting on a slight rise in a midwestern plain overlooking an empty railroad track. It is entitled, *House by the Railroad,* and it was painted by Edward Hopper. At the time of its acquisition, it spoke eloquently of the very real American dilemma of two generations with drastically differing sets of values on a direct collision course. The confrontation was obvious: the hand-crafted warmth of the gingerbread-latticed Victorian home versus the high-speed, impersonal, mechanical momentum of the unseen train. The painting is there today, part of the museum's permanent collection. For most viewers the image evokes vague feelings of nostalgia for a quaint corner of the American Cornbelt; the sense of confrontation and conflict is often completely missed. The train clearly won that confrontation, yet now it seems an antiquated mode of travel. Time has rendered the painting a period piece.

Burroughs lives in such a gaunt, Victorian-style house, built in 1927, and while he may spend his days writing for the space age at the typewriter in his bedroom, there is an antique gramophone on the living room table. On the counter between the living room and the recently rebuilt kitchen is an old-fashioned, clear-glass, milk bottle. A single fading, dust-blue iris is the only touch of color, once Burroughs has pulled down the shades.

He has been back in the United States since leaving England in 1973 and has lived in Lawrence, Kansas, with James Grauerholtz, since shortly after his son's death following a liver transplant in 1981. There is a fitting irony to his living in the Midwest; he was born and raised a few hours' drive east, in Saint Louis.

Public awareness of the Burroughs name grew throughout the early 1900s despite his family's lack of involvement with the company. His father married into aristocracy, to a direct descendant of Robert E. Lee.

Burroughs was born on February 5, 1914. Neither he nor his older brother, Mortimer, Jr., later a successful stockbroker in Saint Louis, knew their famous grandfather, but Burroughs's father, "Mote," told of being beaten if he interrupted the inventor in his study. Burroughs's childhood was unremarkable, other than a marked preference for his mother's company (he was never close to his brother) and his perfecting the skill of toad calling, taught to him by a black gardener ("a lost art, calling the toads," Burroughs recollects).

He was educated first at the John Burroughs School in Saint Louis, named after the American naturalist (not a relative). Later, when he developed sinus trouble, he attended the Los Alamos Ranch School in New Mexico (whose property was expropriated in 1942 as a site for the Manhattan Project). He graduated from Harvard in 1936 and then took graduate courses in anthropology. References to the Kwakiutl Indians, Mayan codices, and Egyptian concepts of immortality appear throughout Burroughs's books, albeit in his own hallucinatory renderings:

> Aztec priests strip blue feather robe from the Naked Youth. They bend him back over a limestone altar, fit a crystal skull over his head, securing the two hemispheres back and front with crystal screws. A waterfall pours over the skull snapping the boy's neck. He ejaculate in a rainbow against the rising sun.
>
> *—Naked Lunch*

I ask Burroughs about his visions, his "hallucinations." "What do you mean by hallucinations?" he snaps. *"Hallucination* is a meaningless word to me, since I see things like that all the time. I very definitely remember seeing a little green reindeer in Forest Park when I was a child—not a hallucination, just another level of awareness. Another time I woke up and saw little men in my bedroom playing in a block house. Many people have these experiences. They are not uncommon." Burroughs says all this with the bored confidence of a professor reviewing the multiplication tables with the class dunce. He does admit to childhood fears of darkness, and of being alone, and nightmares so vivid that he always recalled the advice of an Irish maid who said, "Opium gives people sweet dreams."

At an early age Burroughs wanted to be a writer but he showed the same desultory ambivalence then as he does now. He answers my questions with a Kansas-plains simplicity, rarely expanding. He sits crosslegged at the oaken table, holding a cocktail napkin flat to the tabletop with his right hand, tearing off tiny pieces and rolling them into two-inch-long paper wicks. He then places these in an ashtray where he has absentmindedly left two joints smoking at the same time. "It is tough getting good dope here these days," he says, handing one joint to me. He then continues his compulsive wick making. It seems an unconscious part of his behavior, like his repetitious plucking of a small kitten off the cuffs of his army surplus pants. (He always pats it twice with a heavy, shaking hand, then tosses it several feet to land on the only scatter rug in the house.) I guess that the growing pile of shredded napkin is the remnant of an old junkie habit—making little pipecleaners to ream out the eyedropper used in fixing.

I excuse myself for a moment to use the bathroom, and it seems only outlaw justice that I snoop through William Burroughs's medicine cabinet—all in the line of duty, of course. Door safely shut, toilet flushing for some background cover-up noise, I pry open the cheap motel-mirror front to the cabinet. A double-edged razor blade lies next to a can of shaving cream. On the bottom shelf is an eyedropper and a bottle of eye drops, a perfectly legal prescription item. Just checking.

———————◇◆◇———————

BURROUGHS WENT TO HARVARD by default. "Well, I wanted to go to college; I didn't have anything else to do." After graduation, with a degree in English Literature, came his studies in anthropology, then a six-month stint as a medical student at the University of Vienna—another dalliance. Did he want to become a physician? "Well, no. I am just as glad that didn't work out." The experience *did* provide him with the character of Dr. Benway, who appears and reappears throughout Burroughs's work.

> Nurse: "Adrenaline, doctor?"
> Dr. Benway: "The night porter shot it all up for kicks." He looks around and picks up one of those rubber vacuum cups at the end of a stick they use to unstop toilets. . . . He advances on the patient. . . . "Make an incision, Doctor Limpf," he says to his appalled assistant. . . . "I'm going to massage the heart."
> Dr. Limpf shrugs and begins the incision. Dr. Benway washed the suction cup by swishing it around in the toilet-bowl. . . .
> Nurse: "Shouldn't it be sterilized, doctor?"
> Dr. Benway: "Very likely but there's no time." He sits on the suction cup like a cane seat watching his assistant make the incision. . . . "You young squirts couldn't lance a pimple without an electric vibrating scalpel with automatic drain and suture. . . . Soon we'll be operating by remote control on patients we never see. . . . We'll be nothing but button pushers. All the skill is going out of surgery. . . . All the know-how and make-do. . . . Did I ever tell you about the time I performed an appendectomy with a rusty sardine can? And once I was caught short

without instrument one and removed a uterine tumor with my teeth. That was in the Upper Effendi, and besides . . ."

—*Naked Lunch*

The war forced him back to the United States, but only after a marriage "to help a German refugee get into the States. Never consummated. Her name was Hertsfeld Klappert, from a wealthy Hamburg family. She was a refugee in Yugoslavia, where I was taking the summer in Dubrovnik. I did marry her in the American consulate in Athens. She subsequently got into the United States and lived there for a number of years. During the filmmaking [of *Burroughs*], I was told she may still be alive in Switzerland. I haven't been able to confirm it."

A half year was spent as an army glider trainee near Cold Springs, Texas, where he later moved with his second wife, Joan Vollmer, in 1947. He bounced from job to job: big exterminator in Chicago, private detective, a stint at an advertising agency in New York City (predating Allen Ginsberg's brief ad-agency career). But Burroughs's agency employer ran afoul of the Federal Drug Administration; a colonic called Cascade and an age-spot remover, Endocreme, were found to contain estrogens and subsequently banned. Burroughs was out of another job and devoid of ideas for the future. He was bored stiff, reading Spengler and Korzybski and building inertia instead of a career.

In 1944 he met the entire Columbia University group through Lucien Carr, whom he had known well in Saint Louis, and be began using morphine stolen by a neighbor from a hospital ship in the Brooklyn dockyards. Burroughs was over thirty and seemed, in John Clellon Holmes's words, "a very distant, gray figure;" a wealthy, Harvard-educated junkie who could quote Shakespeare was a walking contradiction the likes of which none of them had ever seen.

"There never *was* a trust fund," Burroughs whines at the public misconception of his wealth, a myth that Kerouac generated in *On the Road*. "It was not a trust fund. Everybody assumed that Jack Kerouac was writing a factual account; it wasn't at all. He had people where they had never been, when they weren't there. You cannot take anything Kerouac has written as being factual. It is fiction. He foisted the goddamned trust fund on me. The actual truth is that my family did send me two hundred dollars a month, which they made working in a gift and art shop called Cobblestone Gardens. First in Saint Louis and later in Palm Beach. Kerouac thought the trust fund was a bit more romantic. He had, in many ways, a Sunday-supplement or *National Enquirer* mind."

We began talking about *The Place of Dead Roads* and how it is religious and straight-line in its message; Burroughs says that he wants to add a sentence at the very end. Borrowing my copy, he turns to page 128, reading aloud: "Kim was aware of the danger from Joe the Dead, but he chose to ignore it. Joe never left the cemetery and Kim was an infrequent visitor there." He hunches over in his bony way, shoulders forward and head down, book in lap, both hands grasping it tightly. With his posture, he looks like a third-grader intent on discovering what Jack will find at the end of the beanstalk, but his voice produces sounds that no child should ever hear. Burroughs reading Burroughs is rude, animal music. His Harvard accent vanishes, replaced by a raw rasp that tears each word living and bleeding from the page, then shreds it a syllable at a time. Burroughs reads with carefully enunciated snarls and hisses: "Besides, vigilance was the medium in which Kim lived. The sensors at the back of his neck would warn him of a hand reaching for a knife, or other weapon." He seems to be in a demonic trance state, a very different William Burroughs than the stoop-shouldered eminence that sat motionless except to shred napkins and toss kittens.

It was this otherworldly Burroughs that Allen Ginsberg encountered in 1944, when he first heard Burroughs's reading of *Twilight's Last Gleaming*. Written at Harvard in 1938, it was an early statement of discontent with life in general, and the United States specifically. In it, the captain of the sinking SS *America* dresses in full drag to get into a lifeboat for women and children only. A spastic paretic with a lisp joins him. Then, to the background music of "The Star-Spangled Banner," he chops off the fingers of people trying to get into the lifeboat while shouting, "Take *that* you thuffering thunthabithes." Ginsberg, who had been keeping diaries and writing since he was eleven years old, had never encountered such a powerful and alien force. His reaction, he recalls, captured his feelings for Burroughs perfectly: "Wow!" Burroughs and Ginsberg's relationship was complex. Over time they played various roles with each other: lover, psychoanalyst, author-agent, muse, and stern parent. With Kerouac, on the other hand, it was Burroughs who was inspired. "When I met him at Joan Vollmer's apartment, he wanted to be a writer. There was no doubt in his mind. He had already written a million words, or so he said. That would be 1944—he was twenty-one. Kerouac was a writer, with the full realization of what that means. He says, in *Vanity of Duluoz,* 'Everything is a fiction. I'm just a spy in someone else's body.' Somebody asked [Jean] Genet when he started to write. He said, 'At birth.' If you are going to be a writer, all your experiences are structured in that direction, so I think that's the essence here, that Kerouac was a writer."

Burroughs credits Kerouac's inspiration and encouragement with rekindling his latent childhood thoughts of becoming a writer. When asked about how he influenced Ginsberg and Kerouac, he says, "It was *much* more the other way. Kerouac gave me the title. He just picked the title out of the air—*Naked Lunch*—this is before I'd written anything. Before *Junkie*. Before Mexico City. He said I would write a book called *Naked Lunch* and that I should be a writer."

While the three men are considered to have formed the core of the

Beat Generation, Burroughs disagrees. " 'The Beat Generation' doesn't fit, because there is no such thing. It is a very loose classification. We don't have literary movements here like they do in France. No cohesive programs. There is nothing that Kerouac, Ginsberg, Corso, and I have in common as writers. It is the fact that we are associated as personal friends and that Jack was the one who first used the phrase that set up this association. It was always much more a sociological than a literary phenomenon."

The biggest phenomenon separating Burroughs from Kerouac and Ginsberg was his discovery of morphine. Burroughs owes his career to addiction. It introduced him to "the whole carny world of the underground" and forced him to live under the tyranny of a force far stronger than that of the individual. His writings continued, in form and content, along the blueprint for shock that was first seen in *Naked Lunch*. His works are virtual celebrations of drug abuse, yet it is another, more universal, theme—sex—that cuts through the social veneer and draws the most attention from readers. Homosexual, heterosexual, multisexual— the incredibly bizarre forms of sex that can be found in Burroughs seem even more bizarre when contrasted with the thin figure of the quiet man across the oaken table from me.

> "Let me hang you, Mark. . . . Let me hang you. . . . Please, Mark, let me hang you!"
>
> "Sure baby." He pulls her brutally to her feet and pins her hands behind her.
>
> "No, Mark!! No! No! No," she screams, shitting and pissing in terror as he drags her to the platform. He leaves her tied on the platform in a pile of old used condoms, while he adjusts the rope across the room . . . and comes back carrying the noose on a silver tray. He jerks her to her feet and tightens the noose. He sticks his cock up her and waltzes around the platform and off into space swinging in a great arc. . . . "Wheeeeee!" he screams, turning into Johnny. Her neck snaps. A great fluid wave undulates through her body. Johnny drops to the floor and stands poised and alert like a young animal.
>
> —*Naked Lunch*

Burroughs's "sex while hanging" scenes have become his literary trademark, a combination of sex and aggression as uniquely individual as a fingerprint. The interpretations of this literary logo are many. Some see it as Burroughs's expression of how thoroughly life in the twentieth century has killed our ability to feel. It is the ultimate mind-body dichotomy, a piece of pure schizophrenia. It is his own update of Hopper's *House by the Railroad*, where life crashes headlong into death and something must snap. Regardless of the interpretation, the image sears the imagination like a branding iron.

It is powerful stuff, yet Burroughs seems disinterested and nonchalant; he is more concerned with heating a bowl of Salmon Buffet for his cats in the kitchen. At times, his conversation with them is more coherent than his conversation with me. "In *Cities of the Red Night* I postulated the whole hanging preoccupation—also themes of love, death, insects eating their mates—as a definite viral illness."

Burroughs has never witnessed a hanging, but he acknowledges the importance, however obscure in origin or meaning, of the image. "I don't know when it first appeared to me. It is an old image. Some call this 'the best kept secret' or 'the most locked closet.' There's an article that mentions me and the Marquis de Sade as the only two writers to explore this area." He then shuffles out of the kitchen, absentmindedly leaving a burner on the stove turned up, glowing red-hot. I watch the cats eat lunch, then turn off the stove, and rejoin Burroughs, who is again shredding a napkin, at the oaken table.

If Burroughs's Kansas life-style seems somewhat pedestrian, the years after meeting Ginsberg and Kerouac were not. He moved from place to place about every two years, and his addiction was inevitably the reason. In 1946 Burroughs ran afoul of the law in New York for forging prescriptions on a stolen pad. His family, splitting their time between the country-club set of Saint Louis and their Sanford Street house in Palm Beach, was always there to provide legal assistance, so that the family name wouldn't receive too much adverse publicity. Invariably, Burroughs kept moving, one step ahead of the law.

By 1950 he jumped bail in New Orleans, fearing that his narcotics-possession case was lost and that he would end up in the Louisiana State Prison in Angola. He had already experienced detoxification at the federal hospital in Lexington, Kentucky, and wanted no more. Burroughs collected his wife, her daughter, and their son, William Seward Burroughs III (born in July 1947 in Conroe, Texas), and headed for Mexico City, where living was cheap and drug prescriptions were easy to acquire. His view of U.S. society grew darker. In January 1950 he wrote Kerouac,

> I fear the U.S. is headed for socialism which means, of course, ever increasing interference in the business of each citizen. Whatever happened to the glorious frontier of minding one's own business? . . . The word liberal has come to stand for the most damnable tyranny, a snivelling, mealy-mouthed tyranny of beaurocrats, social workers, psychiatrists and union officials. The world of 1984 is not even 30 years away.

In Mexico City, his place on Calle Orizaba soon became a regular stop for many of the people he had known in New York. There was a large population of expatriate Americans, many there for the inexpensive life-style and easy access to narcotics.

In the fall of 1951, Burroughs and Joan were visited by Allen Ginsberg and Lucien Carr. Burroughs's wife became deeply disturbed by the fact that Burroughs was spending less time with her and more and more time with young Mexican boys. A few months before, he had written Ginsberg, with whom he was constantly debating the causes and implications of being gay, and stated,

> for Christs sakes, do you think that laying a woman makes someone heter? I have been laying women for the past 15 years and haven't heard any complaints from the women, either. . . . Laying a woman, so far as I'm concerned is OK if I can't score for a boy. But laying one woman or 1,000 really emphasizes the fact that a woman is not what I want either, better than nothing of course. Tortillas is better than no food. But no matter how many tortillas I eat I still want a steak.

Joan had been hooked on Benzedrine during her pregnancy with Billy ("my mother's milk was laced with speed," he would later write) and was now drinking a quart of tequila a day. When Ginsberg and Lucien left Mexico City, Allen recalled that she seemed clearly suicidal.

Two days before leaving, Lucien and Joan went on a wild, drunken drive, tearing through the mountains, seeing how fast the car could go, frightening Allen and the two children until they cowered on the floor of the backseat. The two were so drunk that Joan steered and shifted gears, while Lucien lay on the floor operating the accelerator and clutch with his hands. For Joan the end was near, yet it was Burroughs who provided her with a way out.

Burroughs's life then was filled with ambiguity and confusion. He was thirty-seven years old and well educated. He had a wife, a son, a half daughter, was openly gay and admittedly addicted. He enjoyed the tolerance of the Mexicans and the American expatriates, writing Allen that "the problems and difficulties you complained of in queer relationships are social rather than inherent. Resulting from a social environment in Middle Class, U.S.A. I certainly didn't run into 'problems!' in Mexico . . . needless to say, everyone here who knows me or of me knows that I am an invert and a junkie."

Burroughs knew his intelligence was tuned to a higher octave than the normal man's, but his intellect and emotionality were iced over, cut off from any meaningful outlet by his addiction. He read "self-help" books in an endless, obsessive search for himself, writing to Kerouac that Wilhelm Reich "is the only man in the analysis line *on that beam.*" He built an orgone-accumulator box (there still is one in "the bunker," the renovated YMCA basement in New York's Bowery, where Burroughs occasionally goes to write) and proclaimed "the man is not crazy, he is a fucking genius." He liked Harry Stack Sullivan's interpersonal theories of psychology. He felt that Korzybski's *Science and Sanity* was a necessary cornerstone of intellectual development. In time, he would show the same zeal for LSD as a cancer cure, for Brion Gysin's painting, and for Scientology. But in 1951 he was going nowhere and doing nothing, living in a state of suspended animation amid refugee junkies and underachievers from his own country. On Thursday, September 6, 1951, while walking down Calle Orizaba, Burroughs felt overcome by what Brion Gysin would later name "the ugly spirit." It was an otherworldly kind of dark, foreboding possession that would periodically descend upon him. He began to cry, tears streaming down his face, a dark hood of depression settling in. He and Joan went to a gathering at a friend's house, and Burroughs began drinking hard. He went over to Joan and said, "It's about time for our William Tell act, don't you think?" She stood against a wall of the apartment and balanced a half-filled gin glass on her head. Burroughs shot her through the forehead. The glass crashed to the floor, and the party became a moment frozen in time, as everyone watched while her body slowly slumped into a pile. They had never tried such a stunt before. It was "an absolute piece of insanity," as Burroughs put it.

Mexicans love a good murder; by the time Burroughs arrived at the Cruz Roja Hospital with Joan in an ambulance, the *El Excelsior* reporters were lurking there already, like vultures blessed with precognition. Burroughs told them, in an inebriated state, what had happened. Then he changed his story—twice.

El uxoricida, the wife killer, the newspapers called him, passing judgment before the fact. ENIGMA IN THE DEATH OF THE WOMAN J. VOLLMER BURROUGHS, shouted the headline of a newspaper geared to the expatriate population, where a daily English section was devoted to arrival and departure notices of American socialites, party gossip, and the time and place of Harvard and Princeton Club meetings.

In the very first version given reporters as he walked into the Cruz Roja Hospital, "William made it known that he tried to aim at a target, in the way of a modern William Tell, at a glass of gin he had previously placed on the head of his wife. He missed the target and wounded her." He told the gathered reporters he missed because he was drunk.

As Burroughs was talking to reporters and police, someone from the operating room appeared: As Joan was undergoing emergency surgery, she died. "When informed that his wife had died, he cried bitterly, messing his hair in desperation," the reporters observed. A few moments later his attorney appeared. Burroughs now told the public minister that while he was showing his .38 Star pistol, an accidental shot wounded Joan. The newspapers loved it.

BURROUGHS CHANGES HIS VERSION REGARDING THE DEATH OF HIS YOUNG AND PRETTY WIFE, blared the next day's *Excelsior*. Saying that "the North American had already assumed responsibility for the crime of uxoricide," the paper jumped on the inconsistencies of Burroughs's stories. They visited the place of the shooting and found a "visibly nervous" John Healy still at his apartment on 122 Calle de Monterrey. The pistol was also still there, as were American magazines, ashtrays filled with cigarette butts, three glasses still containing gin, four empty bottles of Oso Negro gin, and a huge pool of dried blood on the floor. Healy reported "not having noticed anything," then added that "he doesn't know them [the Burroughses], and that he was not even a friend of the couple," and that he could talk no more, since his Spanish was quite limited. The investigation moved on to 210 Orizaba in futile search of two more Americans, Herman and Marker.

The day after the incident Burroughs, in custody, read the following curiously constructed statement to a large assemblage of national and foreign correspondents: "My wife had taken a few drinks. I took out my gun to show someone. My wife was seated about eight to ten feet from where I was. The gun slipped and fell, hitting the table and going off. In the beginning I thought it was a joke when my wife fell. I went toward her, where she was lying. I placed her on a chair. Someone called the Red Cross, but Joan did not come out of her fainting stage. Everything was purely accidental. The angle of jealousy that some newspapers have brought forth is absolutely ridiculous. I love my wife and had no reason to be jealous. I did not put any glass on her head. If she did, it was as a joke, and it was not I who tried to aim at the glass." Then, finishing with a flourish intended at ingratiating himself with the strange ways of Mexican justice, he thanked all the officials for treating him with consideration. Further, he explained that the two had been in Mexico City only three days, that he and Joan, who was suffering from infantile paralysis, were on their way to buy a ranch in Panama. (Since the Burroughses had been living in Mexico City since 1949, this statement was probably a suggestion of their attorney, so that as foreign nationals, they would be more leniently dealt with.) It seemed to work.

The Mexican officials stepped in. Burroughs remained in jail until released on two thousand dollars' bail. He retained an attorney, about whom the American embassy told Burroughs's brother, "the fee he is asking is reasonable, and he is the best in Mexico."

The attorney, Sr. Bernabe Gurado, was initially effective, getting Burroughs out of jail "in record time." He had three options: jump bail again and flee, spend time in a Mexican prison for manslaughter, or fight for a lesser charge with Gurado's help. Burroughs waited out a court appearance and the testimony of ballistics experts to strengthen his contention that Joan's death had resulted from an accidental firing while cleaning a handgun. He dove into completing *Junkie*. (Ginsberg feels that the death brought Burroughs's need to write to the surface, as a way of somehow connecting himself to the world.)

Plans were made on the assumption that Gurado could get Burroughs off with only a fine. He wanted to leave Mexico entirely, writing Ginsberg in November 1952 that he had "just decided I don't like Mexicans. Three years in this town and no one I want to say good-bye to when I leave. It seems people get stupider and more worthless every day."

His friends still came to visit, including Kerouac, but Burroughs's sense of hospitality had soured. His apartment was under surveillance, and Kerouac's constant marijuana smoking angered him. "I still like Jack but no one can stand this type of behavior. I have always been considered an easy person to get along with but I can't make it with Jack anymore. Unless he undergoes a dramatic overhauling, I do not propose a repeat visit here or anywhere. Getting money out of Kerouac is like extracting a molar. I always picked up the tab in toto," he wrote to Ginsberg.

As Burroughs awaited the slow turn of Mexican judicial gears, he began planning a trip to the Amazon in search of *yage*, a vine that when boiled and consumed as a tea reportedly produced telepathic effects. Just when a court date with the ballistics experts was finally set up, the ultimate irony occurred: Burroughs's attorney was himself arrested for murdering a seventeen-year-old Mexican boy who had inadvertently damaged Gurado's fishtail Cadillac. The lawyer jumped bail and fled to Brazil. Burroughs jumped bail and fled first to the haven of Palm Beach for Christmas and New Year's 1953, then to the Amazon. "Everywhere I went," he told me, "there was no yage. It seemed the Russians were there in 1927 and took back several tons of the stuff—a means of thought control."

In January 1953 he arrived in Tangiers, then an international free city on the northwestern tip of Africa, the southern boundary of the Strait of Gibraltar. It was a used city, sacked, plundered, and occupied by Phoenicians, Carthaginians, Romans, Visigoths, and Byzantines. Tangiers had been "the brightest jewel" in the crown of England's Charles II, but in the 1950s it had degenerated into a house of financial cards; hundreds of illegitimate banks acted as tax shelters and black-market money changers were everywhere. It was a "B" movie backdrop of dark cafés filled with dark people brewing dark deals. Transients, bohemians, and titled idlers were the social mainstream.

In short, it seemed a perfect setting for a literary gypsy whose life had become an X-rated travelogue. It was a town with American, Spanish, and Arab quarters, yet without an overall nationality. It was neither Africa nor Europe, but a mound of sand whose only significance came from its geopolitical prominence. Tangiers existed for reasons other than itself. A land of endless desert, constant blue skies, and oceans all around, it was solitary confinement without walls, a perfect setting for Burroughs to try to regain his sense of worth.

Burroughs looked for social acceptance in the American expatriate community in Tangiers, but he was shunned by the visiting literary figures he wanted so much to meet. Writing Kerouac in 1954, he described the social scene that he encountered:

> I have generally received a cool reception in Europe and Tangiers. The one time I met Paul Bowles he evinced no cordiality. Since then he has made no effort to follow up the acquaintance. Under the circumstances it is his place to make advances once he knows that I am here and who I am . . . he invites the dreariest queens in Tangiers to tea but has never invited me, which, seeing how small the town is, amounts to

a personal affront. Perhaps he has some idea trouble might result from association with a drug addict. Tennessee Williams and Capote . . . and Brion Howard, a friend of Auden and Isherwood and Evelyn Waugh's . . . are friends of Bowles'. I don't meet them when they come here.

Burroughs, who had never felt out of place being out of place, was finding that drugs and Arab boys were inadequate to pull him out of the depression resulting from his nomadic life-style and his wife's death. He sank into two modes of existence—typing and getting high—and stayed with them for the duration of his life in Tangiers. Out of the drugs, the visions of Morocco, and the depths of his imagination came a growing pile of poorly typed manuscript. It had no structure and no cohesive message. What it did have was a voice that had little precedent in literature.

In the beginning, he typed to escape—a therapy with no direction, with no measure of improvement. Burroughs's alienation was made worse by Ginsberg's failure to write him, which hurt him deeply. His sole dalliance was an Arab boy, Kiki, who evidently cared enough for him to try to stop his morphine addiction. (He once stole Burroughs's pants to prevent him from going down to the street to fill another prescription.) Burroughs wrote Kerouac that Kiki was "a sweet kid . . . so pleasant to loll around with . . . smoking tea, sleeping and having sex with no hurry, running leisurely hands over his lean, hard body, and finally we doze off."

This was the period of time when Kerouac was discovering Buddhism and spent a year of celibacy trying to dig deeply into Eastern thought. Burroughs chided Kerouac, writing, "Buddhism frequently amounts to a form of psychic junk. . . . I may add that I have seen nothing from those California Vedantists but a lot of horseshit. . . . I repeat, *Buddhism is not for the West*. We must evolve our own solutions. . . . I would think twice before giving up sex. It is a basic kick and when it is good as it can be, it's *good*." Still, Burroughs's self-doubts mounted; he wrote Kerouac,

> What am I doing here a broken eccentric? A Bowery evangelist, reading books on theosophy in the public library, an old tin trunk full of notes in my cold water flat . . . imagining myself a secret world controller, in telepathic contact with Tibetan Adepts. . . .
>
> The novel form is completely inadequate to express what I have to say. I don't know if I can find a form. I am very gloomy as to prospects of publication, and I am not like you Jack, I need an audience. Of course, a small audience . . . a writer can be ruined by too much or too little success. . . . I feel myself out of place and unwanted where ever I go.

The "ugly spirit" appeared and dragged him so low that he wrote, "I have been in a profound depression. Convinced I can't write anymore.

What I write is no good. . . . Maybe I will feel a little better when I get my shotgun and kill some living creature."

He made a foray back to the United States to try to get together with Ginsberg ("Seems I can't make it without him"), but Ginsberg was on his way to rewriting the world of poetry and living in San Francisco. Burroughs ended up at his parents' home in Palm Beach. After years of opiate addiction, he was forced to have an operation for the junkie's dilemma, the homosexual's nightmare—impacted bowels.

Back in Tangiers, he read of Dr. John Yerbury Dent, a London physician who used apomorphine, an emetic made of morphine and hydrochloric acid, to cure alcoholics and drug addicts. Then, while standing in line waiting to fill the methadone prescription that fed his fifteen-grains-an-hour habit, with his last allowance check in hand, he had a revelation. He was forty-three years old, in poor health, and apparently no further "evolved" than eight years before, when Kerouac had seen him in New Orleans and written about the chains he and his analyst were using in narcoanalysis. Standing in line, Burroughs felt as though he had sunk to the depth of his fourth personality, the old Negro waiting with everyone else. Always a survivor, he stepped out of line and used his money to buy a ticket to see Dr. Dent.

That Burroughs received a "drug cure" in 1957 is impossible to verify. He went to Dr. Dent ten times, and his stories—in *Harper's* and *The Nation*—of a drug cure by a chemical that allows normal brain metabolism to be established again, thus removing any addictive need, has never been substantiated in medical literature. To this day, though, Burroughs remains as resolute about the cure and its process as any religious convert. Before talking with him, I had called Dr. Sidney Cohen, a Los Angeles research psychiatrist, author of *The Beyond Within: The LSD Story*, and one of the few people to take the establishment side in a series of public debates over drug use with Tim Leary in 1969. ("The greatest enemy of LSD research is Dr. Leary," Cohen had proclaimed, as all research on the drug was abandoned in the public acid crush of the late 1960s.) Cohen told me that apomorphine had once been used in aversive conditioning with alcoholics, but its use as a cure for opiate addiction had never been proved.

For Burroughs, this was blasphemy. "I think I've met Sid Cohen. You see, the medical establishment doesn't want to look at it. That is not unusual. They have always fought every change in treatment. Even Nelson Algren knew nothing about addiction. He was never an addict. *The Man with the Golden Arm* was an interesting book, but my God, it has nothing to do with addiction!"

Regardless of what transpired between Burroughs, Dr. Dent, and apomorphine, he returned to Tangiers and began churning out page after page of manuscript, replete with typographical errors and badly in need of retyping by someone with ten fingers (Burroughs has only nine and a half; he's missing part of his left little finger).

In the spring of 1957, help arrived in the form of one of the world's fastest and most error-free typists, Jack Kerouac. In a matter of weeks, Allen Ginsberg and poet Gregory Corso were there, along with Allen's lover, Peter Orlovsky, whom he had met in San Francisco in 1954. Burroughs and Ginsberg were on good terms by then, and everyone enjoyed the warmth and social openness of North Africa except Kerouac. After retyping Burroughs's pile of pages, Kerouac soured on life abroad and left for New York. Burroughs recalls the assistance clearly. "Jack was a very good typist—very quick typist. He did quite a lot. But he didn't like Tangiers or Europe either. He just got depressed and ran home to his mother."

The timing of Kerouac and Ginsberg's visit to Tangiers was crucial in the making of Burroughs's future. Isolated in North Africa, Burroughs was out of the mainstream of American publishing, yet in the middle of the most productive period of his life. Ginsberg's popularity in the States was on the ascent, and he had a resolute belief in his and Kerouac's roles as spokesmen for a new generation. Kerouac, long suffering from underexposure and general misunderstanding, came to Tangiers on the threshold of fame. An excerpt from *The Subterraneans* was bought for publication by Barney Rosset's *Evergreen Review*. Viking extended an advance—after six years—for *On the Road*, whose publication date was to be September 5, 1957. Kerouac paid for his passage with this money.

The pages of Burroughs's manuscript that Ginsberg brought back to the States soon made their way into an underground University of Chicago journal. It had previously been known as the *Chicago Review*, but when Chancellor Lawrence Klimpton saw the excerpts from Burroughs and Kerouac, he prevented that issue's publication, saying "I will not allow publication of anything that would offend a sixteen-year-old girl." The editors of the *Chicago Review* resigned over the issue of "intellectual freedom," and published all of the outlaw literature in a new publication called *The Big Table*.

The U.S. Post Office seized four hundred issues of *The Big Table* and charged the editors with obscenity. With that government proclamation of "obscenity," *Big Table* immediately became a collector's item, sales of *Howl* soared, and Burroughs, seemingly unfazed, hunkered over his typewriter, nine and a half fingers flailing madly, yet now with some concept of a goal. In late November 1957, now signing his letters to Allen with "and give my best to Peter," he wrote Ginsberg of his view of the world, after fifteen years of drug addiction:

> I am in the groove . . . this theory resulted from necessities of the novel . . . that is, scientific theories and novel are inseparable. What I am evolving is a general theory of addiction which expands into a world

picture with concepts of good and evil. . . . I do nothing but work, given up liquor entirely, writing narrative which comes in great hunks, faster than I can get it down, changes in my psyche are profound and basic. I feel myself not the same person, I'm about to leave Tangiers—I really can't seem to interest myself in boys anymore.

Burroughs left Tangiers for Paris in November 1959. There he was to meet one of the most influential people of his life—Brion Gysin. Born in England of a Swiss father, Gysin was raised in London, then moved to Ontario, then to an Indian reservation in Manitoba. Educated at Downside in England, he ended up in Greece when World War II broke out, then served in the English, Canadian, and American armies. He began exhibiting his watercolors in a gallery in Tangiers in 1952.

Gysin died in 1986, but I visited with him a year earlier in a spartan flat directly opposite the huge, blue, inside-out architectural complex of the Pompidou Cultural Center.

———————◇◆◇———————

Gysin laughs heartily when I tell him of the coin-operated musical pissoir I had found on Rue St. Martin that played Elton John's "Sad Songs." ("Tell Ferlinghetti that one—he did his dissertation at the Sorbonne on 'The History of the Pissoir in Literature,' " he says, chuckling.) Then he begins to relate his fifty-year connection with Burroughs.

"I had actually seen him on a café terrace in Athens in 1935 or 1936; he was with a group of people around the American counsel at that time, married to his first wife. Then, during the war, in New York, he knew some people that I knew, a rather ratty crowd of theater people. His first wife became the secretary to my best friend, John La Touche, who was the·songwriter of 'Cabin in the Sky,' and 'Taking a Chance on Love.' La Touche used to see him and say, 'Don't let him in here; that's your *husband*? Don't let him in!' "

In Tangiers, Gysin began running a cabaret called the 1001 Nights. Burroughs knew of Gysin—Tangiers was small—and had initially rushed into his art gallery, "a very agitated American, talking a mile a minute about the Amazon and being in Mexico City." Gysin and his Arab friend, Hamry, felt that because of Burroughs's having lived in Mexico, he would ally himself with the Spanish population rather than the British. "The two worlds did not mix at all." Hamry was a skilled cook, who came from a family of Moroccan musicians who lived in the hills near Jou-jouka, above Marrakech. In 1968 he and Gysin took Brian Jones, gui-tarist for the Rolling Stones, back into the hills to experience the native musical rites of Bou Jeloud, the Pan god. In December 1957, Hamry brought his relatives to Tangiers to perform at the café. "It was not a one-man café," Gysin recalls. "It was very beautiful—marble patios, sev-eral stories up to the sky, all under the stars. The first of the month, when Burroughs's money would come from Palm Beach, he would splurge by coming to my place. He became a customer, but I still didn't know him. Paul Bowles said one time, 'You really would like Burroughs very much.' "

Burroughs wrote to Ginsberg about the café opening, saying Gysin had a "troup of mountain dancing boys with hawk-like faces and narrow shoulders and bad teeth, looking rather like a bowling team from Newark."

The first real meeting of Burroughs and Gysin, friends to the end, came in Paris in 1958 in the Place St. Michel, right around the corner from what is affectionately known as the Beat Hotel. Gregory Corso had stumbled on the small pension on the Seine's Left Bank, and he had, in his inimitable way, broadcast that 9, Rue Git le Coeur would be the resting place for all travelers he knew. It is still there.

The word *git* appears in no French dictionary. Gysin says, "It is the hotel without a name. It means, 'Here Lies the Heart' or 'Shelter of the Heart'—no two people agree, but it was a shrine and there will be plaques on the walls one day." Perhaps a slang interpretation of Ginsberg's "tenderheartedness," it was where every counterculture vagabond passing through Paris ("except Kerouac—Madame Rashou wouldn't give him a room," Gysin remembers) would stay.

Gysin's paintings—a kind of visual meditation, a calligraphic chant where a similar pattern is repeated over and over—had a startling effect on Burroughs. He wrote Ginsberg in October 1958, from 9 Rue Git le Coeur:

> Brion Gysin is living next door—he is doing painting and writing.
> He regards painting as a hole in the texture of the so called 'reality'
> through which he is exploring an actual place existing in outer space.
> . . . Needless to say, no dealer will touch his work.

Burroughs began to see a relation between the kaleidoscopic imagery, repeated over and over again with minor variations in the pile of his manuscript, and Gysin's art. In late 1959 he felt he had finally stumbled on a method of communicating that could transcend conventional literature and break the antiquated "oxcart of words."

Burroughs recalls those hectic days: "Allen was instrumental in getting *Naked Lunch* published. He had sent the excerpts, finished in Tangiers in 1957, to *Chicago Review;* then *Big Table* came out of that, and Maurice Girodias of Olympia Press heard about this and wanted to publish the book. He had seen it before and thought it too disjointed. I had two weeks to get it ready. There was a pile of about six hundred pages of manuscript, some fairly well typed, and others not at all. One month later the book was on the stands. The one change that was made was that the episode with the two detectives was originally in the beginning, and we moved that to the end."

Burroughs plowed into a sequel to *Naked Lunch,* unfazed by the book's publicity, and the subsequent obscenity trials in the United States, where Norman Mailer testified, "Burroughs is in my opinion . . . a religious writer. There is a sense in *Naked Lunch* of the destruction of soul, which is more intense than any I have encountered in any other modern novel."

In early 1959 Burroughs wrote to Ginsberg:

> I enclose a sample beginning sequel to *Naked Lunch*. . . . I don't know where it's going or which will happen. . . . It is straight exploration like Gysin's paintings to which it is intimately connected . . . we are doing precisely the same thing in different mediums.

Gysin's discovery was "totally by accident," he recalls. "Burroughs was away in London at the time. I was using one of these Stanley blades, cutting a mount for a drawing, and cut through a bunch of newspapers and typewritten stuff. I cut it in slices and fixed it up. When William came back, I said, 'Look, this is something pretty funny when it's pieced together. You'll get a very special kind of laugh out of this; it'll knock you out.' And he read them—you know how he does. Most people put on their glasses to read; William takes them off. He read the thing and said, 'You got a big one here.' " Burroughs, always the nonstop writer, worked out his own version of Gysin's "cut-up" method. He would write in three vertical columns on a pad; one was dream fragments, a second was excerpts from whatever book or magazine he was reading, the third column was a collection of spontaneous images, of whatever he felt or saw at that moment. He would then type all this out, going horizontally across all three columns. Over the next several years, beginning with *Dead Fingers Talk*, written in London, he produced book after book using the technique.

"Life," says Burroughs, as he sits in Kansas with the shades still pulled, "is a cut-up. Every time you walk down the street or look out the window, your consciousness is cut by random factors. Of course, Brion said, 'Writing is fifty years behind painting,' and the painters realized that if you walk around and put what you see on canvas, you would have a jumble of fragments as seen by an individual. The cut-up is even closer than that to human perception."

Material from this phase in Burroughs's writing, or in *The Third Mind*, the book he and Gysin wrote together to explain the technique, can seem even more confusing than the literary light show of *Naked Lunch*, yet he kept at the technique all through the 1960s. Still, it is not surprising that old themes reappear in new writing.

> The boy ejaculates blood over the flower floats. Slow vine rope drops him in a phallic fountain. wire mesh cubicles against the soft inner ribs. Vast warehouse of penis and the shock threw him ten feet to smooth dirt and flak. God with erect penis spurting crystal young cruelty and foe solid. Dazzling terminal caress in silent corridors of Corn God. Erection feeling for descent in the morning sun feels the "Yes" from there by a

mirror on you stripped naked. In the city a group of them came to this last bone meal under the Hanging Tree.

"Pretty familiar."

The Priests came through the Limestone Gates playing green flutes: translucent lobster men and wild blue eyes and shells of flexible copper. A soundless vibration in the spine touched center of erection and the natives moved toward the flute notes on a stiffening blood tube for the Centipede Rites. A stone penis body straddles . . .

—William Burroughs
The Soft Machine

In actuality, the decision of where one book ended and another began was made arbitrarily: He typed continuously, while others edited and published segments pulled from the growing pile. In the 1980s, his work is more linear—an editor's decision—yet when *The Western Land* is published, parts will have already appeared in previous books, and themes are repeated from the past.

———————◇◆◇———————

THE EARLY NOTORIETY OF William Burroughs was not lost on Tim Leary, especially after he'd begun his psylocibin and LSD research at Harvard. Ironically, yet not surprisingly, Burroughs predated Leary in his own interest in LSD and peyote, repeatedly writing Ginsberg in the late 1950s to mail him peyote buttons and to look into LSD. After Ginsberg's involvement with Leary and the Harvard study, he arranged for the two to meet, but only after Tim had mailed containers of the pills (perfectly legal then) to 9 Rue Git le Coeur. In 1961, Leary flew to Tangiers and talked Burroughs into coming back to his alma mater to participate in the LSD studies on creativity.

By this time Burroughs was blossoming creatively, using stroboscopic lighting to induce altered mental states (the Flicker Project); tape recording conversations, cutting them up, and replaying them at different speeds; and taping the sounds from inside an isolation chamber. Constantly trying to find a "way out," or perhaps hoping to stumble on evidence that there was another form of evolution, he wrote an article entitled "It Belongs to the Cucumbers," in which he told of his tape discoveries: "I have gotten words and voices from barking dogs . . . words will emerge from recording of dripping faucets . . . every little breeze seems to whisper Louise." His point was that a similarity exists between patterns found in schizophrenic speech, words spoken in delirium, and the cut-up method. Furthermore, ordinary words and syntax are not sacred objects, but instead often barriers to meaning, used as a means of control. He even wrote of recordings from an isolation tank that repeated an old Latvian phrase, "Heat the bathroom; company is coming."

While both Leary and Burroughs looked forward to the research together at Harvard, the experience, as related to Ginsberg, fell short of Burroughs's expectations:

I have severed all connections with Leary and his project, which seems to me completely ill-intentioned. I soon found out they have the vaguest connection with Harvard University, that the money comes from Madame Luce, and other dubious quarters, that they have utterly no interest in any serious scientific work, no equipment other than a faulty tape recorder, and . . . that I was supposed to sell the beatniks on the mushroom. When I flatly refused to push the mushrooms but volunteered instead to work on [the strobe light] Flicker, . . . the return ticket they had promised me was immediately withdrawn. I received not one cent from Leary beyond the fare to Boston. And I hope never to set eyes on that horse's ass again. A real wrong number. . . . Well, I should have known better than to come here without a return ticket in my pocket. Whenever you hear, 'We don't think much about money on this project,' you're about to get a short count. One thing is sure, Leary isn't getting any short count. $20,000 a year plus expenses. For doing what? Pushing his pestiferous mushrooms.

As the 1960s slowly unrolled, Burroughs's ever-present sense of anger seemed to cool with his growing notoriety. All the world was interested in this thin, patrician eccentric, whose steady stream of writing never ceased to polarize the public, as well as his peers. In a well-publicized writers' conference in Edinburgh in 1962, Burroughs was publicly told by Hugh MacDiarmid, a local poet and hero, that he belonged in jail rather than on the lecture platform. The conference divided into polar camps, with both Mary McCarthy and Norman Mailer speaking out in strong support of Burroughs and his work. Though McCarthy later tried to qualify her support, Mailer sensed a reciprocal feeling of allegiance, and Burroughs says, "I did sense some kinship because of 'The White Negro.' I thought of him as an ally, a friend."

Burroughs, spending most of his time in London, evolved into a cult figure and a sort of muse to rock musicians. The Rolling Stones and Beatles sought out Burroughs. Steely Dan drew its name from *Naked Lunch,* and the term *heavy metal* was used in *Nova Express* to describe the feeling one gets near the terminal stages of addiction.

In discussing the 1960s, Burroughs is careful to qualify his position as that of an outsider, having spent most of the decade abroad. When he mentions "changes," one gets the impression that perhaps just as his anger toward Leary has now turned into friendship, society itself has become a place into which he can fit with less discomfort. It seems that he has been marking time, waiting impatiently for the rest of the world to catch up to him, yet pleased that he is in the lead.

However evolutionary the 1960s were, they fell short of Burroughs's expectations. "We haven't seen any evolutionary changes yet. I am talking about biological changes. We are in a state of arrested evolution. We are not content to remain in this condition any more than a tadpole is content to remain a tadpole. We hope we are working toward a biolog-ical change, and certainly any steps in the direction of increased aware-ness and increased freedom make it an atmosphere in which this can occur. Obviously one direction that evolution would take is emancipa-tion from a very awkward artifact—the human body.

"Still, most of the objectives set forth in the 1960s have been real-ized. People don't seem to realize this when they say to me, 'Do you think the 1960s accomplished anything?' I say WHAT?! They don't seem to realize that forty years ago, four-letter words did not appear on printed pages; that when I was in my twenties and thirties, the idea that a Mex-ican or a black or a queer was anything but a second-class citizen was simply absurd. These were tremendous changes. Then, of course, the end of censorship. The 1960s gave us rock music, and this led to mass meet-ings like Woodstock. It was so different from jazz, being played to very small audiences—a rather terrific factor for social change. You have so many people feeling the same thing at the same time, leading to a feeling of communion.

"Also in the 1960s were changes you don't talk about, like homosex-uality and drug addiction—they became household terms. *Junkie* is now a household word—it sure wasn't forty years ago—and neither was *ho-mosexual*, so that is important.

"There were so many benchmark events . . . Woodstock, Altamont, and the whole acid-culture phenomenon; the Brotherhood of Eternal Love, and Leary and Alpert, and Billy Hitchcock. The attention to East-ern religions. And Kesey's book is important. I first met him at a reading in Eugene some years ago. But as to why these things happened just when they did, I don't think that you'll find an answer."

WHEN BURROUGHS RETURNED TO the States, the 1960s were over. His father had died in Palm Beach in the early 1960s, and his mother, growing increasingly senile in a Saint Louis nursing home, died in 1972. In his mother's will, dated 1965, a sum of ten thousand dollars was left outright to Burroughs, and the same amount to his older brother Mortimer, Jr. The remainder of the estate was also left to the older brother, "not for his own use and benefit, but IN TRUST for my grand-son, WILLIAM BURROUGHS, JR." Laura Lee Burroughs also wrote that her grandson "has resided with my late husband, Mortimer Burroughs, and me for the past many years and he has no other home. This has become a source of constant concern to me." She asked that upon her death, her sons provide a pleasant home for Willy.

After his mother's death in Mexico City when he was four, William S. Burroughs, Jr., was taken to Saint Louis and left by his father to be raised by his grandparents. His father sent him masks from Africa and shrunken heads from the Amazon; Willy collected and kept them all. He saw his father three times in the next ten years; then, when he was fourteen, in 1961, his father asked him to come and live in Tangiers. He did, but didn't really feel comfortable in his father's social circle of "aging faggots with strange accents." Besides, he had developed a serious drug habit of his own, and the place where he knew how to support it best was home, in Palm Beach. Not surprisingly, Willy, the boy whose "mother's milk was laced with speed," was an amphetamine addict. He used to steal prescription pads from doctor's offices and write his own orders for Desoxyn and Dilaudid. In so many ways—being caught forging prescriptions, being sent to the same federal narcotics hospital in Lexington, Kentucky, for detoxification, and writing an autobiographical narrative of his addiction, *Speed*—his life seemed an incredible carbon copy of his father's.

Yet Burroughs does not see it that way at all. "I didn't get any feelings of *déjà vu*" he says. "His experience was really quite different from mine, and in his work no one would say he was influenced by my work." Burroughs also sees no comparison between his first book, *Junkie*, and his son's book, *Speed*. "There aren't any similarities that I can make out. In the first place he is dealing with a whole different kind of addiction, a whole different use of drugs. Speed has nothing to do with junk—just the opposite. The whole context he is talking about is something from the 1960s, but not from my experience at all."

Willy pleaded guilty to violation of barbiturate laws in 1966 and was sentenced to four years' probation. Burroughs came back for the trial, and he and Willy were taken to meet the probation officer, whose name, Mr. Panos, was sloppily pronounced during introductions. Willy later recalled his father, "a long, yellow-toothed junkie, radiating Amazon headwaters and New York jazz scenes," whining in amazement, "Did you say Mr. *Penis!?*"

When Burroughs came back to the United States for good, he and Willy settled in Boulder, Colorado, where Allen Ginsberg runs the Naropa Institute's Jack Kerouac School for Disembodied Poetics every summer. By that time, Willy was an alcoholic drug addict who had had a liver transplant; his life expectancy was uncertain, since his had been one of the first such operations. He can be seen in his father's autobiographical movie, showing the cameraman an eyeless stuffed lamb he had rescued from a trash heap, saying, "I like the symbolism."

Willy was short, unkempt, and pudgy from the steroids used to maintain his liver transplant. He had a large tattoo on his right forearm from his salmon-fishing days in Alaska. He usually wore Levi's, a rope-braid bracelet, a single earring, long sideburns, and a trucker's cap. His physical appearance, husky voice, and southern accent were as different from his father's as can be imagined.

By his early thirties he had written an autobiographical trilogy—as if he knew his days were numbered. Some of his writing is crisp, lively in detail, and vivid; some of it captures the tearful loneliness of Kerouac. He became a gentle, familiar figure on the streets of Boulder and gave some moving poetry readings at the 1979 Naropa Institute Conference.

Willy tested his father constantly—giving away his money to panhandlers; bringing dogs on trips to the mountains, though he knew Burroughs's dislike of dogs; saying, "Hi, Mom," when asked by an Italian interviewer what it was like to be the son of a famous father. He died in 1981, at thirty-four, of a massive rejection of the foreign organ. Burroughs comments drily that "he lived five years after the liver transplant. Apparently the record is fourteen years, but that is very rare."

The year Burroughs returned to the United States, he met his current companion, James Grauerholtz. Grauerholtz read *Naked Lunch* at the age of fourteen and decided he had to meet the author. "I thought I was the only person in Kansas to think about having sex with alien boys," he recalls. Now he screens everyone who comes to interview Burroughs and is openly protective of him, accompanying him on all tours, walking him about the house. Life seems easier now for Burroughs; the dark memories, the years of running from the law, and his addiction are behind him. He has a six-book contract with Holt, Rinehart and Winston, which will assuredly keep his pockets lined, his editors busy, and his public entertained. Age does not seem to concern him much. When asked about his own mortality, he methodically states, "Well, time is running out, of course. But there is no such thing as 'essence' of time. I've said again and again, you aren't your body any more than a pilot is the plane. The body is a complex series of magnetic grids, which certainly could survive physical death.

"What is not a possibility," he growls, "is utopia. It's not a possibility at all; it isn't even necessarily desirable. A well-run, perfectly run society is a dead society. The 1960s stuff about solving world problems through peace and love and nonviolence—I said then that the only way to give flowers to police was in a pot from a high window. The idea that we can all learn to love each other is *booolshit,* plain and simple!"

———◇◆◇———

BEFORE LEAVING BURROUGHS AND Kansas, I ask if I can take his picture. He agrees and stands up for only the third time all day, walking his earth-shoe shuffle, his left shoulder wizened and lower than the right, looking for a suitable backdrop. "For Christ's sake, not in front of the typewriter," he snarls softly. We decide on his sunny backyard, and he walks slowly through the house, pointing out some of his artwork. One large piece was a joint effort with Robert Rauschenberg, a signed and numbered lithograph with "Burroughs" in raised, white-on-white letters along the bottom border. It was a piece of art that might well sell for ten times the value of the building housing it. "And that was done by Brion Gysin, in 1958," he says, pointing to an India-ink design on another wall.

As I follow him out the back door, something shiny and copper-colored sparkles on the lone oval carpet. Perhaps a pencil sharpener, I think, and reach down to pick it up and give it to Burroughs. My hand and mouth open, then close quickly; I put the unfired .22 cartridge into my pocket, a tiny souvenir. Piled high on a nearby chair are used handgun targets, none with holes very far from dead center.

In the sunlight of a late May afternoon, Burroughs's backyard is alive with dancing yellows and greens, filtered through some shade trees. He does his best at posing, simply standing straight and motionless, making no attempts to straighten his thin hair or hide the large cigarette burn in his shirtfront. Through the lens of my camera, I can see he is having considerable difficulty trying to smile. The right side of his mouth twitches upward randomly, then quickly drops down.

Once the trite formality of picture taking is over, he seems to drop all his intellectualizing. Walking me through the house to my car, he stops next to a large piece of barn board leaning against a table scattered with the Sunday *New York Times* and copies of *Gun Digest.*

"And here is some artwork of my own," he says. "A little different." He has taken a tube of yellow and a tube of blue oil paint, pinned each to the board, and blasted them with a small-gauge shotgun. "Hit 'em dead center at twenty feet. See on the back where the shot came through?" He turns the board again. It looks like the aftermath of a Technicolor termite attack.

Standing by my car, knowing my airplane connections were going to be tight, Burroughs seems to hover, in a sad, lost-child kind of way. Like a kid who doesn't want his dad to leave on a business trip, he asks questions of me for the first time all day. "You'll be seeing Tim in Los Angeles?" he asks rhetorically, slowly adding, "I only see him out there—I'd enjoy seeing him more often. He always cheers you up." A shadow of a smile comes and goes. "And what about Hunter?" he asks, as if he and I were a part of a small gathering of aged relatives. "I was to see him when I was doing a lecture in Aspen, but it seemed he had just fallen off his motorcycle. Busted a leg or something."

Burroughs continues, more relaxed than he has been all day, standing beside a porcelain buffalo nearly hidden in the unmowed grass of his small, picket-fenced lawn. "It was given to me by Edie Kerouac. You know, Jack's first wife, Joan's roommate," he adds, as if I, too, had hung out around Columbia in the 1940s. He asks a few more questions about who I'd be seeing and if he knew anyone in Chicago I might talk with. He hovers, as if he wants very much to break free, to be a vagabond again, riding the jet stream, where planes cut white contrails in the blue sky overhead, flying to distant cities, meeting old friends and new people. Yet he knows he is here to stay, rooted in Kansas. As I drive off, he stands next to the ceramic buffalo, one hand in his khaki, army-navy-store pants, the other waving good-bye, like an old soldier saluting the new brigade.

The Beat Goes On

I STEP OUT OF City Lights and onto Columbus Street. North Beach, San Francisco. Fifty years ago the Italian population here used to fill the street in front of A. Cavilli and Company, a bookstore a block or so away, to hear broadcasts of Mussolini's speeches. It was a meeting place for displaced Italian anarchists. Within twenty years it became a meeting place for displaced American anarchists; Café Vesuvio replaced A. Cavilli, and the world's first all-paperback bookstore opened across Adler Alley on the same side of Columbus Street in 1953. The bookstore, named after Charlie Chaplin's man-against-the-machine movie *City Lights*, began by selling Italian anarchist newspapers (*L'Adunata* and *L'Umanità Nova*), and was originally intended to support the publishing of an early avant-garde culture magazine. The magazine, also called *City Lights*, published Pauline Kael's first film criticism and lasted about a year; the original owner went to New York and left the store to Lawrence Ferlinghetti. He began publishing the poetry of a group that became known as the San Francisco Renaissance. It included Michael McClure, Lenore Kandel, Kenneth Rexroth, Gary Snyder, Philip Whalen, Gregory Corso, and Jack Kerouac. But it was the publication of a single poem, by a transplanted New Yorker, that really put City Lights and the San Francisco Beat scene on the map. The poem was *Howl*. The poet was Allen Ginsberg.

Ginsberg: Take One

ALLEN GINSBERG ARRIVED IN San Francisco in 1953. He was twenty-seven years old, with thirty dollars in his pocket, a reputation for good work in the market-research industry, and a letter of introduction from William Carlos Williams to the informal "dean" of the North Beach poets, Kenneth Rexroth. No one on the West Coast had ever heard of him except Neal Cassady, then living in San Jose.

There were still a few years remaining before the wave of vulgar commercialism hit; before Café Vesuvio hired "Hube the Cube" Leslie to sit and look "Beat" in their window, before Carol Doda (still across the street at the Condor) stuffed handfuls of silicon in her breasts and gave new meaning to the term "Grand Tetons." Before all this, Allen Ginsberg met Robert LaVigne, a North Beach artist, whose life-size nude painting of Peter Orlovsky hung in his living room. Ginsberg was mesmerized. Orlovsky, who was living with LaVigne, was then a twenty-one-year-old sophomore at a local junior college. He walked into the room where LaVigne and Allen were admiring his painting, carrying his school books under his arm. Little more than a year later, he left LaVigne for Ginsberg.

As the relationship evolved, it turned out the two had a lot in common. Orlovsky's father had been born in Russia, as was Ginsberg's mother, Naomi. Both Allen's mother and one of Peter's brothers were in mental institutions. But the core of the relationship transcended that; late in 1954, drinking wine in Foster's cafeteria, the two made a vow that each owned the other's body and soul. It gave Allen a sense of belonging that anchored him and allowed his creativity to flourish. The two stayed together for thirty years, until 1985.

LATE IN THE WINTER of 1982 at Passim's in Harvard Square, Ginsberg and Orlovsky were to perform. Ginsberg's secretary had written, saying that Allen would be unable to talk with me for any length of time. I decided to attend the performance regardless, out of curiosity as much as anything.

The last poetry reading I had attended was on a Friday afternoon in the mid-1960s in the living room of my fraternity house in Berkeley. One of the Sig Eps, Dave Vandevere, had somehow gotten a contraband copy of Lenore Kandel's *The Love Book*. To this day, I am not sure how to interpret the writing, but if poetry is intended to expand the consciousness and raise the general level of emotion, then Lenore Kandel proved a master.

Dave stood on a chair in the center of a crowd of about forty guys; his delivery was clear and moving. When he hit the memorable line, "I feel your cock growing strong like a tree in my hand," no potted palm in sight was safe. Hoots and chants of "strong like a tree . . . strong like a tree . . ." reverberated, as forty hormone-driven adolescents grabbed anything with a stem and stomped around the room. At the time I passed off the rather primitive ambiance of that poetry reading to hormonal excess, lack of sexual success, and the general Zeitgeist of a college-fraternity, beer-commercial mentality.

On my way to Passim's, over streets more safely navigated by Hans Brinker, my expectations were that over the past two decades *something* had matured, be it my tastes or poetry itself.

The crowd only half-fills Passim's, but I attribute it to the weather conditions rather than to a waning of Ginsberg's popularity. The audience is mixed. The long-haired, bearded, and denimed people wearing L. L. Bean plaid shirts are older—my age—and clearly have been part of the 1960s, if only by birthdate. The remainder of the crowd is mid-1980s prep.

A handful of young students, all of whom seem to know each other, are discussing who has stolen the last copy of *Howl* from the library. They are all jokingly trying to guess the guilty party, as though playing Clue. Their professor had assigned *Howl* as required reading, just as he had assigned their attendance at Passim's. *Ginsberg Live* was part of the course, like visiting the USS *Constitution* for history class or spending a day at Peabody Museum looking at pre-Columbian basket weaving for Anthro 1-A.

One student relates a tale of two class members who couldn't attend the *Ginsberg Live* show because they have "pulled an all-nighter playing

a Pac-Man marathon—last one awake wins, no matter how many points"—
and both are somewhere sleeping off their efforts. They think it was
Monty who had won, "because he's in such *super* shape, like, he jogs
and only eats fish."

The older crowd discusses a lot of current social issues—the Miskito
Indians and Sandinistas—but education is the hot topic. "It's just that if
you look around the country, the public schools are not good. The place
for alternative education is—right now—in the home, especially for single parents.

"But I don't think it'll be a permanent thing—kids will *reinvent* schools
later on just 'cause they wanna get together."

"I want to start a high school, but it takes money, a lot of money.
But I know some friends in management at Digital, and they are really
behind this—like, in a financial way, too."

The voices go on, and then the door blows open and, along with a
lot of cold air, in comes Allen Ginsberg, Peter Orlovsky, and a young
man who looks a lot like a midget John Denver. Conversations die down,
and everyone wanders to their metal folding chairs, and endures some
ear-piercing feedback and electronic crackle as Ginsberg twiddles with
the microphone, Orlovsky tunes his banjo, and "John Denver" strums
his guitar.

Ginsberg is wearing a navy blazer, white, button-down-collar dress
shirt and rep tie, gray slacks about four inches too long, and a pair of
Dr. Scholl's cloth slippers. From the fifth row of a tiny coffeehouse-
turned-auditorium, it is easy to see that Ginsberg's right eye isn't so much
"shifty," it's just that it doesn't open all the way, especially in contrast
to his left eye, which is round as an *Om.*

Ginsberg takes off his blazer, revealing a Buddhist design that looks
like a four-bladed propeller the size of a small dinner plate, hand-sewn
on the right side of his broadcloth shirt. An Allen Ginsberg designer
shirt? It doesn't seem to make much sense, but after all, he is a Jewish
Buddhist.

Orlovsky, on the other hand, with his ambling walk, his long ponytail, the way he stares dimly and emotionlessly into the lights, even the
way he yawns and picks his nose with no sense of anyone else being
around him, seems to be playing the more traditional "rustic poet" role.

The two of them light into a banjo- and harmonica-accompanied
version of "Airplane Blues," which is an ironic piece about flying from
Denver's smog to New York's smog. Some of it went like this:

> The sun's not eternal
> that's why there's the moon. . . .
>
> Poets full of hatred
> Will outlast any age.

At the end of this ecological hummer, Orlovsky pours some black coffee and begins to smoke. Is it a subtle sideshow with its own message? Poets can be tough to figure.

The kids from the English class are attentive and taking notes. The older group just sits there blankly, as if their attendance were also mandatory, on orders from a more distant professor.

Ginsberg then sings "Birdbrain," which is a handy little antigovernment song composed in such a way that when administrations in Washington change, the lyrics can be altered accordingly, without damage to structure or content. Sing it just right and all the presidents' names come out as two syllables: *Rea*-gan, *Car*-ter, *Fo*-ord, *Nix*-on, *John*-son, *Kenn*-edy. When you get to Eisenhower you run up against a poetic brick wall, but, what the hell, that's old stuff.

Ginsberg's lyrics pick at society's shortcomings—the mistakes, the childishness, the foolishness, the lies. If the audience is expecting a hint of a solution, none is offered.

As he sings and chants, he seems to come alive. His eyes get fiery, and his words come out with a kind of energy that is his very own. He has a deep and full voice, an arresting delivery. His material is the *New York Times* put to music: the destruction of the Amazon . . . . terrorism in Argentina . . . CIA ploys . . . Nicaragua . . . Russian pogroms . . . more Nicaragua. (If we are to believe Ginsberg, Central America is destined to be the Vietnam of the 1980s.)

All of this comes out with a polished professionalism that supersedes spontaneity. The subtle asides, the jokes, are so well rehearsed, and executed with such finesse that at times I feel as though I'm watching the poetic version of a Vegas lounge act. Ginsberg even gets in a plug for his meditation teacher, who will be in town next week.

At break time, I find Ginsberg at the back of Passim's, surrounded by a small number of people handing him books and requesting his autograph. As the admirers scurry off to pick up fliers about the twenty-fifth anniversary party for the publishing of *On the Road* and application forms for Naropa, I introduce myself to Ginsberg. He looks at me, a bit puzzled, until I mention that he and I had corresponded and that Tim Leary had suggested I contact him.

The conversation is brief and uninformative. "How did you meet Tim? . . . How did you get into this writing project? . . . When did you see him last? . . . Where did you go to school? . . ." Orlovsky walks over, shakes my hand with no introduction (no words at all), and walks away, pulling on his ponytail and straightening his taxi-driver hat.

It is time for the second act, and Ginsberg has made it obvious he has little time or inclination to talk. "Maybe in New York. Drop me a line," he says.

After Ginsberg's sociopolitical chants, Orlovsky's off-the-wall poems almost seem a relief. He pounds away, his banjo moving like a woodsman's axe, his ponytail swaying, and his thick, fleshy lips producing a voice that sounds like it was strained through a gravel quarry. He works up a lather, seeming to go into a trance state, as he recites "America's Shit," which is basically a day in the life of a turd. It starts out at Peter and Allen's commune west of Albany, New York, and ends up floating gracefully down the Hudson, past the United Nations (which involves some literary license to get from the Hudson River through the Spuyten Duyvil to the East River), and finally past the Statue of Liberty and out to sea. A cute little scatological travelogue.

Orlovsky brings it up-tempo for his next piece. With booted foot stomping out the rhythm, he and Allen belt out, "You are my dildo, my only dildo—you make me happy when skies are gray," and the two exchange little conspiratorial smirks in between refrains.

The final *pièce de résistance* is Orlovsky's *a capella* rendition of "Good Fuck with Denise." There are no conspiratorial smirks exchanged during this one—actually Orlovsky's trance state has gone one step deeper. He recites, standing stage front, eyes closed, his head back as if Denise's memory is up in the rafter someplace. The audience seems equally displaced; the show ends, and there are no demands for an encore. But it is obvious that to much of the milling crowd, beginning to bundle up for the ice storm outside, the whole show has been an encore, a trip back to a fondly remembered time.

Ginsberg: Take Two:
Rantings in Orono

IT IS THE LONGEST day of summer in Orono, Maine. The woods are filled with bears, the streams are filled with trout, the air is filled with black flies, and my motel is filled with . . . poets!?

The Ezra Pound Centennial Conference is being held at the University of Maine. The reason for my being here is that five days ago Allen Ginsberg wrote me a note with a conference brochure enclosed saying, "Dear POW—I'm overwhelmed by work . . . can't make dates other than those enclosed—Allen G."

All this came on the heels of a Mailgram I sent him, asking for about the fifth time in the last two years if he would be in New York and available to talk. I had reason to be there on very short notice and thought there might be an outside chance . . .

Ginsberg responded to my Mailgram by phoning and asking, "What do you want to talk about?" I reminded him of my project. We talked about our respective publishing deadlines, and he said, "It'll have to be either just before or just after I go to teach the summer course at Naropa in Boulder, Colorado." That was fine with me, and we left it that I'd Mailgram him again later on. I then proceeded with a fumbling attempt to make small talk. It turned out the topic I had chosen for amiable patter was not "small," nor did it result in "talk."

Nearly a year earlier, during my visit with Brion Gysin in Paris, Gysin had been expansive and entertaining, a great source of information about the old times in Tangiers and Paris. He interrupted his comments only to play his new antidrug rock-and-roll rap record. It used the "cut-up" style—randomly placed words to express a single concept: "Junk is no good baby; good junk is no baby; no baby is good junk; is baby junk good no; baby is junk no good . . ." and on and on, all to the accompaniment of two African percussionists. Gysin danced madly, in a state of obvious enjoyment over having bridged the gap between his art and music.

In seeming contrast to this message, whenever things got slow, he would grab some rolling papers and stuff them full of some mind-numbing Moroccan hash that looked like miniature camel turds. At the very end of our visit, he said, "Before you go, I must read this to you. I'll give you the great privilege of being the first person to listen to my encomium: 'My encomium for Allen Ginsberg,' " he began . . .

He read with conviction and warmth, especially in his description of how Allen had magically calmed an angry mob in Italy by intoning a pacifying "Om" amid fistfights and flying beer bottles.

"I haven't heard from *him* yet on the subject—whether he likes it or not. I said I was trying to keep it lighthearted, but that's what I feel about him," Brion said, adding that he had sent the encomium a while back and was expecting some feedback from Allen.

I mentioned this to Ginsberg on the phone, saying, "Mr. Gysin read me his encomium for you. It certainly was well composed and heartfelt, don't you agree?" Unwittingly, I unleashed a verbal onslaught the likes of which I have not heard since I phoned my father and asked if I could skip classes at Berkeley to fly home for my birthday party.

"I do not want to hear about it," Ginsberg raved. For the first of what was to be many times, he shouted into my unsuspecting ear, *"You don't understand! You don't understand!"* Still foaming and fussing, he proceeded to tell me that whatever Brion had sent was for a "festriche": "It's sort of like a literary surprise party. Ask one of your literary friends what it means," he added. I continued bumbling, since I was certain anything Gysin would read into my tape recorder and that had been sent directly to Ginsberg a year before could hardly be much of a surprise.

"Allen, I don't think that we're talking about the same thing. Brion read this to me after he sent it over a year ago."

Whammo! The phone lit up like the White House hot line on the first day of World War III. *"You don't understand! I just told you! You don't understand!* It's for a *festriche.* Get a German dictionary or ask a literary friend [i.e., you dumbshit]." Enough was enough, and I signed off with Ginsberg still sputtering about deadlines and saying that he "wasn't like Tim—I only have two hands and one brain . . ."

The next day I found *festschrift* in *Webster's Unabridged* and discovered that it is "learned essays contributed by students, colleagues, and admirers to honor a scholar on a special anniversary."

Oh.

————————◇◆◇————————

BEFORE LEAVING FOR ORONO I had phoned the motel and left a message for Allen, telling him when I was arriving and asking for a convenient time to talk. On my arrival, I left another note and found out that I was staying in the room between Ginsberg and Olga Rudge, who, the desk clerk informed me, was Ezra Pound's widow. I found that somewhat surprising, since I knew this conference marked the centennial of Pound's birth. Olga Rudge had to be very, very old or a mail-order bride, or both. Later research uncovered that although never legally married, Olga Rudge was Pound's long-time mistress and mother of their son, Omar. She is considered the last living link to the past, since Pound's death in 1973 marked the end of the Modernist poetry period.

That night I bought a huge pizza and a six-pack and tried to find *Miami Vice* on TV while waiting out Ginsberg. I even went so far as to prop a matchstick against the foot of his door to determine if he ever came in or not. He did, late and alone. In my anger at his never contacting me, I contemplated hammering the wall adjoining our rooms until the cheap Utrillo print fell off onto his balding head. I stopped short of theatrics, having developed a warm spot in my heart for the ninety-seven-year-old Olga, who was trying to sleep in the room on the *other* side of me. I had seen her that afternoon in her sunglasses and platinum-white page boy—all four feet eleven inches of her doddering across the motel lobby. She was frail and old, and no doubt needed her sleep. Here I was in some strange reality sandwich, in between two icons of twentieth-century American poetry, not knowing enough to speak intelligently to one and being silently rebuffed by the other.

The next morning I showed up early for the conference's last day and found a couple of visiting poetry professors to talk with before things got rolling. The conference was being held in Nutting Hall, whose name captures perfectly the extent of my knowledge of poetry in general and Ezra Pound in particular. The boundaries of my poetic wisdom are just on the far side of "Casey at the Bat" and certainly far this side of Pound's *Cantos*. I viewed the day as an excellent opportunity for diving in way over my head.

Nutting Hall houses the University of Maine's forestry department, which is analogous to the computer science department at Berkeley or the petroleum engineering department at the University of Texas. In a part of the world known for its inhospitable winters—most buildings on campus are brick—this one is wood. Its foyer is adorned with prizes from intercollegiate competition. Trophy cases are stuffed with plaques etched with, "First Place—Women's Logrolling," and "Men's Bucksawing." Some beautiful, even poetic, wood sculptures were being used by the gathering professors to put coffee cups and elbows on. I approached one woman, who told me she had been teaching poetry at the University of Utah for thirty years. I asked her what her students thought of Ginsberg. "Well, they're very consistent in that, at first, they think he's a complete fraud. You know, just jumping on any political bandwagon that comes along to keep his name current. Then, after a while, if they read him carefully, or especially if they hear him or his recordings, they realize he does have his own voice. But basically he *is* derivative."

Reaching back and grabbing for all I had, I said, "You mean in the same continuum as Whitman and William Carlos Williams?"

"Yes, yes in that stream; he is derivative in that sense. But you have to understand," she added proudly, "I am, above all else, a Poundian." (Later, I overheard the same woman saying she worked for an investment firm in Salt Lake City during the day and taught at night, thereby making her a half-Poundian in my analysis.)

I spoke with another professor, from Scripps College. "My students see Allen Ginsberg as dated, representing an era, very much a period poet. They are interested in him for the same reason they all went to see *The Big Chill,* and I agree, but you have to understand above all else, I am a Poundian."

Wandering off to hear three "Poundian" papers, I found myself thinking about just what the role of a poet in twentieth-century society should be. One paper I listened to discussed Pound's *Cantos* 68, which consists of excerpts taken from John Adams's eighteenth-century treatise on government, which in turn quotes dozens of other writers. Pound put this together in the form of alternating arguments, to express the theme of balance in government. A sort of combination of political science and word salad, it is incredibly demanding of the reader, forcing him to go back and read the original text by Adams before an ounce of sense can be made of Pound. One begins to appreciate the devotion of these "Poundians" and to appreciate also our culture for understanding and accepting them. After all, iambic pentameter will never cure cancer.

As the last paper was drawing to a close, Ginsberg slipped in and sat down across the room, causing a few heads to turn, but no disruption.

Reflecting on the political nature of much of Pound's writing, I harkened back to my very first encounter with Ginsberg.

It was spring of 1965 at Berkeley and I was on my way to an early-morning class, passing the corner of the Student Union Building closest to Sproul Hall. Allen Ginsberg and Art Goldberg, a leader in the second round of the Free Speech Movement—the Filthy Speech Movement—were standing side by side facing Sproul Hall Plaza, which was filled with passing students, shouting at the top of their lungs, "*Fuck . . . shit . . . cunt . . . cock . . . shit . . . fuck . . .*" They each had a megaphone, and it was a truly ludicrous scene, like two cheerleaders for the campus porno debate team. This was not the Free Speech Movement at its best.

I walked over to Ginsberg and shouted, "What kind of poetry is this, Mr. Ginsberg?" There was absolutely no response as he and Goldberg kept up their chanting. He seemed obsessed, unaware of his lack of an interested audience, save me; I shrugged my shoulders and went off to class, genuinely puzzled.

At the end of the last session—a paper on recent critics of Pound—I went over to Ginsberg, who was surrounded by a half dozen people, each with a copy of his recently published *Collected Poetry*. He was dutifully sketching stars and third eyes and signing his name, like any movie star or sports celebrity. When the small crowd dispersed, I introduced myself, carefully enunciating my name while shaking his hand.

"Who are you?" he snapped, with a tone that seemed to say, "I thought I just got rid of the last of these sons of bitches, and here comes another one." He had no recollection of me or my name whatsoever.

"I got your notes, but I thought you were someone Michael had invited." He half-pointed at a youthful-looking figure gazing our way with a smile, his chin in his hands. Michael was his administrative assistant.

"I don't know you and I don't have the *slightest* idea who you are. Who are you?" He peered at me, his right eye squinting even more than usual and his left eye as wide as the ones he had just been sketching. I curbed a lot of impulses and didn't say what I really wanted to say. Instead I reminded him of our half-hour meeting at Passim's, our infamous "festriche" phone conversation, my association with Tim Leary, and his letter to me of a few days ago informing me of this Ezra Pound conference.

Déjà vu settled over me like sudden seasickness. *"You don't understand,"* he shouted angrily. "I can't remember anything! I don't remember people because I meet thirty new people a day. I don't know what day it is, what time it is, or sometimes where I am!!" All this was not spoken *sotto voce*, by any means. It was a minor theatrical production with shouting, flying spittle, and hands poking holes in the sky and pointing at nonexistent objects. My self-introduction had, in an instant, turned him into a raving madman.

"You don't understand" came down the pipe again, and by God he was right, I didn't understand, and I was beginning to get a rolling start at feeling pissed off.

"I have so many demands placed on me!!"

I muttered something in agreement about pressures of publishing contracts, and he shouted back, loudly enough so that a handful of English professors thirty yards away spun around in their Hush Puppies. *"You don't understand. I just told you—I can't remember all the people I meet. My God! The only thing I can remember is who I'm sleeping with!"*

It seemed clear that Ginsberg was not going to be interviewed by someone he did not know. The thought suddenly came to me that the most direct path to Allen Ginsberg was a straight shot to the ego, which seemed a tough target to miss if it would only stand still for a moment.

"You know, Allen," I began, with a voice full of nostalgia, "Hunter

Thompson told me about your organizing the Vietnam Day March in Berkeley. . . . 'That Allen Ginsberg, he has a heart of gold,' Hunter said." Immediately Ginsberg's head dropped, and his beard sank into his chest as if he'd suffered an acute attack of narcolepsy. He stood there, head hung low, then slowly lifted his gaze to about the level of my kneecaps and said very quietly, very peacefully, and very slowly, "Hunter . . . Hunter. How is he these days?"

I began to tell him that Hunter was last seen driving off into the jaws of a rogue tornado in the Florida Keys, but then I noticed that Ginsberg wasn't even listening. He seemed lost in time, as if the memories of twenty years past—all the odors and sounds and sensations—were overwhelming his consciousness. I think if I could have magically produced some finger cymbals and a joint, I could have gotten my interview right then and there.

From this state of semireverie, Allen decided that we should talk in November. He told me about some papers in his own private collection at Columbia that I should see and that he would write me a letter for access. He was helpful, even gracious, and gave me his New York City phone number to call for the letter.

I shook his hand, held my arms out to the side, stepped back one large step, and asked, "In November will you remember who I am?"

I was close enough to the door to slip outside and fade into the crowd, just as the final chorus began. *"I just told you . . . don't you understand? . . . I can't remember."*

Take Three:
Ginsberg's World

GOING TO MEET WITH Allen Ginsberg at his East Village apartment, a few weeks after Orono, it seemed a wise idea to pull out all the stops—to wear the same yellow flower-print aloha shirt, the same Levi's, and the same white Astroturf shoes with the pink-and-blue shoe laces. "If he doesn't recognize me," I thought, "maybe he'll remember my tasteful outfit."

Entry to Ginsberg's is a rite. Many total strangers come by, having found the address through the underground grapevine, but you have to know the rules to get in. Ginsberg needs peace and quiet and safety in the middle of this noisy and carnivorous city. He has been mugged here before. On the Lower East Side, in the 1980s, a small, bespectacled Jewish man is a minority and possibly an endangered species.

The buildings were not well kept up. A couple of tall black women in black leather and black high heels slid by. On this warm summer morning, blacks and Hispanics milled around on the sidewalk aimlessly, passing brown paper bags, shouting across the street in *linguache* or patois.

Walking south on First Avenue, I passed three pudgy Hispanic men, each wearing football jerseys and camouflage pants—sort of like a little Sandinista intramural squad, only with bottles tucked under their arms instead of balls. A fourth approached as I walked by, toward the corner. They were overjoyed to see him, speaking in excited Spanish, as they swarmed around him on unsure legs, looking through glazed eyes.

143

I turned the corner and suddenly, in two steps, the teeming streets of San Juan or Havana seemed far away. On the north side of the street were old apartment buildings, a few warehouses, and the Sisters of Salesia Convent. On the south side was Public School 60, which was being refurbished. Directly across from Ginsberg's was a large Roman Catholic Church. It was eleven o'clock, and the church carillon was filling the otherwise silent and empty street with peals of metallic sound. The reverberation made it seem as though every window, doorway, and garage were ringing its own little bell.

As the last echo was slowly replaced by the distant sounds of First Avenue, I began the standard operating procedure for entry to Allen's. I had phoned ahead, which was step one, giving my approximate arrival time. Step two was planting my feet in the middle of the street, tilting my head back, cupping my hands, and shouting, "Al-len . . . Al-len . . ."

Pop! Like a beatnik cuckoo clock, out shot his balding head. "I'll drop you the key," he said. "You know it's Apartment Twenty-three."

Four stories above, Allen held out his hand and dropped what appeared to be an old, navy-blue sock. Inside it was a key. Climbing clockwise, I reached Apartment 23 and was confronted with three different locks. While I was fumbling helplessly, the door sort of fell open, and Allen Ginsberg appeared, saying, "Let me spare you the trouble. The key doesn't work, and besides, the door isn't locked."

Figuring that step four in the Standard Operating Procedure was a response to this little Zen koan, I said, "Of course. That's why there are so many."

Allen seemed pleased that at least my intellect was capable of a little Oriental mind-gaming. His voice and general demeanor were so orthogonally different from what I'd experienced at Orono that I was caught off guard. I suspected that Ginsberg thought I had come to do some work with his secretary, Bob Rosenthal, and had not the slightest idea who I was. Following him down the hallway and into the kitchen, I noticed that he walked as if there were little suction cups on the bottom of his slippers requiring him to exert an extra amount of lift. If he were a marionette, you would guess that the person pulling the strings had bad arthritic hands.

Allen has lived and worked here since 1975, when he hired his chief of staff Bob Rosenthal, who was living next door with his wife and knew of the vacancy. It is one of those great, indestructible brick-and-wood walk-ups, with fourteen-foot ceilings and plenty of wall space for hanging posters, pots and pans, and bookshelves.

He leads me into the kitchen. A butcher-block table serves as the epicenter of activity. There is a gas stove and a wall hung with heavy

cast-iron pots and pans. Across the room is a sink and long wooden shelf with cupboards above. Ginsberg's muses are in this room. Over the doorway to the hall is a poster of Rimbaud. On another wall, peeking over the top of a large box of Wheaties (breakfast of champion poets) is a full-bearded Walt Whitman. There is also a framed, official NASA photograph of the space shuttle, poised on its launch pad, with a comforting full moon in the background. If you take the photo out of its frame, you see that there is a poem written on the back—a poem to Allen Ginsberg from a NASA astronaut; that ends with the line: "The weight of the world is not love but hate."

Allen did not show me the photo or the poem—Harry Smith did. I was introduced to Harry in the kitchen, just as Bob Rosenthal shouted out from the adjoining room that Allen was wanted on the phone.

Ginsberg took me by surprise when he told Harry, in detail, my name and why I was there. (This lent considerable credence to the aloha-shirt theory of cognitive recall.) At first glance, Harry Smith looks like just another face in the mission soup line. His broken, horn-rimmed glasses are taped together over the nose, his ponytail looks like a year-old squirrel nest, most of his teeth are somewhere out on the trail, and his left big-toenail is so purple it seems to radiate as he *slap-slaps* around the bare wooden floors. You *know* you've seen his face in the soup line. His appearance is as forgettable as his name, yet there is an aura about him.

As we chatted in the kitchen while waiting for Allen to return from the phone in his office room, Harry exuded a happy gregariousness, exhibiting an interesting, if abstract, intellect. (Later, after Allen made a midafternoon sortie and brought back Harry's two quarts of Colt 45, he mumbled more and his conversation meandered. I decided that this was probably the Harry that accidentally turned his big toe bright purple.) Harry lives in Allen's refurbished pantry, underneath three ten-foot-long shelves lined solid with his lifelong collection of tapes.

Harry, now in his late sixties, never mentioned that he was the first person to record Charlie Parker or that he recorded and edited the classic *Anthology of American Folk Music*. He *was* excited about his current project, which involved a new way of "listening to the world." One microphone is stuck out onto the street side of the apartment and another is stuck out onto the more peaceful courtyard side in a sort of urban stereo.

"Then what I do," Harry said, knocking his cigarette ashes into the ashtray like a Gene Krupa rim-shot, "is take all the sounds and speed them up so I can edit them. I have found surges in sound, punctuated by a single bird call or a single dog bark, that are pure beauty. These surges—these waves of energy—are really fascinating. So far I have recorded during two full moons and a summer solstice—about one hundred twenty hours in all."

I asked Harry what was the best way to listen to it, meaning shoul

you use earphones, or maybe it should be heard in a huge indoor auditorium, or . . .

"I'd say with heroin," he replied. "That's probably the best. After all, it *is* one hundred twenty hours."

Finished with the phone, Allen returns, sitting in the chair silently vacated by Harry, who pads off. He asks me what, besides writing, do I do for a living? I remind him that, as Leary had been, I am a clinical psychologist.

"So you make people better?" he asks. Five little words that seem to scream out for a one-syllable answer, but I can't find one.

"I'm not in a clinical setting anymore," I begin. "If you really want to know why not, I'll tell you someday when we have lots of time. I'm more of a historian than a chiropractor—I do selection evaluations for companies to get the right guy into the right position." There seems a strange and awkward echo in what I am saying, but if there is any discomfort, apparently I am the only one sensing it. Ginsberg seems genuinely interested and completely relaxed. His gentle, modulated voice almost makes me feel as though I am receiving the attentions of a wise man simply interested in becoming wiser.

After a long discussion, Ginsberg leads me around the corner and sits me down to study a thick file of correspondence at his desk. (On the wall, done in red calligraphy, is a framed mantra of his current guru, Chögyam Trungpa, the founder of Naropa. Translated, it says, quite simply, "AH.") The material Allen presents to me concerns the period 1973 through 1975, when Tim Leary was imprisoned in various federal penitentiaries around the country.

One night, late in 1973, Ginsberg had received a phone call from Joanna Harcourt, who was the only person who could see Leary at that time. She said she was concerned over his well-being and had been asked by Tim to call Allen secretly and ask for his help.

The rest is underground history. As documented in the dossier he put before me, Ginsberg had organized a group to raise fifteen thousand dollars on short notice and investigate the vacuum of silence into which Tim had disappeared. He managed also to hire an attorney to look into possible breaches of Constitutional rights.

Whether or not his activities—and they were intense—had an effect on Leary's release in 1976, Ginsberg's efforts for a friend and colleague in arms seemed remarkable. I comment on the energies he had directed against the brick wall of the FBI.

"No, it wasn't really beyond the call of duty," he says and gives a little shrug, implying perhaps that such a cause is what life in the counterculture is all about.

Allen's modesty regarding his efforts to help Leary seems real, yet there is a distinct edge in his voice when he asks me about Joanna Leary. There is speculation that the U.S. government planted her in an attempt

to manipulate Tim into disclosing more information than necessary to attain his parole, especially about the possibility of Communist funding of the Weathermen.

"She stole money," Ginsberg says in disgust. "She stole money that I had raised for Tim's defense. Isn't that illegal? It's certainly not right, but isn't that illegal? Is there a statute of limitations? If Tim considers it old business, I do not. Peter, find out if she can still be sued—I'd really like to sue her." He says all this very slowly, with clear concern.

I tell him that I had only met Joanna once, right after Tim had been released from prison in San Diego, and had found her charming.

"Charming?" he says, heating up. "Charming! How can you say 'charming'? I don't know *anyone* who thought she was charming." And he spins around in his slippers, shaking his head in disbelief.

"Allen," I say to his back, as he walks away, muttering, "put my impression in proper perspective. Half the day I spent with her was at a veterinarian's, after I had run over her dog. My car wouldn't start, so I had to jump-start it downhill, and I flattened her Shih Tzu—just a dislocated hip it turned out. Maybe I felt her Shih Tzu was charming; I don't know. All I know is that she was in tears for about two hours. I felt horrible, and Tim laughed like hell when Joanna took one of the Valiums the vet had prescribed for the dog. So, anyway, I've got a weird experience to base my impression on."

Ginsberg turns and calmly gives me a nonverbal reprieve—a quick nod and a low grunt—and wanders out to get some lunch.

The desk in Allen's room is next to the window on the street and near the foot of his bed. Against the other wall, on the floor, are his two prayer pads, for meditation. They are made of a bright-red Chinese fabric that matches his framed mantra. Curiously, on the wall directly in front of the prayer pad is a large poster with instructions on "How to Meditate," giving the different breathing techniques to reach the seven stages of consciousness. Since Ginsberg has been a Buddhist for decades, this chart on the wall seems a little odd, like going into the cockpit of a 747 and discovering the pilot reading the instruction manual.

The serenity of the room, with its desk, bed, prayer mat, and bookshelves (one whole shelf on Kerouac with three different copies of *On the Road,* one half shelf of Pound), is smashed every hour, as the Catholic Church's bells sweep through the entire apartment like a musical storm.

After the last bell rings, there is an hour of quiet study time, interrupted only by pigeons, squacking and flapping down past the window. Then someone shouts three times in a strong, gravelly baritone, "Al-len . . . Al-len . . . Al-len."

Not sure, but thinking I am alone in the apartment, I do nothing. After a few minutes I walk around to stretch my legs and find Harry Smith in the workroom. I mention the caller on the street, saying that it must be a common refrain on his "Listening to the World" tape.

"You wouldn't believe all the people who stand down there and yell for Allen," he says. "Most of them have just gotten out of their straitjackets. The first thing they do is come here and yell for Allen. Some just stand there and read poetry—can you believe it? Dodging cars and reading poetry. Now that's the Big Apple for you."

Just then the unlocked door bangs open and a trim, middle-aged man with a gray beard bounces in saying, "Why the hell don't you answer your window, Harry?"

Harry introduces me to "Lucien," and I ask if he is Lucien Carr. He is. And the man who had played a major role in the lives of Kerouac, Ginsberg, and Burroughs ceases to be just a photo in a book and comes to life.

Lucien wants to go see a photo exhibit by Robert Frank, a close friend of his and Allen's. It was written up in the Sunday *Times* he is carrying, folded up as if to swat a passing bee. "Where the fuck is Ginsberg. I told him when I'd be here," he growls.

"You've known Allen for fifty years," Harry slowly counters, "so why be surprised if he's half an hour late? Or half a day? Here, let me put some music on for you," and he slides over to a cassette player and puts on something that sounds like a bad night in a maternity ward.

Later, when Allen returns and Harry is deep into his malt liquor, I take a photo of the two old visionaries hamming it up over the *New York Times*.

LUCIEN CARR WAS PROBABLY the single most important catalyst in bringing together Burroughs, Ginsberg, and Kerouac. Carr was born in New York but raised in Saint Louis, where he met two men, a little older, who had gone to Harvard together—William Burroughs and Dave Kammerer. The relationship between Carr and Kammerer slowly progressed toward pathology. As a fourteen-year-old, Carr went on nature hikes guided by Kammerer, who fell obsessively in love with him. He followed Lucien to New York City when he enrolled at Columbia in 1943 and refused to leave him alone. He would climb up the front of buildings to get into parties where Lucien was; he would sit on the fire escape outside Lucien's room to watch him sleep.

Kammerer and Burroughs had lost touch, but ran into each other at the Harvard Club in New York, used by each as a place for leaving and picking up messages from friends, many of whom were poor students without telephones. Both were living in the Village; Burroughs on Bedford Street and Kammerer on Morton Street. Together with Lucien, they began to socialize, sharing steak dinners and new books. They were from families with some money, but both Kammerer and Burroughs had jobs, though not precisely what one might expect from a couple of Harvard graduates. Wartime wasn't really geared toward climbing the career ladder; Kammerer was a janitor and Burroughs a summons server and part-time bartender.

In 1943 Carr was a good-looking, eighteen-year-old kid with a lot of energy, a lot of ideas, and a philosophy that hammered together equal parts of Rimbaud, Yeats, and Dostoyevski into something he called the New Vision. It was Carr's strong literary and philosophical bent that helped persuade his dormmate at Columbia, Allen Ginsberg, to forget about growing up to be a labor attorney and start writing more. Ginsberg had met Carr by following the strains of the Brahms *Trio Number One* down the dorm hall and into Lucien's room.

One of Carr's classes at Columbia was a sketching course taught by George Groz. Here Carr met an art student, Edie Parker, who lived with her boyfriend, Jack Kerouac, when he was not at sea in the Merchant Marines.

Through Edie, Kerouac met Carr at the West End Bar on 114th Street and Broadway, a favorite hangout for students. Although initially jealous of the friendship that had developed between Edie and Lucien while he was away at sea, Kerouac came to appreciate Carr's spunky impulsiveness and his intellectual energies: "A mischievous-looking little prick," Kerouac called him.

Ginsberg met Kerouac through Lucien. Their first encounter, at the apartment shared by Jack, Edie, Joan Vollmer Adams, and occasionally Celine Young, Lucien's girlfriend, was somewhat less than propitious. Reportedly Ginsberg said, "Discretion is the better part of valor," to which Kerouac responded, "Ah, shut up, you little twitch."

On August 14, 1944, the relationship between Carr and Kammerer turned ugly. Kammerer made what the Columbia *Spectator* later called "indecent advances" toward Carr while they were sitting by the Hudson River in Riverside Park. Carr responded by stabbing him in the heart and killing him with his Boy Scout knife.

Carr weighted and dumped the body in the Hudson River and went to Burroughs for advice. Burroughs advised him to call a lawyer, turn himself in, and claim self-defense. Instead of immediately turning himself in, Carr went to Jack and Edie's place. He and Jack proceeded to idle the day away, having a few beers, seeing a movie, disposing of the murder weapon down the sewer, and visiting the Museum of Modern Art.

When Carr did turn himself in, both Burroughs and Kerouac ended up in jail for being accomplices after the fact. Burroughs phoned home, got bail, and left for Saint Louis. Kerouac phoned home and got rejected. His father refused to go his bail, saying, "No Kerouac ever got involved in a murder." The alternative source of bail money was Edie's father, who ran a successful Buick dealership in Grosse Pointe, Michigan. However, she couldn't get money from her father unless they were married.

On August 22, Kerouac and a plainclothes policeman left the Bronx jail for the afternoon. They picked up Edie and Celine and went to City Hall. With a cop as witness and Celine as bridesmaid, Jack and Edie began a marriage that produced a twenty-five-hundred-dollar bail and that lasted less than two months. (In the mad swirl of the summer of 1944, Edie's other roommate, Joan Vollmer Adams, became Jean Vollmer Adams Burroughs.)

Lucien Carr (after a trial during which he constantly gripped a copy of Yeats's *Visions*) was sentenced to two years in the Elmira Reformatory. When he was released from Elmira, Carr's New Vision was tainted, but he never forgot his friendships, formed out of the enthusiasms of adolescence, and he put up with a lot of Kerouac's alcoholic abuse in his later years.

If Carr's vision had been "reformed," his friends' visions had been revised and refined and were soon to become the heartbeat of American counterculture: Ginsberg's collected early poems from this period later appeared as *Gates of Wrath*; Kerouac was busy writing his first novel, *The Town and the City*, and had begun collecting cross-country travel experiences for *On the Road*. Burroughs was writing *Junkie* and growing marijuana on a farm in southeast Texas.

Carr took a job with UPI, which he still has. He maintained his friendship with all, appearing as a character in six of Kerouac's books. (The Kammerer incident became the focus of a novel—never completed—by Kerouac and Burroughs entitled *And the Hippos Were Boiled in Their Tanks.*)

One must wonder at the incredible serendipity of all these connections. *What if*'s inevitably rear their ridiculous heads, underscoring the fragile beginnings of this new generation.

What if Lucien Carr had been roomed on the fifth floor of the dorm at Columbia instead of the seventh? What if Allen Ginsberg had already heard Brahms's *Trio Number One*—or had disliked it? What if Burroughs and Kammerer had used someplace other than the Harvard University Club as a postal drop? What if Carr didn't have his Boy Scout knife with him on August 13, 1944? What if? What if? The reality is that all this *did* happen, and the New Vision rolled on, with or without its impresario. Later that summer of 1944, Kerouac wrote a letter to Ginsberg that captured his interpretation of the "vision" and outlined the youthful energies and ambition that were to fuel the next quarter century of American counterculture.

Kerouac saw more than coincidence that his wedding day fell on the same day Paris was liberated. He was possessed with living out Lucien's concept of the "new vision," stating that a small flat in Montparnasse would be fertile ground for it to blossom. With typical boundless drive, he spoke of seeking all knowledge, all life, and all power. For him, the new vision was the ultimate art form and it appeared as writing; he urged Ginsberg to look at *Finnegan's Wake, Ulysses,* and the *The Magic Mountain* for inspiration.

Kerouac's plan had him quickly establishing his own fortune, Ginsberg setting aside his legal labors, and Lucien completing the trio of visionary writers living in Paris—a time-honored tradition for fledgling American artists of all kinds.

However, it did not work out that way. Instead, by staying closer to home, a very *untraditional* "new vision" began to take shape—on the roads and in the cities of their own America.

Today Carr retains his spunky humor. Ginsberg had missed the *Times* article about the Robert Frank exhibit and Lucien chides him for his oversight, circling the relevant paragraphs just as one would expect a wire editor to do. "Christ, Allen, you're working too hard. You don't read the papers anymore. Now here, read this," he says, handing him the paper and shaking his head in mock disbelief.

Ginsberg reads the article, impressed that Frank had two exhibits simultaneously, and comments that "he didn't invite me to either." Eyes rolling heavenward, Carr walks out of the room to look through Harry Smith's umbrella collection.

The late-afternoon weather is beginning to look ragged. Allen and Lucien, with Harry's help, drag out a half-dozen umbrellas, fussing over which was whose, and should we wear raincoats and jackets, or hats and no umbrellas, like three obsessive mothers dressing their kids to meet the school bus.

At one point Harry demonstrates the relative merits of a particular umbrella by opening it and holding it over his five-foot body. He looks like a designer mushroom, his head obscured by gaudy red, white, and blue stripes. All that is visible are his cut-off Levi's and his bare feet. Carr growls, "For Christ's sake, Harry, hasn't anyone ever told you it's bad luck to open an umbrella inside?" But Harry is lost in thought, suddenly needing to know what time Allen was going to be back. "By eight o'clock, Allen? By eight-thirty?"

"Since when do I have to make an appointment to get into my own fucking house?" Allen asks of the ceiling. But Harry says *he* has an appointment and wants to be able to get in. "Of course, of course," Allen says calmly, "I'll be back by nine o'clock."

The problem of umbrellas and foul-weather gear is settled with the rough-edged amiability found among old, true friends, and Allen and Lucien leave for the photography exhibits.

My back is aching from sitting at Allen's desk in his old wooden chair. I ask Harry if he has any aspirin as I begin running water into a wineglass with a blue Columbia University seal on it. He finds some aspirin and hands them to me, saying, "I don't have any, but here's some of Allen's. The way I see it, what's mine is mine, but what's Ginsberg's is the world's."

Take Four:
The Sorcerer's Apprentice

I HAD BEGUN TO think of Allen Ginsberg as a series of events: chanting in the center of the cyclone that was the Free Speech Movement; singing and reading at Passim's; shouting in a public display of temper at the University of Maine. While he had seemed far more peaceful during our summer meeting in his apartment, Ginsberg still seemed larger than life, an energy force with a beard, glasses and a temper.

However, as he sits across the table from me, doodling on the blank white paper table mats at K and K's Polish Restaurant on First Avenue, he seems peaceful. He seems, finally, an individual rather than a social abstraction.

Maybe it was because I had the routine down. Before going out to dinner I had stood in the middle of his street, now winter-dark in early evening, shouting up at the top of my lungs, "Hell-oo . . . All-en . . . Hell-oo . . . ALL-en." After I'd caught the key in the sock and hiked up the four flights of old worn marble stairs to Apartment 23, Ginsberg met me at the door. He was barefooted and in mismatched pajama tops and bottoms, his hair looking like a terrified tumbleweed. He motioned for me to come in, saying nothing as he gestured for me to put my bag down in the kitchen. Then turning, he shut off the gas flame under a huge pot of boiling rice and meat, all the time saying clipped things like "Yeah . . . uh-huh . . . nope . . . maybe . . . then what . . ." into a cordless phone.

He came to the end of his conversation, stuffed the antenna down into the receiver, put it flat on a tabletop, and said, "Isn't this wonderful? A cordless phone. Now I can carry on a conversation, do five other things at the same time and *really* get confused!"

Ginsberg hadn't gone to bed until 5:00 A.M. and had slept all through the day. He had been up the previous night going over a thick pile of contact sheets of black-and-white photographs taken during his recent cultural-exchange tour of the Soviet Union. "I cannot trust my memory anymore," he said in serious tones. "I have been back a couple of weeks, but I've been so busy . . . it just hasn't gotten done and if I don't do it now, I will forget." He flipped a few of the sheets to the back side, where he read his small handwritten notes: "This is with Yevtushenko in Moscow. . . . This one is at the Gorki Institute, and this is with Arthur Miller and William Gaddis and I *think* it was taken in Tbilisi, but I'm not sure. . . . I've got to check some other notes on that one," and he briefly rustled through some papers. Ginsberg is a consummate collector and documents his every move. Housed in the rare manuscript library on the sixth floor of Columbia's Butler Library are the Ginsberg Collection (correspondence) and the Ginsberg Deposit (more personal writings and records). He retains Bill Morgan, an artist and professional archivist to catalog and arrange the ever-increasing library.

A diary kept when he was a ten-year-old in a Paterson, New Jersey, grammar school is there, as is correspondence with nearly every literary and political figure imaginable in his lifetime. Ginsberg seems to have been aware from a very early age of his ultimate niche in history.

Letters from the early Columbia University days with Kerouac and Burroughs are there. The late 1950s, when he began to receive public notice, are documented by correspondence from Kenneth Rexroth, Lew Welch, and with Norman Mailer.

The 1960s come alive with notes to Robert MacNamara and President Johnson, and from Hunter Thompson:

> I am including your poem "To the Angels" in my book [*Hell's Angels*]—
> got a copy from the *Berkeley Barb* and want to pay you for it . . . you
> gave me one [copy] one night last winter when I boomed into your Fell
> Street apartment in a jabbering pill frenzy . . . anyway, I'm stone broke
> and desperate which means I can't pay you anything for the use of the
> poem . . . selling my bike to move into a new apartment . . . the
> Chinese evicted me from this last week, maybe because the neighbors
> reported it as a Hell's Angels hideout.
> —Hunter S. Thompson to Allen Ginsberg, July 1966

Ken Kesey wrote from Puerto Vallarta, Mexico, where he was holed up facing a deadline, the plastic wrapper from a packet of Codeinetas, or Mexican codeine, still stapled on the back, nearly twenty years later. From the relative quiet of the mid-1970s, Tim Leary wrote long, academic treatises on the "utopian city" while locked up in the bowels of the American penal system. The chronology of Ginsberg's incredibly busy and complex life is all there—including notes scribbled from phone calls in the middle of the night ("Joanna called 2:30 A.M. . . . says to say nothing to Kunzler").

It is a life that has now, incredibly, bridged seven decades of American cultural evolution and shows no sign of letting up. He keeps as busy a schedule as the executive vice president of a billion-dollar company. His archives, to date, include well in excess of two hundred thousand items. That translates to eleven pieces a day, every day of the week, since he was ten years old. Some interpret his obsession as a mere documentation of his self-worth; perhaps, but it is also documentation of American culture.

GINSBERG EXCUSED HIMSELF, TO change from his pajamas into something more appropriate for dinner on the Lower East Side of Manhattan. I wandered through his kitchen, still under the stern gaze of Walt Whitman and Rimbaud, but without the chattery presence of Harry Smith, who was now living with someone in Brooklyn.

"I just heard a great tape that Ed Sanders and the Fugs cut," Allen shouted from his bedroom. "The really terrible thing about their album is"—here he paused momentarily to try to find a bottle of Brylcreem to pacify his protesting hair—". . . is that to get their album played on any radio station would take about three hundred thousand dollars—in payola! That's how business in *that* industry is done."

"Hey, Allen," I said, in mock seriousness. "I went to five different fish stores today. I tried like hell to buy you some sixteen-year-old male sturgeon, but the guys at the market just looked at me funny, so I come empty-handed—no gifts—dinner will have to do."

"Sixteen-year-old sturgeon?" he asked in mild disbelief. "Who told you I'd want that?"

"Bob Rosenthal," I answered, referring to an earlier, fuzzy phone conversation I had had with Allen's secretary regarding what I could bring as a holiday gift ("When Ram Dass came, he brought a pineapple," Bob had told me).

"Oh no. You got it confused," Allen said with a straight face, while brushing his hair straight back and putting on his omnipresent navy blazer. "It was a sixteen-year-old male virgin."

ON THE WAY TO the smorgasbord of small ethnic restaurants along First Avenue, Ginsberg told me about the necessity of housing his archives at Butler Library for lack of space at home, and about the rent control that keeps his monthly charge near three hundred dollars. "When rent control finally disappears, I guess my place will go for about fifteen hundred dollars a month. By then I'll be seventy-five years old, toothless, in a wheelchair, and completely unable to do anything about it except shout. And they'll carry me out, dump me on the street, and say, 'Well, fuck you. You've had it good for the last twenty years.' " And he shrugged his shoulders passively.

Inside the Polish restaurant ("It's brand-new. I've never been in here before. Let's try it."), Allen waves hello to two couples sitting near the door. "What's the food like? Is anything good?" He is all seriousness as he visually rummages through the contents of their plates.

After the waitress finally arrives to take our order, Ginsberg begins talking about Leary's imprisonment. He pulls a pen from inside his blazer and begins doodling on the white paper placemat. "Peter, if you can just get all of the Freedom of Information Act material, if you can show that Joanna *was* a narc, and that the FBI planted her to get information out of Tim, then you'd really put that whole era of government repression in proper perspective. Doesn't Tim want to sue?"

His doodling is getting larger and larger, a sort of series of intricate concentric rings that approaches the size of a saucer by the time we are joined by Barry Miles (the British biographer of the Beatles, Mick Jagger, and now Allen Ginsberg). Allen is in for another long night, going over his life with first me and then Miles, as he is known.

"What do you two think this is?" Allen asks, tapping his pen on the doodle, now completed, with the addition of two vertical projections at the north and south poles, each with a little orb on top.

"It's the cross-section of a cabbage," Miles says, making a karate-chop motion with his hand and pointing to the dish of shredded red cabbage in the middle of the tiny table.

"Nope, your turn," he says, pointing his pen at me.

"Let's see. . . . It's a Polish restaurant. You know what I ordered for dinner, so I would say this is an infinite circle of kielbasa links." We both look at Allen for the final decree.

"You're both wrong. It's a cunt," and he chuckles wryly, while inking in the center.

There is a clear element of absurdity to Allen Ginsberg, in both his life and his writings. His occasional goofiness seems somehow a key to his creative processes, his ability to regress and see the world with a child's naïveté, his seeming total disregard for how his thoughts and actions might be interpreted by those around him.

IF THE DEFINITION OF a poet is, as Randall Jarrell put it, "someone who manages, in a lifetime of standing out in thunderstorms, to be struck by lightning five or six times," then Allen Ginsberg fills that bill. In the summer of 1948, while reading Blake's *Songs of Experience*, he felt the presence of Blake himself and heard the poem "speak itself" in a grave, oracular tone that he understood to be the Master's voice. It was as profound an experience as he has ever felt, and trying to reconstitute that experience, or some approximation of it, became a lifelong pursuit.

"It wasn't a hallucination," he points out nearly forty years later. "I didn't see anything, really. It was more a change of consciousness . . . a new vision, a new awareness . . . and it *still* mystifies me."

He shakes his head slowly in disbelief; having spent four decades trying to comprehend the meaning of that mystery, witnessed at an early age. "I still don't know what was going on there."

He experimented with a variety of approaches to try to rediscover "an alternative modality of consciousness. Those were the terms I used then, I think." In 1952 a store on Tenth Street, off Second Avenue, sold peyote buttons from Magic Gardens, Texas. Ginsberg tried them. A few years later a druggist in Chicago provided mescaline; nitrous oxide came from a Berkeley dentist. In 1959, at a Stanford University study on creativity, Ginsberg met Gregory Bateson, the anthropology professor of Esalen's Richard Price and Michael Murphy, and subsequently experimented with LSD. By the time he was asked to address the Group for the Advancement of Psychiatry, in 1960, on the relationship between creativity and altered states of consciousness, he was a veteran of the psychedelic experience, a virtual elder statesman of underground pharmacology.

One member of the GAP conference was a psychologist from Harvard, who informed Ginsberg that another faculty member was experimenting with drugs and creativity. Allen wrote the professor, saying he would be honored to participate in his research.

One week later, Ginsberg answered a knock on the door of his and Peter Orlovsky's Tenth Street apartment and met Timothy Leary. Nearly thirty years later the two remain close friends.

What Leary sought from Ginsberg was advice and assistance. Should LSD be kept a cult secret or democratized? If the answer were the latter, could Ginsberg's bohemian, underground, and artistic connections be used to help spread the gospel of the coming "New Age" of awareness?

Before Leary and Ginsberg's meeting, which is perhaps the single most important interpersonal linkage in making the sixties what they were, Allen had politicized his drug experiences, publicly joining forces with Ashley Montague and Norman Mailer in 1960 to advocate the decriminalization of marijuana. "So it was more the politics of drugs, or mindchanging substances that I was interested in, and that's what Tim was interested in, too," Ginsberg remembers. "Actually, I think he asked me, 'What would be the result of large-scale use on the culture?' The other thing he was definitely and directly interested in was whether LSD should be used only as Huxley had suggested to him—hermetically, hierarchically set up—or whether it should be dispensed freely.

"Democratize it, I thought. I was afraid that if he made it hermetic, he'd have little cults of power. I probably used that term, because Gregory [Corso] had written a poem called 'Power.' "

Leary could not have agreed more. When it came to the 1960s version of networking, Allen proved invaluable. He introduced Leary to the creative bohemia of greater New York. Then, once the gap had been bridged between beatnik and flower power, Leary often set the stage for Allen to chant and sing. They tended to balance each other out and, in the process, began to appeal to a growing audience. Ginsberg felt that psychedelic drugs could be a catalyst to extend the vision. "So, I thought that by traveling along the same, older network of poetry connections, or cultural connections of high-class bohemia and jazz, that it would spread through the culture and people would transmit the sensibility as well as the acid itself."

Ginsberg took Leary on a personal tour of Manhattan, introducing him (and handing out psilocybin pills) to the Pulitzer Prize-winning poet Robert Lowell, publisher Barney Rosset, Dorothy Norman (a contemporary of the photographer Alfred Stieglitz), and two jazz musicians, Dizzy Gillespie and Thelonious Monk. The idea of wandering through such a pantheon of cultural heroes and simply handing out potentially disorienting chemicals borders on the incredible; yet it happened. Leary's idea was not so much to assess the drug's effects on creativity as to cultivate a following among established artistic and intellectual circles (and their patrons). He felt it would help prevent him from being singled out as culpable should the experiment of a generation run upon the rocks.

Not all of the results were positive: Thelonious Monk asked for more psilocybin—neither he nor any of his band members felt any effect at all; Barney Rosset had an anxiety fit, trembling in a corner saying, "I pay my psychiatrist one hundred dollars an hour to keep this away from me"; Dizzy Gillespie wanted more, "for my whole band"; and Robert Lowell predated the Beatles, saying, "*Amor Vincit Omnia.*"

In December 1960, Ginsberg and Orlovsky went to Harvard and stayed at Leary's house in Newton. After ingesting a handful of Sandoz pills, Allen and Peter came downstairs, stark naked, and announced that the world was "one" and that it was their duty to take peace to the new generation. They attempted to telephone Burroughs in Paris, Mailer in New York, Kennedy in Washington, and Krushchev in Moscow, but they had to settle for Jack Kerouac on Long Island. They urged him to come to Newton and sample the experience, which he did. Ginsberg remembers that Leary "seemed very bouncy and open" and that Kerouac "caught it" calling him "Coach Leary."

After their visit to Newton, each was asked to write a letter describing their experiences and any lasting insights or behavior changes that they might have discovered. In January 1961, Kerouac wrote a letter to Leary that Ginsberg still keeps in his office.

In it, Kerouac carefully described his magic carpet, floating sensations during the LSD sessions. After returning home, he and his mother had talked for three days and three nights and Kerouac found a new depth to his love for Mamêre. It had been on Friday the thirteenth that the usually superstitious Kerouac had chewed the pills, yet he prolonged his ecstacy and excitement for an entire week (noting Kennedy's inauguration on Friday the twentieth) in a typical manner: drinking Christian Brothers port on the rocks.

Revealing his background as both an ardent Catholic and star football player, he signed off by first referring to Leary as a Jesuit priest, asking when they could get together for touch football, and embellishing his signature with a drawn crucifix. While Kerouac might not have simulated the "new vision" of 1944, his Harvard experience with LSD had been quite positive, profoundly religious, and deeply insightful.

For Ginsberg, however, LSD was somewhat of a dead end. He simply did not achieve the visionary vantage point he had expected (with the exception of a short LSD session in Wales, in 1967, when he produced the poem "Wales Visitation").

His expectations, at the beginning, were very high; he felt the country was on the verge of blasting off toward inner as well as outer space. "I had experienced the Blake visitation, or whatever you call it," he remembers, "so I was interested in that particular breakthrough. I thought that if everyone in America had it, it would build up some kind of critical mass and open up a lot of seriousness and sublimity and spirituality; the realization that the whole hard-edge, negative psychology of business, war, competition, and suspiciousness would melt. There would be a different attitude toward people, and different attitudes toward society and different attitudes toward being alive. It would be much more open. Like Kerouac's sense of mortal poignancy . . . a sense of wide-open, nonjudgmental, nonprejudicial inquisitiveness."

In theory it made sense, but for Allen, the practice didn't quite work. Ironically, the man who introduced Timothy Leary to the world of the beatniks became frightened by LSD. When he had taken Leary to meet Robert Lowell and Dizzy Gillespie, he "chickened out," not taking the drug until later at Leary's house in Newton.

"I was always a little paranoid, for fear that if I took acid, I would reveal my basic ignorance and idiocy. Most of the time I substituted common sense and singing . . . as my social contribution," he says.

"With acid I went through two bum trips, basically, and with psilocybin I also went through bum trips, and I never did get out of it until 1967 or so. . . . I was very hesitant and chary about taking acid all that time." He now feels he was simply overanxious, grasping too eagerly in an attempt to re-create the Blake visitation. He saw LSD, the chemical high, as a "moral fault."

During the sixties Ginsberg and Orlovsky were abroad a great deal—in the Amazon, Paris, and especially India. Ginsberg became more taken with Buddhism and chanting and breathing exercises as an alternative to the drug high. Now he says, "I'm not a very good Buddhist," while bumming another cigarette. "I don't sit enough. But I don't think there is that much of an opposition between Jewishness and Buddhism. It's like saying, 'Are you Jewish or a New Jerseyan?' You can be both."

Ginsberg's conversion coincided with the 1960s fascination with Indian gurus and Eastern mysticism. But he explained what he was doing in simpler terms—getting high legally. He had none of the aloof, Indian mystique that the foreign imports did, but he was immensely popular.

The press followed him as if he were a Pied Piper of Peace. He was articulate, and generous with his time. He was a bellwether to those who wanted to be in the right place at the right time: the Free Speech Movement in the fall of 1964; the Filthy Speech Movement a year later; the Vietnam Day marches in late 1965; and the ultimate pre-Woodstock happening, the 1967 Human Be-in in San Francisco's Golden Gate Park.

Ginsberg seemed to be everywhere—and to know everyone. His long relationship with Neal Cassady helped ensure that East met West, and began a nationwide counterculture festival. Cassady had become the bus driver for Kesey. Through Cassady, Ginsberg first met Kesey and experienced the scene at La Honda.

> Cool black night thru redwoods
> cars parked outside in shade
> behind the gate, stars dim above
> the ravine, a fire burning by the side
> porch and a few tired souls hunched over
> in black leather jackets. In the huge
> wooden house, a yellow chandelier
> at 3 am the blast of loudspeakers
> hi-fi Rolling Stones Ray Charles Beatles
> Jumping Joe Jackson and twenty youths
> dancing to the vibration thru the floor,
> a little weed in the bathroom, girls in scarlet
> tights, one muscular smooth skinned man
> sweating dancing for hours, beer cans
> bent littering the yard, a hanged man
> sculpture dangling from a high creek branch,
> children sleeping softly in bedroom bunks,
> And 4 police cars parked outside the painted
> gate, red lights revolving in the leaves.
> —Allen Ginsberg, December 1965
> "First Party at Ken Kesey's with Hell's Angels,"

It was a scene similar to, and yet wildly different from one Ginsberg had experienced before, at Millbrook, New York, where Leary, Richard

Alpert, and Ralph Metzner, a Harvard psychopharmacologist, had their experimental commune on the twenty-five-hundred-acre Hitchcock family estate, an hour away from Ginsberg in New York City. "Millbrook was much more sedate and expansive, not half as rough and ready and wild and American, and as gung-ho as La Honda," he says. "It was another generation. It was more like a psychedelic circus [at La Honda] than a psychedelic community, though they both had strong central family relationships with kids and wives."

Ginsberg was well known on the West Coast by the time Kesey, the Pranksters, and the Free Speech Movement at Berkeley began to unhinge the American public's general definition of "a college education." His reading of *Howl*, on October 13, 1955, at San Francisco's Six Gallery had no doubt helped to pave the way for all that was to follow. In reading *Howl*, Ginsberg opened up a can of consciousness for which the world was not quite ready. The poem reflected his own consciousness, which had recently undergone a similarly wrenching transformation.

When he arrived in San Francisco in late 1953, he was in a state of mental turmoil, tormented by the progressive psychotic deterioration of his mother and confused over his homosexual tendencies. Further, he still had William Blake to contend with, a haunting source of motivation that drove him to search, to inquire, to learn. He had been in and out of psychotherapy since 1944 and, in fact, had once spent some time in an institution, though the circumstances surrounding his admission were somewhat unusual.

In 1948, he was working as a copy boy for Associated Press and sharing his apartment with two men and a woman who were supporting their heroin habits by theft. They began storing increasing amounts of silverware, appliances, and clothing in the apartment. Ginsberg, who worked nights, cast a naive and romantic eye on the whole operation until the building security guard began to take notice. He then decided his apartment was no longer safe and asked his underworld roommates to drive him and his papers (even in his early twenties, Ginsberg was an omnivorous collector) to a relative's house on Long Island. During the drive, in a stolen car filled with contraband and driven by a felon with eighteen previous arrests, a wrong turn was taken down a one-way street. A high-speed police chase ensued, and the car flipped, spilling Ginsberg and his papers onto the street. His picture appeared on the front of the *Daily News*, accompanied by an article calling him a "student genius who was plotting out big criminal scenes."

After conferring with a law professor and his father, he pleaded insanity, citing the Blake "vision." He was sentenced to nine months in the Columbia Psychiatric Institute.

"I was pretty much in my right mind, actually, as the doctors later said," Ginsberg recalls. "I was just *so* intellectualized. . . . I had no idea. There were people coming up from having transorbital lobectomies, but I wasn't in that kind of a situation. They weren't even giving me any medicine. I was just getting occupational therapy and hydrotheraphy and psychiatry. I was happy to get some free psychiatry."

Serendipitously, the first person that Ginsberg met in CPI was Carl Solomon. He had landed in the "bughouse" for harmless, yet aberrant, behavior (throwing potato salad at CCNY speakers, demanding a lobotomy for his twenty-first birthday). His uncle owned Ace Books, and years later on Allen's suggestion, he first published Burroughs's *Junkie*. Solomon introduced Allen to the works of a number of writers, including Jean Genet, whose underworld activities and homosexuality were as intriguing as his writings. The two developed a close intellectual relationship; Ginsberg, in fact, dedicated *Howl* to Solomon.

After his stay at CPI, Ginsberg went home to New Jersey, where he wrote a letter to William Carlos Williams requesting an interview with him for a newspaper article. From Williams, living in nearby Rutherford, New Jersey, Ginsberg got encouragement to continue writing poetry. Williams urged him to simplify "rather than fake something which sounded arty."

For a while, Ginsberg led a split life, writing poetry and working in marketing research first in New York, then in San Francisco. Once in San Francisco, Ginsberg found a psychotherapist, Philip Hicks at the Langley Porter Clinic, who finally asked the right questions. At the time, he was involved with a woman, as well as with Peter Orlovsky; and he was trying to write poetry while doing market research for Towne, Oller and Company.

Ginsberg told Hicks he wanted to be a gay poet. Hicks said, "Why don't you do what you want to do?"

Shortly thereafter, Ginsberg, then thirty, wrote a memo to Towne, Oller and Company, recommending that his position be replaced by an IBM computer. He left his girlfriend for Peter, immersed himself in the thick of the San Francisco poetry scene, and enrolled at Berkeley in a graduate program in English.

Allen recalls, "We [he and Peter] had finally come to some kind of compact or agreement, and that was the first time I had a sense of a secure love relationship. I felt accomplished, fulfilled, grounded. I felt I was not just a lonely nut trying to find love that was impossible. . . . I felt confirmed in my inclinations."

His new sense of freedom helped him initiate the writing of *Howl*, along with a letter from Kenneth Rexroth. "He wrote about a poem I had written," Ginsberg says now, "saying that I was being academical with my poetry and hadn't progressed very much. I was depressed and figured I wasn't going to get anywhere anyway, so it didn't matter what I wrote. I could write whatever I felt, without thinking about being published."

Rexroth's critique was the next to the last straw; the final precipitant was Kerouac, according to Ginsberg. "Kerouac influenced me more than anybody . . . for his ebullience, spontaneity, personal self-confidence, breadth—for the run-ons—the Melvillian run-ons. The final blow was when Kerouac came around and said I was wasting my time in school, that I ought to be studying Sanskrit."

A few weeks later, *Howl* was finished. At the initial reading, Kerouac was in the small audience, passing a jug of wine and verbally punctuating Allen's delivery as he would a long saxophone solo or drum riff; the new poetry was spoken jazz:

> I saw the best minds of my generation
> destroyed by madness, starving
> hysterical naked,
> dragging themselves through the
> negro streets at dawn looking for an
> angry fix,
> angelheaded hipsters burning for the
> ancient heavenly connection to the
> starry dynamo in the machinery of
> the night
> —*Howl*, Part I

'I thought it was a good . . . uh . . . expression," Ginsberg says now. "It had a little verve, breadth and inspiration. I thought that was needed 'cause people were too tight-assed or too worried and careful about their poetry. So this was a little more open. But Kerouac had done that a lot before."

The entire social pantheon of Ginsberg's existence appeared in *Howl*, including Burroughs, Kerouac, Carr, and Cassady. Each stanza refers to a specific person and incident; Allen and his biographer are still trying to match sections with names.

> who burned cigarette holes in their arms protesting
> the narcotic tobacco haze of Capitalism,
> who distributed Supercommunist pamphlets in Union
> Square weeping and undressing while the sirens
> of Los Alamos wailed them down, and wailed
> down Wall, and the Staten Island ferry also
> wailed,
> who broke down crying in white gymnasiums naked
> and trembling before the machinery of other
> skeletons,
> who bit detectives in the neck and shrieked with delight
> in policecars for committing no crime but their
> own wild cooking pederasty and intoxication,
> who howled on their knees in the subway and were
> dragged off the roof waving genitals and manuscripts,
> —*Howl*, Part I

News of his reading appeared in the *New York Times*, but the first person on the scene was Lawrence Ferlinghetti. He telegramed Ginsberg the next day, offering to publish Allen at City Lights. Ferlinghetti then summed up his impression of what *Howl* portended by quoting from the letter sent by Nathaniel Hawthorne to Walt Whitman upon the publication of *Leaves of Grass*, one hundred years and eighty-five days earlier: "I greet you at the beginning of a great career."

IN 1956, THE APPLAUSE for *Howl* still reverberated, Allen's mother died, precipitating *Kaddish*, a eulogy, written in two days' time, and whose last line was Naomi's own, from inside Pilgrim State Mental Institution —her handwritten response to reading *Howl*: "The key is the window, the key is in the sunlight in the window—I have the key—get married Allen don't take drugs—the key is in the bars, in the sunlight in the window."

Howl hit America where it hurt ("America how can I write a holy litany in your silly mood?"). In the summer of 1957, City Lights' Ferlinghetti and his manager, Shigeyoshi Murau, were arrested for selling obscene literature; the ACLU defended them. With their subsequent acquittal, it had been proven in the Establishment's courts that this new poet and this new consciousness were at the very least, not illegal. The ruling that a book was not obscene if it had "the slightest redeeming social importance" opened the doors for the publication of works by D. H. Lawrence, Henry Miller, William Burroughs, and others, providing a significant legal precedent. The September 9, 1957, issue of *Life* proclaimed, BIG DAY FOR BARDS AT BAY: TRIAL OVER HOWL AND OTHER POEMS.

BUT IT WASN'T JUST Ginsberg's *poetry* that began to attract attention. In response to a heckler at another 1957 reading, Ginsberg took off his clothes to illustrate "man's naturalness and vulnerability in an increasingly contrived and dangerous world." Later, in New York's Jackson Church on Washington Square, twenty members of the Russian delegation to the United Nations stared incredulously, then filed out the side door, as Peter Orlovsky undressed to emphasize the personal nature of a diary he was reading. Ginsberg became known as the "naked poet" (capped by his unclothed role in the 1965 underground movie *Ciao! Manhattan* about a day in the life of Edie Sedgwick). His boldness began to garner him strong allies.

In 1960, Norman Mailer wrote:

I sometimes think
that little Jew bastard
that queer ugly kike
is the bravest man
in America
—"Ode to Allen
Ginsberg"

When asked about the poem, Ginsberg says, "That's about my saying publicly that I'm gay. He thought that was brave. To him it seemed brave, because it seemed so alien and horrible. He had written some prose about a dream about an orgy, where he was penetrated and enjoyed it. He has some kind of funny bullfight relation with the soul.

"Actually, I'm basically a coward, the kind who thinks, 'I could go to *jail* for that.' "

His self-perception of courage aside, Ginsberg's lifelong social and literary quest is at least financially rewarding these days. Random House (which rejected his collection, *Empty Mirror*, in 1952) has tendered a six-book contract with a six-figure advance. Ever the nonmaterialist, he has placed the funds in the Ginsberg Foundation, a charitable, tax-exempt foundation set up by his attorney brother, Eugene. Ginsberg is more than busy and he seems to thrive on it, drawing inspiration from a new generation. One of his original sources of inspiration, Peter Orlovsky, has fallen on difficult times recently. A long-time substance abuser, he was committed to Bellevue twice in the winter of 1985 after he terrorized Ginsberg's office staff by chasing them with a meat cleaver. He is currently in a Buddhist retreat in Vermont, Allen says.

AROUND MIDNIGHT, BACK AT Ginsberg's apartment, I leave him as I found him earlier that day, phone in hand, walking around the room, making short comments to an unseen caller. "Yes, May in Los Angeles, August in Boulder. . . . No, I don't have the time. . . . Of course there's a deadline . . ." In between snatches of dialogue, he rummages through his desk for an address or a phone number.

Walking down the dimly lit, old marble stairs to the cold street, Allen's comments on rent control come to mind. I envision a seventy-five-year-old Ginsberg, with less hair, white on top and through his beard. He is being evicted while lying in his bed, still directing a team of young assistants who surround and carry him, like a bespectacled old Malay sultan. He dictates a letter. He schedules a reading. He turns away an obnoxious interviewer. He is read some anonymous letters containing "new poetry—unpublished, as yet." As the eviction procession moves down the stairs and into the street, his cordless phone rings and he begins to talk.

It's tough to find a good poet these days, tougher still to keep him down.

The Six Years War

GOING TO COLLEGE AT Berkeley was never really my intention, but every other school turned me down. Perhaps that sense of rejection helped me fit in well enough to run the entire four-year gauntlet and graduate. It was a success of considerable proportions, given the dark forces, magnetic distractions, and bottomless confusions that were the essence of the University of California's Berkeley campus in the 1960s.

For four years I studied here, then left, only to find the rest of the world a flabby bore by comparison. I came back just in time for the darkest hour, to realize that time refuses to stand still regardless of how hard you drug it. Then I left for good.

Yet here I am again, my back to the campus, standing on the north side of Haste Street. Across the way on the wall of a Mexican restaurant is a 150-foot-long hand-painted mural. In the tradition of David Siqueiros, José Orozco, and Diego Rivera, it is the history of revolution, a mural of the Six Years War that established this campus as the counterforce to anything labeled establishment. It is a dense, complex, op-art headline, graphically showing the central events that shaped the campus from late fall of 1964 to the summer of 1969. From left to right, the Free Speech Movement flows into the Vietnam War, punctuated by the Summer of Love of 1967, and capped by the riots and the final battle for People's Park.

A larger-than-life Mario Savio addresses a crowd of thousands surrounding a trapped campus police car with a handcuffed protestor inside.

Look closely: On the hood of the police car is a copy of Savio's "put your bodies on the gears, the levers . . ." speech. Behind is Sproul Hall, the campus administration building that made sit-ins American. On the second floor of the student-occupied building are the huge letters *FSM*, for Free Speech Movement, under an American flag. The Ionic columns are, in the mural, hollow and open at the bottom. Government money and bombs pour out of the columns into the second stage of the Six Years War, the protest against U.S. intervention in Vietnam. A half-dozen young men in three-piece suits are shown graduating, exiting Sproul Hall. Gradually, their heads become less rounded and more boxlike until they evolve into television sets with LBJ, Nixon, Reagan, a bar of soap, and a Vietnamese woman with a carbine strapped to her back on the screens; it was the world's first prime-time war. Picket signs announcing Vietnam Teach-in Today and Stop-the-Draft Week appear around a boy burning his draft card, as your eyes move slowly to the right, through the tumult of 1965 and 1966.

Abruptly, and without artistic explanation, there is a vividly colorful rendering of Telegraph Avenue during the few months of aimless gorgeousness that was the hiatus from frenzy; the strangely illuminated and parenthetical summer of 1967, when the operative form of protest became a life-style of peace. Its credo, and indeed, the mentality of a generation, seemed to be "believe it and it will exist." In the mural, everyone's hair is much longer, and the entire avenue seems wrapped in a gauze of marijuana smoke and magic soap bubbles.

Driving down Telegraph Avenue amid the psychedelic carnival are two microcosms of the outside world. In a new four-door sedan rides a very middle-class, very frightened couple with a terrified child in the backseat. They are strangers in their own land, furious yet not comprehending, and quite fearful for their child's future in a world of pushers and panhandlers and street musicians with no underwear, people whose view of the future extends only as far as their next joint, free meal, or benefit rock concert. If you listen carefully, you can almost hear the Jefferson Airplane.

The car behind is a VW bug with an interracial couple inside. They are reveling in the middle-class repugnance they inspire. They have become the children their parents warned them about, and they love it.

Suddenly things turn ugly. In a photo-realistic insert a man lies dying on a Telegraph Avenue rooftop; three Alameda County sheriffs are still training their shotguns on him. An eight-foot-tall helmeted, gas-masked Blue Meanie hovers above a scene of riot. The once-peaceful main drag of Berkeley is now the scene of the battle over an acre of land that the university owned, and the street people wanted. It took another four years of on-and-off skirmishes before People's Park was finally "liberated," as they used to say. The mural ends in a frenzy of bucolic cooperation; people of every age, sex, and ethnic background are shown in an idyllic denouement to the 1960s: tearing down the fences, ripping out the asphalt by hand, planting trees and gardens, pounding giant conga drums, dancing wildly, and worshiping the skies above in a kind of ecumenical earth stomp.

Just up the street, a mural's length off Telegraph Avenue, is the real People's Park. It can be entered from any point, but just past the mural is a sort of unofficial entranceway, complete with a hand-painted wooden sign and a bulletin board announcing upcoming events.

After having spent a half hour inspecting and photographing the mural, I move toward the entrance to take some shots of the park itself. It is late afternoon, and the recent Pacific rainstorm is now merely a mound of clouds over the Berkeley hills, reflecting some sorely needed sunshine.

I had no idea that I might be construed as an interloper here; boots and Levi's, unshaved face, eyes pinwheeling madly from four days of nonstop research in the library—my disguise seems perfect. But when I pull out my camera, all hell breaks loose. As I focus on some gardens being cultivated in the sunlight, twenty people begin to run toward me. They are shouting, swearing, and waving their hands for me to get out, like a band of Masai warriors who fear the camera will steal their souls and keep them from their promised afterlife.

I dodge a few errant rocks and clumps of dirt; then the gardeners, except for three, turn and run in seventeen different directions. I put away the dreaded Pentax and discover that it is not a concern for the "afterlife" that caused people to run amok.

"Every fucking manchild here's got a record as long as your arm or a warrant out on his ass, man . . . and you come 'round here look just like a narc with your stubble and your shitkickers *and pull out a camera.*" This from an agitated black woman barely five feet tall. "What the fuck you expect them to do—pose? You keep that black box in your bag or I'm gonna *own* myself a new camera in about five minutes." She gestures in a palsied kind of way behind me, and sure enough, she has more friends than I do. A slow circle of angry humanity forms around me, mostly black men, all holding hoes, rakes, and shovels.

Keeping the Pentax out of sight seems to settle things down, but one blond man in his midthirties alternates between trying to panhandle me for a quarter ("I'll split it with my sister here," he says pointing at the agitated lady) and telling me about his brother, who was killed in the Battle of People's Park. All this is tough for me to follow, torn as I am between keeping watch on the cordon of palace guards and listening to the blond guy talk between gulps on a quart of beer. These people are not the victors of the 1960s, they are the victims—and they rule People's Park.

It is not a particularly comfortable scene, but in a sad way it is grotesquely informative. I give the guy a quarter, then walk toward Bowditch Street up the middle of the park listening to a minor squabble break out behind me over the price of my safety ("fuck you, sister; you ain't getting nothing—that narc gave this quarter to *me!* Fuck you, fuck you, fuck you").

THE MURAL OF THE Six Years War captures the dynamics of the struggle heard around the world, but it leaves a lot untold. When one scratched just below the surface that was the 1964 Free Speech Movement, the Berkeley campus seemed a more than likely candidate for student unrest; It was a rumbling volcano whose eruption had been getting predictably closer as each year passed.

The issue of free speech was not new to the fall of 1964; as early as 1934 the entire campus had been declared off-limits to political fundraising, campaigning, and the recruitment of volunteers for off-campus activities. This ruling created controversy and confusion, since the hotbed for soapbox speakers and pamphleteers was a twenty-six-foot-long strip of sidewalk where Telegraph Avenue forms a T intersection with Bancroft Way, just beyond Sather Gate, across Sproul Hall Plaza. It is the main entrance to the campus, a heavily trafficked area, halfway between classrooms and campus housing, fringed by bookstores and cafeterias. On any schoolday, an academic village of more than twenty thousand inhabitants streams across the strip, coming, going, or just hanging around. The university owns the Bancroft Strip; there are two small brass plaques in the sidewalk that state in unequivocal terms, Property of the University of California—Permission to Enter or Pass Over Is Revocable at Any Time. But what takes place on that little stretch of land is free entertainment. After sitting through hours of lecture on Plato's argument over whether the basic question of justice is to be good or to be strong, or seeing a nonstop black-and-white slide show on basket-weaving patterns of the Hopi Indians, the average student came to feel that he *deserved* the kind of nonacademic action found only on the Bancroft Strip. Jugglers, mimes, evangelists, radicals of every stripe—this was therapy that was sorely needed, and it was a tradition as old as anyone could remember.

The biggest problem involved enforcement of university policy, that is, putting the threat, spelled out so concisely on the two plaques, into action. In 1934, when the campus ban on fund-raising and campaigning went into effect, students protested to such an extent that a small area on campus was set aside for "free speech." Logically, it was called Hyde Park. However, the university, for the most part, turned a blind eye to what continued to go on on the sidewalk parallel to Bancroft Way. The free therapy was tacitly allowed to proceed.

As time went by, real-world issues crept back on campus. In hindsight it seems that the academic year 1962–63 was the last year when anything on the campus—or the world in general—retained a traditional nature. During the fall of 1962, everyone carried transistor radios to class to catch the L.A. Dodgers/San Francisco Giants National League play-off series. Football at Cal took on a new aura of promise as Craig Morton, in his first varsity start, set a new school total-offense record of 285 yards against Penn State. (Still keeping within the larger confines of tradition, Cal lost 23–21.)

In October 1962 the biggest demonstration seen on campus was for a group called SINA, the Society for Indecency to Naked Animals. The head of the organization told a large gathering that his organization had run tests on animals at the Ohio State Fair Grounds and had "found horses with Bermuda shorts ran better and were more gentlemanly in their conduct than those without."

At this point in time, the devil's triumvirate of sex, drugs, and rock and roll had not appeared. At Cal, lockout for women was at 1:00 A.M. Contraceptives were not available for students at the university's Cowell Memorial Hospital until 1966. (However, every year at the Cal–USC Trojans football game, dozens of helium-filled prophylactics could be seen floating across Memorial Stadium.)

Drugs were still mainly in the hands of poets in North Beach. When State Attorney General Stanley Mosk addressed the campus that fall, he was repeatedly interrupted by a nonstudent, Lenny Glaser, a Bancroft Strip regular and a minor cult hero who gave Mosk and the crowd of hundreds their first hint of the future by shouting that the marijuana laws were "a political tool"; that marijuana, peyote, and mescaline are not habit forming; that Sigmund Freud introduced cocaine to the West and that Coleridge had used opiates to write "Kubla Khan." The crowd hissed and booed Glaser. The campus drug was still beer, although Berkeley had the lowest number of bars (and highest number of churches) per capita of any U.S. city with a population over one hundred thousand.

As for rock and roll, it was Glen Yarbrough, the Christy Minstrels, and Peter, Paul, and Mary singing "Puff the Magic Dragon" that brought thousands at $2.50 a head to fill Harmon Gymnasium. The twist and the limbo were the moving forces in the world of dance. Joan Baez had left Big Sur, but would be waiting in the wings for two more years before becoming the musical doyenne of the Free Speech Movement.

On Labor Day weekend of 1963, days after Martin Luther King's "I have a dream" speech, this was the campus environment I entered. There are few experiences in life as packed with exhilaration as that felt by a seventeen-year-old with a college letter of acceptance in one hand and a one-way airline ticket in the other. That fall there were probably about five million kids like me, fresh out of high school, with our flattops, Levi's, and penny loafers, humming the lyrics to the Four Seasons' "Walk Like a Man." The first slap in the face came at something called Cal Prep, a three-day-long introductory weekend to the campus and its traditions, where Clark Kerr said what all university presidents were saying to the baby-boom generation: "Look to your right; look to your left; in four years only one of you will still be here." What he didn't say, and could not have known, was that in four years one of those three would probably be in Vietnam and the other spaced out in some drug frenzy.

For a registration fee of ninety dollars a semester (just up from seventy-five dollars), the record enrollment of 25,033 students at Berkeley in 1963, was getting the best education money could buy. But the university was not quite yet prepared for the knowledge-hungry hordes. The last dorm unit to be constructed, with the endearing name Unit III, was ready for everything except meals: Three times a day all its residents streamed up Durant Avenue to the cafeteria at Unit I. At freshman mixers or fraternity rush parties, they were the ones who took their two-by-three-inch name tags with "Hello, I'm . . ." printed in the upper-lefthand corner and wrote in "all fucked up" underneath.

In Washington, D.C., President Kennedy was sponsoring a new Civil Rights Bill and had encouraged Martin Luther King's march on Washington; the campus speakers that fall reflected the times. Eight thousand people came to hear Malcolm X speak about black supremacy; James Farmer, head of CORE, also spoke. Thousands crowded in a half hour early to hear James Baldwin say, "the danger in America is that there has always been one thing to *not* think about—*me.*"

Other events on the fall speakers' schedule included *Playboy*'s Miss July, Carrie Enright ("I don't drink, I smoke only Marlboros, and I do not want to have any affairs before marriage"), and someone considerably more sensual—Madame Ngo-Dinh-Nhu, the beautiful and powerful Dragon Lady of Vietnam.

Vietnam, at that time, was a nonissue, the subject of much sophomoric humor. There was a frequently told joke about the increasing number of spectacular public suicides in South Vietnam: "What kind of mileage does a Buddhist monk get? A whole lifetime to the gallon." It wasn't really funny, but even Madame Nhu referred to them as "barbecues."

It seemed that regardless of the intrusions of civil-rights leaders and foreign heads of state, there was a sense of protectedness in this academic village. Berkeley was a world unto itself. It was as if the endless line of speakers was but a smorgasbord, a taste of what the real world might be like if you ever left campus. Then, suddenly, on a Friday afternoon in November (I was riding in Gary Robinson's 1958 Chevy Impala, getting ready to go skiing on early snow at Squaw Valley), the news of Kennedy's assassination brought the outside world much, much closer.

Almost everything shut down. Even the Big Game with Stanford was postponed. In a world turned upside down, heading to the bars, the porno shows, and the carny world of North Beach seemed somehow logical. A small handful of us went, just to avoid thinking of the future, just to drink and talk. There was far more drinking done than talking. No one knew what to say.

———————◇◆◇———————

IN THE FALL OF 1964, my sophomore year, an open letter to the student body appeared in the *Daily Cal* that sent shivers through the heart of the administration. As it turned out, the next three months would ultimately prove to be the cornerstone for a decade of student protest, a milestone in time wherein the silent generation was totally eclipsed by a new, noisy activism.

The letter was from Slate, a radical off-campus group known for its picketing of Charter Day and its yearly "supplement" rating professors and classes. This year there was an addendum to the supplement, a pitched call to action: "Students . . . should begin an open, fierce and thorough-going rebellion on this campus . . . the university does not deserve a response of loyalty and allegiance from you. There is only one proper response to Berkeley from undergraduates: that you *organize and split this campus right open!"*

Later the same week, the university released a statement that because of growing misuse of the Bancroft Strip it would, as of the following Monday, September 21, be off-limits to off-campus politics, specifically the solicitation of funds for off-campus activities. The brass plaques made a brief appearance, as the university reminded students who really owned the Strip. In the absence of Clark Kerr, the "off-limits" order had been reluctantly issued by Katherine Towle, a woman with impeccable credentials for handling tough situations. She had been the first director of the Women's Marine Corps and the first woman named dean of students at the University of California.

The chairman of Slate said that "the university is moving counter to making it a marketplace of ideas, which it should be." Those most upset were those who daily manned the tables along Bancroft Way. This was an election year, and the Young Peoples Socialist League and the California Students for Goldwater both threatened civil disobedience for the following Monday.

Over the weekend some rather startling events took place. The Golden Bears played good football, upsetting Missouri 21 to 14; and the university administration played bad poker, giving back the Bancroft Strip with certain conditions. The conditions included moving the free-speech, or "Hyde Park," area from an isolated spot behind the student union to the main entrance of Sproul Hall. Off-campus organizations were still banned from the strip, but moving Hyde Park gave the students a kind of visibility they'd never dreamed of.

The students personally impacted by this new order accurately saw the concession as a chink in the enemy's armor, a drastic miscalculation by the university of the depth of the students' conviction.

The activists attacked like piranha, setting up tables illegally and picketing the strip. As the crowds watched, the university did nothing, a further indication to the students that the administration could be had. Picket signs were fast becoming a counterculture art form: Bomb the

Ban, Ban Political Birth Control, and UC Manufactures Safe Minds were favorites.

The decision to move Hyde Park proved a critical error. On Wednesday, the first of a seemingly endless series of student gatherings began. At that time they were called free-speech "vigils," and they soon attracted all kinds of people who had no idea of what "freedoms" might have been trampled: It was perhaps the best place on campus to meet people. Typical of many, one girl told the press that she came "to see what the well-dressed college girl wears to an all-night vigil." Around three hundred stayed all night, snuggling on the steps and grass outside Sproul Hall exchanging telephone numbers, class notes, an occasional revolutionary concept, and singing songs straight out of Martin Luther King's hymnbook. The vigil never formally ended, and "the steps people," as they came to be known, became as much a part of Sproul Hall as its Ionic columns.

The next Monday the university, perhaps snapping under the pressure of hearing "We Shall Overcome" repeated for the three thousandth time, slapped down their second hand of bad poker. More concessions, but again with mixed messages. Dean of Men Arleigh Williams threatened possible suspension, probation, or expulsion for students defying the Strip regulations; at the same time, Chancellor Edward Strong gave back more territory, allowing distribution on the Strip of buttons, bumper stickers, and "yes" and "no" straw voting on propositions and candidates. To the rapidly crystallizing ranks of protestors, this was read as a clear sign that the administration was confused. "We'll settle for nothing less than a total victory," was the cry from Sproul Hall steps, literally right under the noses and ears of the administration.

The last day of September, things got serious. The university continued to pick nits, the students dealt only in broad concepts. The administration focused on details: the collection of funds and political "advocacy." The students gathered irreversible momentum behind a simple slogan—the generic war cry of the 1960s—"Free Speech." It covered anything.

At noon on the thirtieth, Friends of the Student Nonviolent Coordinating Committee (SNCC, or "Snick") and the Campus Congress of Racial Equality (CORE) set up tables *and* began collecting funds. It was a clear test case, and the university took the bait. As dozens of the "noninvolved" gathered to watch what was rapidly becoming the most dramatic and entertaining free theater on campus, two administration representatives approached the tables, took the names of five students, and told each to appear in the dean of men's office for "disciplinary action" at 3:00 P.M. that afternoon.

Precisely at 3:00 P.M., the five—Brian Turner, Donald Hatch, Mark Bravo, Elizabeth Gardiner, and David Goins—appeared in Arleigh Williams's office at 201 Sproul Hall. It is not clear precisely what "disciplinary action" Dean Williams had planned; he didn't have the opportunity to talk much. The five offenders had brought along 495 friends and a document they'd all signed stating that they shared the blame with the original five. It was an incredibly, almost magically, clever maneuver. And it was an action that helped inspire student activism elsewhere in the country. The concept was seen as a symbol of hope for the tiny student, formerly powerless against the anonymous university bureaucracy. As Mario Savio put it later that night after the university refused to readmit the suspended five, "We want equal action, and that is *no* action, because they can't take action against all the people who are here." He was right: after adding Savio's name to the list, the administration simply went home Wednesday night and left Sproul Hall to the students. Thursday brought not only a new month but a new level of action.

Things of a political nature on the Berkeley campus usually begin at noon; it gives the kids time to go to at least some of their classes or maybe sleep off an all-night strategy session. October 1 was no exception. After a noon rally on Sproul Hall steps, a nonstudent, Jack Weinberg, began collecting funds at a CORE table at the foot of Sproul Hall steps. A campus police car pulled up to the table as hundreds of demonstrators chanted, "Arrest us all! Arrest us all!" The university policeman left in search of reinforcements, then returned and was trapped with Weinberg inside his car for the next thirty-two hours. The crowd chanted, "We shall not be moved,' and all three thousand meant it.

The roof of the police car was high ground, and Savio worked the crowd masterfully. The symbolism could not have been more perfect. At 2:30, they voted to send some of their troops into Sproul Hall, trapping Associate Dean of Students Peter Van Houten and Arleigh Williams inside their offices. A policeman attempted to trap the trappers by locking Sproul Hall shut, but the students packed the doorways open and captured him inside as well.

Near midnight, on the grassy knoll at the southwest corner of Sproul Hall, a hundred people, predominantly from dorms and fraternities, gathered to shout obscenities at the protestors, lobbing eggs and singing choruses of "Mickey Mouse" in response to the demonstrators' "We Shall Overcome."

Clark Kerr stepped in for Chancellor Strong (who would soon take a permanent leave of absence for health reasons and be replaced by Martin Meyerson). Police were mobilized; 450 gathered along Bancroft Way for mass arrests. Fearing the worst, protest leaders shouted through bullhorns, "Loosen your tie and unbutton your collar. It will make you look like a beatnik, but it's for your own safety."

No arrests were made. Kerr, the ultimate arbitrator, negotiated a six-point agreement, and everyone went home for the night. The agreement called for the two sides to sit down and talk. The protestors agreed to a moratorium on demonstrations and to stop collecting money for off-campus organizations while the details of the arrangement were hammered out. Things seemed so good that on the fifth, Savio spoke on the steps, saying, "Let us agree by acclamation to accept this document and rise quietly and with dignity and go home." Across the plaza, leaflets were handed out announcing a dance Tuesday night in Pauley Ballroom featuring "instruction in the Waltz, Rhumba, the Swing, plus lessons in the latest dance crazes, directly from Liverpool." With the air filled with "I Want to Hold Your Hand" and "Please, Please Me," how could anybody want to protest?

All through October and November (when the FSM was formally organized and filled out applications for on-campus status), the administration and FSM members haggled, with minor success, and primarily succeeded in setting up joint student-faculty committees to make the university more "responsive" to the needs of the students. On one point the administration gave no ground: Eight individuals (including Mario Savio) were still suspended, but an *ad hoc* committee would hear their cases.

In early November things started to unravel: The moratorium ended before a final agreement was reached; fund-raising tables were set up as thousands thronged Sproul Hall Plaza. Then came a reprieve and a sense of vindication for the FSM, as the system-wide Academic Senate voted to criticize the university's handling of the matter and to reinstate the eight. Further, on November 20, the Friday before Thanksgiving, the regents of the university voted with the Academic Senate to reinstate the eight and expand the allowed activities on Bancroft Strip; money could now be raised for "legal" off-campus organizations.

It seemed as if the October sit-in had really done the job. The FSM wanted a more personal university, one that treated students like people. Their prime focus was on redemocratizing the university. They did not want it to be used as a public utility of big business or the defense department. They wanted to see their professors from less than five hundred feet away across a crowded lecture hall.

The irony, in light of events that were to follow, is that FSM's goals parroted the Godkin Lectures given by university president Clark Kerr at Harvard in April 1963. His presentations were on the topic of "the multiversity," how to administer mass education of a high standard.

Kerr criticized professors that were too caught up in fund-raising and gaining influence to the detriment of undergraduate teaching. He even predicted the ugly side effects that could arise if the multiversity were unsuccessful: Students would feel neglected and depersonalized to such an extent that they could be moved to revolt. For his tireless efforts to provide high-quality education for the masses, Kerr was awarded the 1964 Alexander Meiklejohn Award for contributions to academic freedom from the American Association of Universities.

However awarded, Clark Kerr was not on the Berkeley campus to implement his arbitration skills when the Bancroft Strip was closed down in September; he was flying back from Tokyo after a summer economics project in Russia.

One point deeply irritated Kerr when he got to Berkeley and saw what had happened as a result of the Strip being closed. Five years before, he had sniffed trouble in the university's policy of not enforcing the ban on politics on the Bancroft Strip. He had actually sent a memo requesting the secretary of the university to get the regents' approval to deed the title to the Strip over to the city of Berkeley. For reasons unexplained, the memo was lost, and a movement was born.

———————◇◆◇———————

THE MONDAY FOLLOWING THE Thanksgiving holidays, the now-notorious eight students returned to campus to find that Chancellor Strong had reversed the regents' reversal. Some of the students, including Savio, were again suspended. On Wednesday, December 2, one thousand people packed Sproul Hall in protest. It was as orderly as it was entertaining; old movies were shown, a rabbi came in and gave Hanukkah services, classes in civil disobedience were taught, and a delivery boy from La Valle's Pizza walked through the hallway shouting the last name of a hungry protestor. At 3:00 A.M. on December 3, Chancellor Strong appeared and said, "Please, go." The response was another chorus of "We Shall Overcome." He left, and several hundred police were ordered in by Governor Edmund G. Brown (against the advice of Kerr and Strong); they dragged off the eight hundred sit-ins. The graduate students and teachers went on strike. The next Monday, President Kerr called a meeting at the Greek Theatre and announced a peace proposal. At the end of his speech, Savio ran on stage, grabbed the microphone, and attempted to call an FSM rally. He was tackled by a policeman and hauled offstage in a hammerlock. The crowd went nuts. The Greek Theatre, an open amphitheater, shook like a runaway freight train. To preclude an angry riot, Savio was allowed to announce the meeting. The next day, in the heaviest voting ever on a system-wide issue, the Academic Senate overwhelmingly (824–115) backed the FSM plan to broaden political freedom. The rules went into effect, after further gnashings of teeth, in the spring semester of 1965.

The FSM had established itself nationally, receiving support for their national defense fund from Lawrence Ferlinghetti, James Farmer, Bertrand Russell, Jessica Mitford, and Norman Mailer. But by the end of March 1965, the FSM was, for all practical purposes, dissolved, though occasional rallies were held to raise funds for the legal defense of the eight hundred (whose prosecution was led by Deputy District Attorney Edwin Meese III). In April, Mario Savio announced he had dropped out of school and was leaving the FSM because of its "excessively undemocratic character." He spent the next year studying physics at Oxford.

Until the fall of 1965, things were quiet on the Berkeley campus. One could almost imagine the entire FSM saga as a blip on the screen of history, an unexplainable anomaly, leaving us with little more than the anachronistic phrase "Don't trust anyone over thirty." And yet, it left a legacy for other movements with other goals. The precedent of civil disobedience and nonviolence learned from the civil-rights movement was shown to be effective on campus as well. As the events evolved, the FSM proved a paradigm for protest of any sort. Most significantly, though, when the pressure and confusion of the Vietnam War mounted to psychotic proportions, the example of personal conviction as moral imperative set by the FSM became the loyalty oath for a generation. Had the war come first, the generic blueprint for student disobedience would have been quashed for security reasons. But it didn't happen that way.

———————— ◇◆◇ ————————

IT WAS NOT UNTIL sixteen months after Madame Nhu's speech that the specter of Vietnam really hit Berkeley. One reason for its relative insignificance was the preoccupation with the FSM. It must be remembered also that from December 1961 to the end of 1964, a total of only 243 Americans had been killed in Vietnam. Prior to the emerging campus concern over Vietnam, there was a brief interlude, a ludicrous expansion of the free-speech issue that provoked Clark Kerr's and Martin Meyerson's resignations: the Filthy Speech Movement. A nonstudent, John Thomson, was jailed for parading on the Bancroft Strip carrying a protest sign that read, Fuck. Thompson explained that his mother had ordered him to carry the placard and that he was sorry to have caused trouble. The ACLU noted an interest in the case. Former Slate and FSM leader Art Goldberg announced a noon protest rally the next day. Goldberg went on to say that Thomson's sign was simply a logical extension of free speech. Serendipitously, his point was accentuated by an annual campus-approved charity fund-raising campaign, the Ugly Man Contest. Students bought votes for their favorite candidates; as a publicity gimmick, the actress who played "Pussy Galore" in the latest James Bond movie, *Goldfinger*, was entered in the election. What Goldberg couldn't fathom was why John Thomson's Fuck sign got him arrested, when ten feet away people were allowed to go on selling "I Like Pussy" buttons.

The next day a fund for Thomson was set up on the Strip behind a sign reading, Fuck Defense Fund. Once again, it was free entertainment. Two were arrested for manning the table. Two more went into the basement of Sproul Hall to the campus police office, one reading *Lady Chatterly's Lover*, the other holding a hastily hand-printed sign saying, Support the Fuck Clause. Both were arrested. Kerr and Meyerson resigned on March 10, stating, "What might have been regarded earlier as childish bad taste has become to many the last straw of contempt."

An eighty-five-year-old Oakland real estate developer, Fred Reed, publicly announced his removal of a $2 million endowment to the university until authorities "have demonstrated they are running a university, rather than a bunch of children." Ronald Reagan, preparing for the state Republican primary, told an audience, "Preservation of free speech does not justify letting beatniks and advocates of sexual orgies, drug usage, and filthy speech disrupt the academic community and interfere with our universities' purpose." After being informed that Cal still had a football team, he further endeared himself to the campus by asking, "What do they use for cleats—nails pushed through their sandals?"

It was a brief and foolish saga. By mid-March, Kerr and Meyerson had withdrawn their resignations; by mid-May, Art Goldberg had been expelled for a year. But the Berkeley campus was now an established magnet for organized protest. Jerry Rubin's Vietnam Day Committee (VDC) had no difficulty attracting Bertrand Russell (who sent tapes), Benjamin Spock, Senator Ernest Gruening, Kenneth Rexroth, Norman Thomas, Paul Krassner, and Norman Mailer to speak on the presidency of Lyndon Johnson. It was late May, classes were over, the weather was perfect, and Vietnam Day was a successful thirty nonstop hours of discussion.

The summer of 1965 brought the Watts riots, the world's first naked picket line, sponsored by the Sexual Freedom League ("Love Thy Neighbor" was their motto); and the Jefferson Airplane. Bell-bottoms, hip-huggers, and long hair—the school uniform for millions—started to become common in the fall of 1965. These were days of grandeur for Major General Lewis B. Hershey, the aging, half-blind director of Selective Services. In early October, he stated, "I cannot see an end to the draft. Student deferment may not be extended." A week later, a new style of war protest was begun by twenty-two-year-old David Miller of Manchester, New Hampshire, as he burned his draft card on the steps of the Induction Center on Whitehall Street in New York City.

"Misdirected adolescents—I think they should be spanked," said Hershey as he left for his weekly poker game with J. Edgar Hoover. The Westwood Village draft board in Los Angeles stopped giving student deferments in late October, and a thick pall settled over the Berkeley campus.

As the fall semester moved on, a barely controlled panic was beginning to become a bond between students, who increasingly tended to "feed their heads" (as the Jefferson Airplane urged in "White Rabbit"), as an antidote to the fear of getting them blown off in Vietnam. Drugs were an escape; drugs with music were reverie; drugs with music and sex were ecstasy. The catch-22 to all of this was that passing grades, an absolute necessity for draft deferment, were very tough to get without a clear mind. Ironically, many students smoked and drugged their way to Vietnam.

All the various currents of discontent seemed to come alive by late 1965, making the entire Bay Area a complex, confusing—and thoroughly exciting place to live. The Students for a Democratic Society (SDS) sponsored a Black Africa Rally in the Greek Theatre and got more than they'd contracted for; Stokely Carmichael attacked white power, calling the University of California the "white intellectual ghetto of the West" and warning white society to "move over or we're gonna move on over you." Even the SDS seemed confused. In the middle of November, half the group picketed a speech by Igor Rogochev of the Russian embassy; the other half picketed the picketers.

A former *Ramparts* writer, Jann Wenner, began writing a weekly column in the *Daily Cal* called "Seamy Signs of Rock and Roll." Wenner, now publisher of *Rolling Stone*, revealed where the strangest music and most bizarre happenings were. (At one point, in a review of some galley proofs from Hunter Thompson's soon-to-be-published book *Hell's Angels*, he dismissed Thompson as trivial, "another hippy journalist.")

---------⟡◆⟡---------

ON OCTOBER 16, A VDC-SPONSORED march on the Oakland Army Terminal ran into the jagged patriotism of the Hell's Angels. Four hundred helmeted Oakland Police and National Guardsmen had lined up to stop the marchers and ensure order. The Angels, led by Thompson's roommate, Tiny, somehow got through the police barricade and incited mayhem, tearing up people, signs, sound systems, and swinging at anything, like leather-jacketed sharks in a blood frenzy. Tiny smashed a Berkeley cop over the head with a bottle, then flailed into the crowd with a bullhorn. Another policeman suffered a broken leg. In all, the Angels seemed better organized than either protestors or police. They led three charges through the no-man's-land separating the two groups, the last an all-out human wave, locking arms and running head-down into the crowd of students, who parted like the Red Sea (most of the Angels wore spear-topped Kaiser Wilhelm helmets). Back on campus, the John Birch Society took up a collection for Tiny's bail—few causes went unnoticed in those days.

The VDC was determined to mount another march; their goal was to reach the army terminal itself. With Thompson's, Kesey's and Ginsberg's help, they entered into negotiations with the Hell's Angels, a threat far more serious than the police. Preliminary meetings were held in Spartan Stadium at San Jose State, in a drenching rain in early November. It was Allen Ginsberg versus the Angels. The five-foot-six-inch poet probed suicidally, asking, "Why do you want to attack us? For right-wing money? For public sympathy? For kicks? Or have you struck a deal with the Oakland police to take the heat off you by kicking us around? I don't understand."

Toward the end of the meeting, as two dozen Angels would be seen through the rain leaping high into the air, jumping down to start their bikes into deafening explosions, an Angel named Quack took the microphone and in a flat, nasal voice, said, "I ain't very good with words like these gentlemen. I'm trying to explain why I despise these marchers. I believe these guys are living a lie. It's like when you go around a corner on a motorcycle. If you don't push that thing as fast as you can, you're living a lie—a joke. They're all cowards," he shouted, waving a burly arm at the crowd of drenched students. "We *despise* them!"

As the meeting broke up, another Angel grabbed the microphone and said, "See you the twentieth." No one laughed. A couple of minor miracles were worked before the twentieth, however, and the Angels didn't even make an appearance. One of the things that kept the march from becoming a nasty bloodbath was Allen Ginsberg's "To the Angels." Copies were distributed to all at the stadium, and it was later published in the *Berkeley Barb*. It was a piece of honesty that helped turn the tide:

> BUT NOBODY WANTS TO REJECT THE SOULS OF
> THE HELL'S ANGELS
>   or make them change—
>   WE JUST DON'T WANT TO GET BEAT UP
>
>   The protest march is trying to point out
>   that the terror in Vietnam is making
>   same terror here inside our country
>   loosing publicly the same cruel psychology that'll
>   give approval to busting yellow head gooks in Vietnam
>   This is infecting peaceful human relations here
>   allowing for public mass persecution of people
>   who disagree with
> the
>   growth of mass hostility mass hypocrisy mass conflict
>   The mass of marchers are not POLITICAL, they're
>   PSYCHOLOGICAL HEADS
>   who don't want the country to drift into the habit of blind
>   violence & unconscious cruelty & egoism   NOT
>   COMMUNICATION—with outside world or lonely
>   minorities in America
>   such as yourselves
>   and ourselves
>   AND the negroes
>   AND the teaheads
>   AND the Communists
>   AND the Beatnicks
>   AND the Birchers
>   AND even the so called Squares

Ginsberg was a visible presence on campus that year, having received a six-thousand-dollar Guggenheim Poetry Fellowship. His classes, in 123 Wheeler Hall, were jammed long before the discussions began. But it was a night at the Oakland home of Sonny Barger, Hell's Angels' chapter president, that gave the students the chance to protest in peace. Ginsberg, Kesey, Neal Cassady, and Hunter Thompson, along with several Angels, talked philosophy, played Bob Dylan and Joan Baez records, smoked dope, chanted mantras, and dropped acid.

"Again, being a coward, I didn't take any acid and everybody else did," Allen recalled years later. "So I was the goodly saint. Kesey, Cassady, and a couple of others all got zonked on acid. We got into some political arguments with the Angels, which I initiated, and Kesey very wisely got me off my high horse. Then I started singing the *Prajnaparamita Sutra,* and that was very soothing and pleasant."

The high, white miracle came soon after, when Ginsberg confronted Barger. "That goddamed Ginsberg is gonna fuck us *all* up," Terry the Tramp said later. "For a guy that ain't straight at all, he's about the straightest son of a bitch I ever met. Man, you shoulda been there when he told Sonny he loved him. . . . Sonny didn't know *what* the hell to say."

The VDC march was saved, and Barger took his still-powerful sense of patriotism directly to President Johnson. On the Friday before the march, he called a press conference, stating that the Angels would not resist the marchers. Reading aloud from his telegram to the president, he volunteered the services of the Angels, "a group of loyal Americans, for behind-the-lines duty in Vietnam. We feel that a crack group of trained gorrillas [sic] would demoralize the Viet Cong and advance the cause of freedom."

The VDC march on the twentieth of November drew nearly as many people as the Cal-Stanford game, played the same day. The army terminal was never reached; instead the protest went on for three hours at De Fremery Park. Speeches were made, signs displayed, dope was sold, soap bubbles blown, Frisbees tossed, and addresses exchanged—all to the accompaniment of Country Joe and the Fish singing the "I Feel Like I'm Fixing to Die Rag":

> Come on, Mothers, throughout the land,
> Pack your boys off to Viet Nam;
> Come on, Fathers, don't hesitate,
> Send your sons off before it's too late;
> You can be the first on your block
> To have your son come home in a box.

———————◇◆◇———————

> The summer had inhaled, and held its breath too long;
> The winter looked the same; as if it never had gone . .
> And through an open window where no curtain hung,
> I saw you . . . I saw you . . . Comin' back to me.
> —Jefferson Airplane
> "Comin' Back To Me"

The calendar year of 1966 had its beginning and end in the "anniversary services" for the December 1964 FSM sit-in. The stuff in between was a crescendo of pure schizophrenia that only stiff doses of strong drugs could wrestle back into a semblance of reality. By the magic summer of 1967 that is precisely what had happened. The death pall of Vietnam, where troop levels escalated from 184,000 in late 1965 to 478,000 by June 1966, was an ever-present backdrop to the whirlwind of daily life in a culture in transition.

The first FSM anniversary was done in Mario Savio's absence—he was studying physics at Oxford. In solemn tribute to the smashing of the old consciousness, the students reenacted the sit-in, broadcast tapes of Savio's famous speech ("There comes a time when you've got to throw your body on the gears of the machine . . . on the levers . . . to indicate to people who are running it that unless you are free, the machine won't run"), sang "We Shall Not Be Moved," filed into Sproul Hall, up the stairs, past the dean of students office and out again. Sproul Hall Plaza was as packed as Times Square at midnight on New Year's Eve and as hushed as Saint Patrick's Cathedral during prayer.

By the time the second anniversary came around in December 1966, campus life had taken a turn toward more militant activism. The key incident involved, again, card tables for distributing materials. An off-campus table handing out antidraft literature was removed by university officials while the table next to it was allowed to remain. The ensuing week-long strike shut down the university. Nonstudent organizations were not allowed to have tables, it seemed, while government agencies were: The table allowed to remain was a Navy recruiting table. In retrospect, putting a Navy recruiting table in the student union was a lot like selling soul food at a Ku Klux Klan rally.

The strike at the now-politicized campus was endorsed by four hundred faculty members, twelve hundred teaching assistants, picketed with Fly Navy: Burn Babies signs, and mediated by the new chancellor, Roger Heyns. The strike ultimately resulted in greater student representation in rule making and the firing of Clark Kerr ("It was not politically motivated," Ronald Reagan said from Sacramento), who reappeared on campus in April as a professor of business administration and economics.

A sign of the changing times, the Strike Committee adopted the Beatles movie *Yellow Submarine* as the symbol of their movement. Traditional religion took a nosedive in 1966; *Time* magazine asked, "Is God Dead?" On the eve of the Beatles' U.S. tour, John Lennon stated, "Christianity will go. It will vanish and sink. I needn't argue about that. We're more popular than Jesus right now." In response, the American Bible Society released figures showing that, in 1965, 150 million Bibles had been sold as opposed to only 13 million Beatles albums. The campus abounded with fundamentalist evangelists, such as Hubert Lindsey; the more hip countered by handing out leaflets reading, "May the Baby Jesus Open Your Mind and Shut Your Mouth."

If there was a breach in the ranks of traditional religion, it was probably because of the new spirituality. God was not dead; he was just showing up in brand-new places. Timothy Leary, interviewed in the September 1966 issue of *Playboy*, delivered his message of the LSD-induced confluence of love, self, and divinity; the Beatles' *Revolver* album quoted verbatim from his "Psychedelic Prayers" in the cut "Tomorrow Never Knows."

On November 30, 1966, students voted 4 to 1 for the issuance of birth-control devices by Cowell Memorial Hospital. The book *The Psychedelic Experience,* by Leary, Alpert, and Ralph Metzner, was reviewed in the *Daily Cal* thusly: "to go tripping without this book is roughly equivalent to trying to reach the moon without a spacesuit." A laundromat on University Avenue announced that their machines all used "LSD— low-sudsing detergent."

The Grateful Dead ("the loudest, longest band in the world") began playing for Ken Kesey's "Trips Festivals." The founder of the Dead took his inspiration from a surprising source, an individual he had met at Kesey's. Jerry Garcia said, "Until I met Neal Cassady, I was headed toward being a graphic artist. . . . He helped the Grateful dead become the kind of band we are. He presented a model for how far you could take yourself with the most minimal resources. . . . Neal had no tools. He didn't even have work. He had no focus, really. His focus was just himself and time."

Kesey's Trips Festivals had begun in Santa Cruz in 1965 and evolved into mass celebrations, gathering places where cauldrons of Kool-Aid were labeled Electric if laced with LSD. Few, if any, knew whether the signs had been switched, or if perhaps both vats were laced, or neither. Fewer still cared; most people showed up already laced. Nor were many sure what was being celebrated, other than life itself. These were pagan rites, with hundreds of people experiencing the same drugs, the same strobe lights, and the same music. The last acid test took place on Halloween 1966, after Kesey had returned from months on the lam in Mexico and LSD had been declared illegal (on October 6).

The Halloween festival was the end of the fun; possession of LSD was now a misdemeanor and selling was a felony. Jail was not a middle-class experience. Kesey called the Halloween happening at Winterland Ballroom a graduation from LSD: "The class motto should be 'Cleanliness Is Next.' It's time we did something with our experience." Kesey, who had gone "beyond literature" to explore alternative consciousness, was now going "beyond LSD." Regardless of the law, or Kesey's influence, LSD continued to be made all over California in mobile labs. It became the fuel that fired the summer of '67, and it was a whole lot easier to get than good grades or a draft deferment.

———————◇◆◇———————

THE RISE OF THE LSD black market involved a perfect union of technology and finance. The technology came in the person of a former radar technician and electronics wizard named Augustus Owsley Stanley III, who became known to millions around the world simply as Owsley. He was a short, manic, myopic entrepreneur who talked so fast that few could understand him and who reportedly made himself a millionaire by age thirty selling his "Owsley" acid.

He began his ventures into the world of underground pharmaceuticals in 1964, when he helped his girlfriend produce a pound of methamphetamine as a project for her freshman chemistry class at Berkeley. His lab was busted in February 1965, but nothing of legal importance could be found; all the drugs were in the trunk of his car. (Owsley's speed, tinted green, probably saved more undergraduates from flunking out of Cal than any cheating scam imaginable.) At about the same time as his methamphetamine bust, Owsley had begun doing electronics work for the Grateful Dead and became initiated to the world of LSD. He literally joined the band, living with them in Pasadena in late 1965 and early '66, and changed his chemicals.

Owsley took the money he had made from selling his "greenies" and made the last legal purchase of lysergic acid in the United States, from Cyclo Chemical Company, a transaction duly noted by the U.S. government.

Eventually, the demand for LSD so far outstripped supply that Owsley had to turn to someone with deeper pockets and a better knowledge of the world of high finance to fund his expansion. He was prone to spending money quickly, and in Kesey's absence he was virtually supporting the Grateful Dead and their camp following, an expensive proposition.

In early 1966 Owsley went east, having heard about Millbrook from Richard Alpert, to investigate the East Coast market potential for LSD and the Grateful Dead. He stayed awhile at Millbrook and then, while driving to New York City, Owsley was stopped by a state trooper (alert to cars seen on the Hitchcock property) for a tail light that supposedly wasn't functioning. As Owsley opened the door of his car, a ball of hashish rolled out, prompting the trooper to search the vehicle and impound, among other things, the key to Owsley's New York safe-deposit box.

Owsley was at a manic peak. He called Alpert, who called in the well-heeled and well-connected owner of Millbrook—twenty-six-year-old Billy Hitchcock. Hitchcock was a stockbroker at Lehman Brothers, where his father had been a partner. With his wealth and family ties, Billy was capable of opening thick bank vaults with a single telephone call. His father, Tommy Hitchcock, known as the Babe Ruth of polo, had been killed in 1944 in England test-flying a P-51. His death made Billy and his three siblings heirs to an immense sum of money. Billy's mother was no piker either: She was a Pittsburgh Mellon, and her father, William

Larrimer Mellon, founded Gulf Oil. The family also started Alcoa Aluminum and the Mellon Bank. In the mid-1960s, the Mellons were reportedly worth five billion dollars. Billy reportedly received about seven million dollars a year from the interest on a trust, ultimately controlled by his mother, Margaret. Tall, plump, puppy-dog friendly, and driven by a deep-rooted need to make more money, Billy Hitchcock was the perfect partner for Owsley.

After retrieving his money from the safe-deposit box, Owsley took it to Hitchcock's office for investment purposes. Billy was deeply involved with Fiduciary Trust, a Nassau, Bahamas, subdivision of the Robert Vesco–Bernie Cornfield Corporation, IOS. Unzipping the bag, Owsley dumped $225,000 in cash on Hitchcock's desk.

Hitchcock had already experienced the spiritual side effects of LSD during numerous sessions with Leary and Alpert. During the early days at Millbrook, when things were more scientifically controlled, LSD sessions were tape-recorded, transcribed, and analyzed. In the middle of one session, after a long, long lull of silence, Leary's sonorous voice asks the ultimate question of "seekers": "What knowledge do you wish?" After an even longer silence comes Billy Hitchcock's answer: "How can I make more money on the stock market?"

As Owsley piled the rectangles of green bills higher and higher, Billy experienced another side effect: greed. In short order, he left his wife, his twenty-five-hundred-acre estate, and his job as a stockbroker. He moved to Sausilito, to be close to the LSD action and far from his mother. The economics of LSD, as Owsley had so graphically illustrated, were as mind-boggling as the substance itself. While the raw chemicals could be expensive and hard to find, a small lab set up in the basement of a house in Windsor, California, and run by chemists that Hitchcock kept on monthly retainers, produced a reported twenty million dollars' profit in six months' time. Billy Hitchcock became the banker to the Bacchus of LSD. His precise role in the mass production of the drug is somewhat cloudy; he plea-bargained at his trial and was granted immunity by the government for testimony against his chemists.

It took until 1973, when the government hit Billy with three separate indictments covering his financial behavior from 1965 through 1971, for all this to come to light. In brief, he had traded forty million dollars of his money (sources not reported) through a Nassau bank, which quickly relocated to Switzerland and was run by his friend, Freddy Paravicini. The entire deal was done with no collateral, the largest-ever breach of SEC Regulation "T," which dictates how much money you must have to borrow against—then a sizable 70 percent of one's total investment.

The government had begun to collect surveillance data on the chemists in 1966 before LSD was illegal, often pressuring chemical companies to divulge the names of their cash-on-the-barrel customers. The defense argument revolved around relatively petty legal points concerning technical definitions of the chemicals that they had been making. In order to present a picture that might result in more lenient sentencing, the chemists' defense painted Billy as the "mastermind" of the LSD operation rather than the banker.

For the testimony against the chemists, Billy was slapped lightly across the wrist and fined $543,800 in taxes for "evaded income." He simply sat down and wrote the IRS a check. The chemists went to jail. Hitchcock later told an interviewer that he thought he was helping the economic development of the Apache Indians on their reservations. ("I had *no idea* what those guys were making," he professed.)

Owsley paid $143,000 in fines and spent two years in Lompoc Prison. Then he moved to the south of Australia, where he still lives, making cloisonné and gold jewelry and painting psychedelic patterns on small rocks.

There is a final irony in the all-American union of Billy Hitchcock (born on the 4th of July) and Augustus Owsley Stanley III. If Billy had consulted a history book instead of the Tarot cards, he would have discovered that possibly the worst person in America to help him develop a monopoly on *anything* was Owsley. Owsley was the grandson of a Kentucky senator, Augustus Owsley Stanley I, better known in the early 1900s as the "Trust-Busting Congressman." The Stanley Committee, with Owsley's grandfather as chief investigator, led an all-out attack on U.S. Steel, thirty million dollars of which (Union Steel) had been owned by the Mellon family. The investigation caught the nation's eye, as Carnegies and Rockefellers and Roosevelts were paraded before Congress to testify about the monopolistic growth of big business. The result was legislation that reoriented how the Mellon family did business—the Clayton Anti-Trust Act, authored by Augustus Owsley Stanley. The act put teeth into the vague Sherman Act and remains the primary legal weapon for countering monopolies of any type. Billy Hitchcock and Owsley III were doomed by their heritage long before they met.

———————— ◇◆◇ ————————

THE SUMMER OF 1967 WAS a Brigadoon time warp. The air seemed filled with an incredible amount of aimless creativity and harmless zaniness. For several months, the radical and activist segments of campus life seemed to disappear, leaving in its void the hippie culture. In essence, it became a movement by default; they were, for a while, the only show in town, and a colorful one at that. Thousands seemed to be reading Tolkien and Hesse, and selling keys of marijuana to buy a VW van so that they could go build a log cabin in the Sierras.

"The hippies are valuable," Vice-chancellor William Boyd said at an Inter-Fraternity Council speakers program. "Their community is a laboratory from which we may discover secrets from a world in which human relations will be more absorbing than jobs." Then, pointing out the basic difference between hippies and the rest of the world, he added, "We have made work sacred, the object of our lives. The hippies have had the courage to forego work."

The spirit of play was everywhere. Across the bay, as Haight-Ashbury prepared for an avalanche of humanity—perhaps as many as a quarter million—the city of San Francisco even had the foresight to make all these strangers feel a bit more welcome by naming as public-health director a physician by the name of Ellis D. ("LSD") Sox.

When the Beatles' *Sergeant Pepper's Lonely Hearts Club Band* album hit the stands in June, the party began in earnest. For $2.66, you got great music, lyrics celebrating drug use, and you could cut out and wear the enclosed mustache while amusing yourself trying to find the faces of Bob Dylan, Oscar Wilde, and Edgar Allen Poe on the cover. Pushing materialism to edge-city, John Lennon painted his Rolls-Royce with flowers and psychedelic insignia. (In the late 1970s the car was exhibited at the Cooper-Hewitt Museum in New York as a kind of cultural anachronism, a period piece of bent materialism.)

Even the basic human needs, food for instance, took on new dimensions. Two organizations collected, cooked, and doled out restaurant leftovers daily in Golden Gate and Berkeley parks. The Diggers in San Francisco and the Provos in the East Bay served up enough bread and stew daily to feed a wave of unemployed and disinherited domestic immigrants. (The Diggers took their name from a 1600s' English social-reformist group who wanted to abolish money and ownership of private property. A noble idea, but somewhere along the way the purity of the movement was lost: Digger pioneer Emmett Grogan died of a heroin overdose in 1978, and cohort Peter Cohon changed his last name to Coyote and established himself as a Hollywood actor.)

———————◇◆◇———————

RELIGION, RECREATION, SEX, MUSIC, food—it was all so magically easy. In the summer of 1967 the whole world seemed to be changing; even professors came to class barefoot, with flowers in their hair. A single image stays etched in my mind. I see a couple, locked in embrace, barefoot, with hair of equal length, fused together with no concern but themselves. In the distance is Berkeley Park, where music plays, Frisbees fly, and the odor of marijuana mixes with Creole cooking. (The Provos' "head chef" was a former cook at Antoine's in New Orleans.)

If you knew the rules, life was good and life was cheap. I spent the entire summer living on the roof of my fraternity house in a sleeping bag and eating at Berkeley Park. I spent $4.00 on vitamins and $2.30 on gasoline for my Triumph 650. I had bought the motorcycle a few years earlier as a means of combining cheap thrills with cheap transportation. The few times it actually ran, it filled both bills quite well.

The true "goodness" of those days of slanted sunlight and spiced stew at Berkeley Park came not only in the price ("It's free because it's yours: price $0.00," was the Provos' motto) but also in the music (Steve Miller Blues Band, live every Sunday) and in the quintessential anti-establishment gesture of peace: two hundred happy, well-fed frolickers with less than a dime among them smoking dope one hundred yards in front of the Berkeley police department.

The message of that summer seemed clear: that in an age of conspicuous consumption, it was not only possible to live off society's excess, it was great fun. While it seemed like the ultimate in self-subsistence, you were actually still entirely dependent on others. Little had changed. The ultimate question of just how long it could last had yet to be answered. It was after one of those Sundays in the park with sunlight and spice that I left; before the Haight-Ashbury drug pushers started killing each other; before the LSD and marijuana were laced with strychnine and paraquat; and, generally, before reality stepped in.

The magic, the mania, the whole hippie scene, ended very quickly for a couple of fundamental reasons: There were no leaders, just a lot of followers. Leary was embroiled in legal hassles; Ginsberg, more of an adviser than a leader, was in Wales; and Kesey was serving time.

The strangest force leading to the disappearance of the hippie counterculture was the absorptive resilience of mainstream American culture. When the Jefferson Airplane made an ad for Levi Strauss and Company in May, singing "White Levi's" to the tune of their classic hit, "White Rabbit," the end was in sight. In a year there was no culture for the hippies to be counter to. It was a case of "We have met the enemy and they have bought us." Yesterday's cult eccentricity became today's high fashion. There was money to be made in this counterculture thing; within months, housewives in Peoria were wearing headbands to PTA meetings; brokers on Wall Street grew their hair longer, sported paisley neckties, and wore bell-bottomed three-piece suits.

The return to materialism and capitalism took only months, not years. The work ethic might have taken a summer vacation, but it came back to Berkeley with a vengeance in the fall, and it is still there, lining Bancroft Strip with food carts and covering the sidewalks of Telegraph Avenue with crafts and jewelry stands.

THE BATTLE FOR PEOPLE'S Park in the spring of 1969 was a rerun of the FSM, only this time someone was killed. The warning signs of unrest had, once again, been obvious for some time. In May 1967, a study noted that of the 27,500 students enrolled at Berkeley, 263 were blacks, or less than 1 percent. Bobby Seale, chairman of the recently formed Black Panthers, claimed that predominantly black Oakland police force had recently been doubled—with white cops. "We are out to defend ourselves, not to kill white people. But if I catch a cop brutalizing a black person, I am going to kill him." Seale was true to his word.

When the university banned *Soul on Ice* author Eldridge Cleaver from speaking on campus in October 1968, Moses Hall was trashed by an angry mob. The world was in an ugly mood following the assassinations of King and Kennedy, Nixon's election, and the endless war in Vietnam.

The Third World Liberation Front (TWLF), uniting Afro-Americans, Chicanos, Asians, and Native Americans, was formed. Their demands for a black-studies program were made on January 15 and approved by a weary and wary university administration the very next day. It was not enough. The TWLF led a campus-wide strike that went on for six weeks, bombed Wheeler Auditorium, and barred nonstrikers from campus. A sign hung at Sather Gate that read, "Through These Portals Pass the Best-Educated Scabs in the World." Police and tear gas were used to disperse strikers, who demanded a black-studies department, a college of ethnic studies, and admission of more nonwhite students.

The ethnic issue reached its zenith when the American Indian Ad Hoc Board of Regents claimed the ninety thousand acres of land granted to the university by the Morrill Act plus forty-three million dollars they said was owed them. Henceforth, the campus was to be known as Tecumseh University.

In April, goals were redefined. Under the leadership of former Slate and FSM member, now Rutgers Law graduate, Art Goldberg, energies focused on a couple of acres of land the university had purchased for $1.3 million in 1967. On a warm Sunday, April 22, 1969, two hundred street people joined forces with students and began to rake, shovel, and plant the land, claiming squatters' rights. Their manifesto stated, "Your university's land title is covered with blood. . . . your people ripped it off from the Indians a long time ago. If you want it back now, you'll have to fight for it." And, of course, they did.

National Guard helicopters spewing tear gas buzzed the lower Student Union Plaza. Pepper-gas canisters and rocks were thrown back and forth daily, like a savage game of Hot Potato. Even the weather was evil: It rained for thirty-nine days straight, and an immense earthquake was predicted. Creedence Clearwater Revival played "Bad Moon Rising" down on University Avenue, and it seemed as if they knew their astrology.

During one massive, leaderless movement toward the park, a police car was overturned and torched and the windows at the Bank of America were smashed. The air was charged. Someone threw a brick from a Telegraph Avenue rooftop, hitting an Alameda County sheriff. He spun and fired a pump-action riot gun three times. Two people several rooftops from where the brick had been thrown were injured, and when one, James Rector, unexpectedly died the following Monday night, the campus became an armed camp. Governor Reagan declared the campus to be under Emergency Law. It was a hellish scene: a university fighting against itself. No one even tried to make sense of it; teenage students placed flowers in the gun barrels of teenage National Guardsmen. When one guardsman, Michael Felciano, dropped his rifle, removed his helmet, and quietly sat down in the middle of the Bancroft and Telegraph intersection saying, "I can't take it anymore," he spoke for millions.

The People's Park conflict came, and went, and came again over the next three years. The university built playing fields and a parking lot on the land, but they were boycotted. In the spring of 1972, in response to President Nixon's mining of Haiphong Harbor, a small army of people, with no interference from the university, tore down the fences and ripped up the asphalt by hand.

———————◇◆◇———————

THE UNIVERSITY HAS BEEN pretty quiet since People's Park, but quiet more like a well-fed, caged bear that takes an occasional swipe at its zookeeper, than quiet like a mouse. The undergraduates staged a weeklong gala twenty-year memorial of the Free Speech Movement in the fall of 1984. "Celebrate Your Heritage," proclaimed a huge banner hung from the student union, and they did just that. Discussion panels, films of the 1960s, a "hootenanny," and, of course, a noon rally on Sproul Hall steps were highlighted by an appearance by Mario Savio.

Perhaps it was the 1984 "refresher course" that jump-started the engines of student protest. In April 1985, protesting civil-rights issues in South Africa, 158 people (including 83 students) were arrested for sitting-in at Sproul Hall. When booked, each one gave his or her name as Steve (or Stephanie) Biko, after the slain black South African student in whose name the student union has been rededicated. All charges were dropped after only a few months. "I guess they figured they couldn't find a jury in Berkeley that would convict them," said defending attorney Stan Dewey.

———————◇◆◇———————

SITTING ON THE STUDENT union steps in late summer, I notice that the latest *Daily Cal* features *Bloom County;* "house for sale" ads proliferate; the Grateful Dead will be playing at Donner Summit; and *Burning Spear,* a black-power newspaper, is looking for help ("Did you ever want to work on a *radical* newspaper??").

The fog is burning off to the west as noon approaches—the hour of awakening for Sproul Hall steps, directly in front of me. Bancroft Strip is lined with carts serving Mexican, vegetarian, Middle Eastern, and American foods. The daily crowds are beginning to gather.

Three orange-and-white Hare Krishnas in their inevitable high-topped black tennis shoes begin a finger-cymbal-and-drum-accompanied mantra, a *ching-chinga ching, bonk bonk manja manja luta luta* sutra whose frenetic intensity is actually drowning out the six guitars and thirty voices of the Body of Christ Christian Fundamentalist choir from Boston that is trying to get its message heard from the steps.

The crowd thickens as a pair of jugglers set up shop, flipping bowling pins back and forth, higher and higher, until people are walking underneath a kinetic bridge. Two teenagers with guitars begin singing 1950s rock-and-roll songs right in front of me, and the "campus greeter" makes his first appearance of the day. He is unofficial, of course, yet he puts much energy into his work, shaking hands, slapping backs, and shouting hello to perfect strangers.

To the north, just this side of Sather Gate, a couple in their late forties, she in a pleated skirt and monogrammed sweater, he in a Ralph Lauren polo shirt and tasseled loafers, are quite obviously enjoying a tour of the campus with their seventeen-year-old daughter, no doubt a prospective student. As the small family unit enters the thick of the Sproul Hall Plaza menagerie, the parents' eyes are suddenly locked straight ahead, trying to deny the existence of all this. A lone man with a megaphone appears on Sproul Hall steps, dodging through the choir, announcing an anti-apartheid rally for noon tomorrow. The couple acts like it's their first day in a nudist camp, looking neither left nor right. The daughter, however, begins to beam, to radiate curiosity.

They pass right in front of the 1950s rock-and-rollers, who hit a new chorus, belting out, "I never want this special feeling to end . . . let's do it over—over and over again," and they moan with orgasmic delight.

The daughter walks a few steps ahead; her parents are now visibly concerned, their jaws tight as machinery. They exchange worried, angry looks and futile gestures; the noise level drowns out conversation.

At last, the "greeter" sees them. He is unshaven, barefoot, wearing grimy Levi's. A lit cigarette butt dangles from the corner of his mouth; his T-shirt reads, "Eat the Rich." He stands in front of the new arrivals and begins to do a combination of ta'i chi movements with the upper part of his body and a get-down, low-down, dirty-boogie, hip grind from the waist down, shouting greetings while somehow keeping his cigarette in place.

The parents are stunned and spin in tight circles, trying to escape. My sense of duty rises to the fore. Putting down an avocado-and-bean-sprouts-in-pita-bread sandwich, I begin running through the crowd toward them, waving my arms to get their attention. I want to tell them that this is not just a carnival, it is turbo-charged free speech; that this is free entertainment, not sin; that there are all those Nobel Prize winners behind the walls of the campus; that there is *no better education on earth* than what is at their feet! I pull up short, first thinking my antics would lead them to believe I had more fever blisters on my brain than the "greeter," who is now doing free-form aerobic exercises in front of the Hare Krishnas. But the real reason for my stopping and disappearing into the crowd—an easy thing to do here—is their daughter's eyes. I've caught just a glimpse, yet I saw in them what I myself felt two decades ago: an excitement, an aroused curiosity, an instinctual knowledge that no place else could ever be like this. I didn't talk to her parents because it was so obvious. Okay—*make* her go to Stanford. She'll be here every weekend, and there's nothing you can do to stop her.

The Longreach Ranch

THE ROAD FROM THE Bay Area north to Ken Kesey's in Oregon passes the Longreach Ranch, frequented during the 1960s and '70s by Billy Hitchcock, Owsley, Tim Leary, Richard Alpert, Mickey Hart of the Grateful Dead, and Terry the Tramp of the Hell's Angels, among others. Longreach is stuck way up in the hills, off Route 128 above the Russian River, three hours' north of Berkeley. From 1967 to 1973 it was the Pentagon of the illicit LSD wars. Even now, every so often, some battered, starry-eyed stranger will hike up the steep and twisting gravel trail to the main house, knock on the door, and ask if he can "go out behind where I left my stash . . . about fourteen years ago." In doing so they risk their life: This is No Tresspassers Private Property Beware of Dogs country, where marijuana is now a cash crop that rivals wine in total income.

The land was originally purchased in the 1880s for a twenty-five-dollar gold piece by the Lotti family, immigrant Italian wine-growing homesteaders. But recently it was a far more potent substance that brought people together at Longreach, which the locals still refer to as Doctor Hitchcock's. The gold-leafed logogram of the Brotherhood of Eternal Love is still on the wall just inside the "back" house. It is about eighteen inches high—a gold-painted Buddhist symbol for eternal love—and it looks like a stylized propeller with an angel hovering above it. It shines as freshly as when it was painted in 1967. (A flashlight was used to capture the enlarged silhouette of a neck pendant worn by one of the inner-circle members of the Brotherhood.) For this loose network of La-guna Beach surfers-turned-international-consciousness-raisers, the "back" house was where strategy was made, deals drawn up, and cash ex-changed. The woods, thousands of sturdy walnut trees, were literally laced with acid stashes. The family living there now is one part of a consortium of six who purchased the property for ninety thousand dollars in 1973 from the government and the law firm of Surrey, Karasik and Gould. It was auctioned off in an attempt to reclaim legal fees and back taxes on members of the Brotherhood, who made lots of money, but neglected to tell the IRS.

When the family living there is not discovering new ways to use wal-nuts (the bread tasted fine, but the dog ate all the cookies while we were inspecting the logogram), they show the property to potential buyers. For $985,000 it can be yours, and it comes furnished with Timothy Leary's piano and a 1927 wood-paneled, brake-and-shoot Rolls-Royce station wagon, nostalgically named "Sir Henery."

Many vestiges of Longreach's counterculture days are still around. While out picking walnuts recently, the owners tripped over a watertight con-tainer the size of a large eggplant, filled with enough of Owsley's "Orange Sunshine" LSD tablets (identifiable by its color and shape) to flip out half of Marin County. This happens frequently, they told me. Reassur-ingly, the walnut waffles and muffins tasted normal—no aftereffects.

Always Going Beyond

FINDING WHERE KEN KESEY lives is simple; it's finding when Ken Kesey lives there that's tough. Two years earlier, I had made this same trip from Berkeley north to Oregon and I must have made a dozen phone calls trying to verify our meeting. Faye Kesey was vaguely encouraging, saying "he *seems* to be headed back in this direction. Calling him between noon and one would be your best chance." Finally, it was Kesey on the phone speaking in a low, monosyllabic way, as hazy as Faye. Saying, "Yeah . . . well . . . not the weekend . . . gotta be somewhere sometime . . . I'm not sure just when . . . I'll check with Faye . . ." We finally agreed on a time. Then Faye got back on the phone to give directions, "two and one-half miles past the gas station. We live in a red barn with a star on the side." This time Kesey wasn't there, so I'd have to be satisfied with driving by, but as I passed familiar landmarks, memories of my last visit came flooding back . . .

BEFORE HEADING TO KESEY's I stopped at a gas station Faye had mentioned. I figured the small mountain back roads wouldn't have a gas station open at night. The station attendant looked to be in his twenties; I asked him directions to Kesey's, which confirmed Faye's. Then, curious, I asked him *who* Kesey was. The attendant said, "I'm not real sure. He went to school with my mom; that's how I know where he lives. I think he writes books and stuff, but I don't really know."

"Books and stuff." As I drove the last two and a half miles, my mind chewed on the kid's comment, and I searched for a scenario with which to explain Kesey to someone his age. What I came up with was this:

Author John Irving smashes sales records, wows critics, and cultivates millions of fans with his first big book, *The World According to Garp*. It is made into an equally successful movie. He then proceeds to place a second gleaming jewel in the Triple Crown of American Fiction with *Hotel New Hampshire*. It is a curiously different book, filled with incest, lesbianism, and anarchism. Next, as his burgeoning public slavers in anticipation of the third gem, as critics wait cynically, the hero of hardbacks pulls the literary rug out from under everyone. A public statement is made that he is "leaving literature behind." He descends upon Boston and New York, preaching the use of drugs, living life for the experience of living life. Mocking convention, he breeds a camp following, a circus Day-Glo clowns. They buy a bus, paint it very strangely, and drive across the country, acting very strange. The once-loved writer takes the two-thirds-completed Triple Crown and its assurance of immortality and mortal wealth and casually tosses it out the back of an old school bus.

Something very much like this happened once before, more than twenty years ago. President Kennedy was alive and on the New Frontier. Young men wore crewcuts. The Kingston Trio harmonized. Blacks and whites ate, drank, and lived separately. In February 1962, within days of John Glenn's first American orbital flight, a young author burst open the American literary consciousness with his first big book, *One Flew Over the Cuckoo's Nest*. Kirk Douglas starred in the Broadway production. Reviews were great, sales soared, and the future seemed limitless, sky-high, far-out. Within a few years he had done it again, with *Sometimes a Great Notion*. There were a few complaints: "It's too ambitious, overwritten, complex," some said. But most offered praise: "A fascinating story," "a turbulent tale," "a towering redwood in the fiction wilderness."

And then the huge tree crashed, sending shocks and splinters across the entire country. Ken Kesey went "beyond literature," the Merry Pranksters evolved, drug use mushroomed, the Hell's Angels and Hunter Thompson were temporarily tamed, and then the law closed in.

———————◇◆◇———————

NOW, MORE THAN TWENTY years since that young star first shined in the West, it's quiet up here in Oregon. Real quiet. It's been real quiet since 1968; the silence is so old that it can vote and go to war. It has been quiet since Ken and Faye Kesey drove the bus up to the eighty-acre farm and set up house in the big red barn after Ken finished his jail time.

The star is the sign. It is shiny aluminum, inserted into a cut-out with a deep-blue ring around it. All this against the red of the barn. It's big, maybe six feet across, like some westward-migrated Pennsylvania Dutch hex sign with a pituitary problem. It is a very American star.

It's quiet out back of the barn, off the shed where the bus, bubble-topped, gutted, and graffiti-covered (the sign on the front still reads, Further; on the back, Caution: Weird Load), sits silent and alone.

Especially at night it is quiet, when the farm animals are hunkered down and Ken Kesey sits silent and alone, writing his novel on Alaska. Through the long northern winter nights, he sits at a small desk. It is Spartan and clean in the little room. There is a paperback book—something by Jack London—propped open, a red candle in a bottle of generic beer. An old typewriter with a lightning bolt decal sits by, ready to turn into black and white the millions of random thoughts that spurt and sputter and clamor to be articulated. The small two-burner wood stove keeps his coffee warm. Kesey's mind churns and cranks and puffs and sparks like the great Prankster bus itself, trying to jump-start the rusty engines of creative output. He tries new combinations. He experiments with old ones, looking for the right key, the right lock, until the light of dawn.

He sleeps until noon. But he says he has started something out there in the room with the zappo typewriter and the single red candle. Sometimes at night, if you listen real close, you can hear it rumble, see it crackle and spark like blue neon, then feel it purr real nice and smooth and sweet for a while like a crisp new Mercedes sedan. Then it starts to cough, pop, and miss, all out of tune. And the silence settles down thick and close in, like the ground fog rolling in slow through the pines.

———————◇◆◇———————

GOING TO MEET KESEY, I anticipated a gruff bear in the second decade of hibernation; over the hill, and under the influence. As I pull onto his property, I notice that stereo speakers and colored lights are everywhere—hung in trees, on the roof—just the way it was at La Honda twenty years before. A blue-and-yellow macaw croaks, "Good-bye," as I enter the barn. Faye ushers me through the vast interior—one big room with a TV and a wrestling mat—to a big round wooden table by the back porch. In front of the TV is a bus bench pulled from *Further*. The decor is sparse, yet functional. On the porch, Faye calls to Ken as he drives around on a small tractor, pulling bales of hay down by the duck pond for the sheep.

He fits in well out here on this rolling, green farmland. His silver hair is thick and fleecy. His chest, his neck, are thick, like one of the bulls wandering amiably down by the duck pond. He comes over and says hello, not smiling, not even looking at me. He shakes hands, and I introduce myself. Then he sees the cattle getting through the fence. He turns and runs, splay-footed on legs too skinny for his bulky old wrestler's torso, and shoos the cattle back to where they should be. He seems like the gruff bear I anticipated.

Just as I begin to think I have traveled two thousand miles to try to interview some burnt-out backwoods hermit, Ken Kesey comes back, whistling, singing, smiling. He says, "Did you know that it was the red-winged blackbirds who wrote the Gillette Razor jingle?" He whistles just like a blackbird, sings a few bars of "Look sharp, feel sharp," and a laugh leaps out of his Pendleton-covered chest. It's a Randle Patrick Mc-Murphy laugh that warms us all, that sinks through the chilly Oregon drizzle just like a straight shot of tequila.

He sits down on the porch, eyeing the wayward cattle, rolling a pathetic stubby joint out of stems and seeds. He lights up with a kitchen match, takes two little hits—still looking straight over the duck pond—and then he exhales. He puts the joint down. It goes out, but he doesn't notice or seem to care. He turns toward me and smiles, warm like the laughter, only more sunlight than thunder. He looks like a 210-pound, five-foot eleven-inch Paul Newman.

"Do you have any kids?" He asks this in a very serious and direct way, and I answer, somewhat puzzled, "No. Just a parrot and a Persian cat." Kesey is not interested in my menagerie. "You have got to have kids," he admonishes, almost as if he was scolding one of his own. "You cannot know," he enunciates, carefully saying *cannot*, instead of *can't*, "you will *never* know what life is until you have kids."

I wasn't sure if I totally accepted his secret of life, but if there is a resident American expert on bridging generations, Kesey is the man. Born in 1935, his life and career span the Beat Generation of the 1950s, the acid-consciousness revolutionaries of the 1960s and '70s, and the future.

I ask him about his youth. "I used to have a ventriloquist show here in Eugene as a kid," he says. "I still work magic tricks," and so saying he rolls three fifty-cent pieces around his fingers and makes one disappear. "In every high school, there was always the weird kid, interested in stuff nobody else was interested in. He was always doing tricks, studying the stars, or reading science fiction. He was always boiling strange things. He usually had a bad complexion, and the girls weren't big on him because he was weird."

This was the young Ken Kesey, boiling strange things, reading *Childhood's End* and *Magic Mountain* between wrestling matches and work at his father's dairy.

"When you do magic, it has to do with real power. I am a power junkie. I love power," he says. "For one thing, I think it is not corrupting, like some people think; it is purifying. People who think they have power yet do not are corrupted. People who really have power are humbled by it."

Power, magic, drugs—whatever the label for Kesey, he always seemed to want to "go beyond." And there was an inherent charisma about him that made others want to go along.

When he got to Stanford in 1958 (by winning a literary competition), he was a twenty-two-year-old grad student, married, and having difficulty supporting a family. He was self-assured, but not really cocky. Those around him got a feeling that Kesey knew he was going to do big things, even if he hadn't the slightest idea how or what. It was as if even before he tasted his first peyote button, he realized he was in concert with "the larger forces."

That sense of confidence appears in a letter Kesey wrote to Curtis, Brown Literary Agency as a senior in college in June 1957:

> . . . I am currently twenty-one years old, a senior at the University of Oregon in Radio TV, living with my wife, Faye, also a student here, and our four month old white and brown beagle pup . . . (At) the University of Oregon . . . I appeared as a magician and hypnotist around town and did once a week ventriloquist shows for cash . . . I played football and was on the wrestling team, lettering three years . . .
>
> Finally, this last summer, along with sports, studies, fraternity work, deer and duck hunting, forty hours a week at the local creamery and writing some TV plays, I wrote a novel about school and sports as I have observed them in four years.
>
> From here? I'm not sure. I'm starting another novel and probably will write another TV play I've been thinking on. I'm still going to keep shooting for the big billing. I've got a lot of faith in my resources, some day someone will tap them. Perhaps they just need a little more aging before the tap is inserted.

At Stanford University, Kesey had the opportunity to age his resources. Though the reading public usually considers *Cuckoo's Nest* to be his first effort, it was actually Kesey's fourth: *The End of Autumn, The First Sunday of September,* and *Zoo* (about the beatnik scene in North Beach) never saw the printer's press. There was also an earlier version of *Cuckoo's Nest,* printed by Stanford University Press as *McMurphy and the Machine.*

Kesey was formally enrolled as a student at Stanford for the academic year 1958–59, but also hung around Perry Lane auditing Malcolm Cowley's class. At that time he was involved in writing *Zoo,* a portion of which won a Saxton Grant from Harper Brothers Publishers. Kesey was notified of the award in late November 1959 by Elizabeth Lawrence, of Harper, who warned him that "the Grant does not carry any assurance of publication." Further she was concerned that Kesey had projected the book as two volumes. "I hope not," Ms. Lawrence wrote, "for sequels are usually disastrous."

With a major publishing house showing serious, if guarded, interest in *Zoo,* Kesey gushed back to Lawrence in early December 1959. "I was very pleased to hear from you on behalf of Harper Brothers. The letter is a first of its kind, and whether anything comes of it or not I shall cherish it always among my pile of short story rejection slips."

Hard at work through the winter and spring of 1960, his confidence grew, buoyed by Malcolm Cowley's encouragement. In early May 1960, he wrote Harper, sending the completed manuscript and requesting that it be submitted for the annual Harper's Prize.

Harper replied in late June: Everyone had read *Zoo*, and Elizabeth Lawrence called the book "one of the most interesting entries," adding that all who had read it assured her that it was certainly "publishable . . . fresh in its handling of language and easily the best statement (if that is the word) we have seen on the Beats and their world." She then added, almost parenthetically, that her letter could be added to Kesey's growing pile of rejection slips.

Pained, but with his competitiveness undaunted, Kesey wrote back in early July that "it is with equal regret (no, that's understating it) that I send this letter in answer to your rejection." Kesey burned the *Zoo* manuscript and moved on to his next project.

Vik Lovell, a Perry Lane neighbor and psychology graduate student, played a significant role in Kesey's career when he suggested that Kesey might be interested in the experience, as well as the money, that came from being a participant in the MK-Ultra, CIA-funded research on mind-altering drugs. It was seventy-five dollars a night, and yes, they paid you! Under the influence of psilocybin and LSD, Kesey saw for the first time what mental patients chronically felt: the oppression of consciousness. The dedication to *Cuckoo's Nest* reads, "To Vik Lovell—who told me there were no dragons, then led me to their lairs."

Lovell recalls Kesey as "a young, all-American fraternity man. He didn't drink and he didn't smoke, but he was kind of reckless and adventurous. I really know of no long-range plans that he had, other than being an actor, and he went to Hollywood and actually gave it a shot."

Lovell not only introduced Kesey to the drug experiments but was also with him as a student in Malcolm Cowley's creative-writing class. It was not a large class—about fifteen. They would meet in Jones Hall around a large oval table and read their compositions to each other for critique. Cowley had never heard language used in fiction as Kesey was using it. He was acquainted with the new generation, but not with the new chemicals. It took Cowley some time to understand the changes in perception that Kesey was experiencing, but it took him very little time to recognize *Cuckoo's Nest* as a valuable contribution to American literature.

(Not all of Kesey's inspiration came from the visionary effects of psychedelic drugs. Other writers played a role in confirming that what Kesey saw was an oppression of consciousness. "When Burroughs's *Naked Lunch* appeared on Perry Lane," Vik Lovell recalls, "it was incredibly influential to all of us in saying, 'There are new directions.' Especially Kesey. Ken read *Naked Lunch* a great deal. He was very much influenced by it. I recall us standing up, reading sections to each other so that we could *hear* the sound of it. We were amazed by it.")

Kesey now finds a wonderful irony in the fact that the U.S. government provided him with a crash course in mind-altering drugs. "There was something American about the government conducting these experiments at the Veterans Administration (VA). This was the same consciousness as Lewis and Clark must have had heading into unknown territory. My metaphor is this: that the government discovered a room and none of them wanted to go in, so they hired these students. As the people came back out of the room, the government saw the changes and stopped the experiment about two-thirds of the way through. One of these days they will finish it.

"When we first took those drugs in the hospital, it was like the books God keeps. You had heard about the Bible and the Akashic Records, but suddenly you had a glimpse of them. These were the real books. These weren't kept in the school library, these were the *real books.*" Kesey repeats this for emphasis, then slowly continues, reciting his experiences as a twenty-two-year-old kid, as though they had happened yesterday.

"So we wanted to see these books and we took more and more drugs, until finally, at one point, God said, 'You want to see the books? *I'll* show you the fucking books,' and it was like a big hand grabbed us by the back of the head and held us there for twelve hours. We were in absolute hell because we saw ourselves; we saw all the stuff we had done, mistakes we had made, our indulgences, our cruelties. That was hell."

What he experienced in the VA experiments was just the beginning, a tease. He knew he wanted to see more. After unsuccessfully trying to get an extension on his fellowship, he began working for Leo Hollister, who was funded to continue LSD research at Stanford. In learning to see the world through the eyes of the inmates in "the nuthouse," Kesey began to see that evil was at the core of human behavior.

"Evil is more important than good," he says. "Unless you have something big and scary, you never get to know the hero. When a big evil comes, something will rise out of the populace to take it on. But without the evil it is just drab stuff. I saw the looks on these people's faces [in the mental institution] and realized that Freud was full of shit. Something really dug deep in these people's minds, and it wasn't the way they were treated when they were toilet trained; it wasn't the way their father rejected them when they were thirteen. It was something to do with the American Dream. How the American Dream gave us our daily energy and yet the dream was perverted and not allowed to develop fully. *Cuckoo's Nest* was supposed to be a revolutionary book. It was supposed to be about America, about how the sickness in America is in the consciousness of the people. Not the government, not the cops and *not* Big Nurse," he concludes, indicating his still-smoldering anger over the movie version of his book.

Finishing *Cuckoo's Nest* while working nights in the VA hospital, Kesey supplemented his supply of in-house chemicals with mail-order peyote buttons (from the same "Magic Gardens, Texas," concern Allen Ginsberg had found in the early fifties). He stayed on another session at Stanford as a nonstudent in order to complete his manuscript. He didn't like Cowley's replacement, however, and encouraged the creative-writing students to boycott Jones Hall and the new instructor (Frank O'Connor, who didn't feel comfortable with Kesey's use of Chief Bromden as the narrative voice of *Cuckoo's Nest*).

With his manuscript finally completed, Kesey headed north with his family to work on the family dairy, then on logging trucks to get some background for his next novel. Like *Cuckoo's Nest*, it had begun with a short story, entitled "Spring Rain."

"When I finished at Stanford, my old teacher, Malcolm Cowley, took the manuscript, and I thought, 'That's it; I made my run,' and I came back up here to work in my brother's creamery. I went right to work on my next novel. I didn't 'expect'; I didn't even think about it. I was going good. All I knew was that once you were moving good, you had better keep moving, and I just kept moving, working on my second book. When the reviews and stuff started coming out for *Cuckoo's Nest*, as time went by, I realized, 'Boy! I have written a great book!' But, it didn't occur to me when I was writing it. I had no idea it would be taken like it was."

By the time *Notion* was completed, Kesey had moved back south, and the Perry Lane crowd took to hanging out at La Honda. The attraction of a good-looking, all-American, two-book author was overwhelming, and people began to materialize around him. Those who had known him in his prefame days felt it was a self-fulfilled prophecy. Most of them hung around to see what was going to happen next among ponderosa pines alongside Route 84. Others learned of Kesey by proxy—reading his books or through local newspapers. The number of connections grew. Vik Lovell introduced his therapist to marijuana, then introduced his therapist to Kesey. Richard Alpert was teaching with Leary at Harvard, but also hanging out around Stanford. At the Nepenthe Bar (literally "a place to dull pain and sorrow"), where Jack Kerouac had gotten obnoxiously drunk on martinis after his ill-fated "dead-otter" visit to the Esalen baths, Lovell ran into Alpert, who was there watching the fog roll in with Allen Ginsberg. The counterculture was, as Burroughs had said of the beatniks, initially a social network, only later did it become a "movement."

As Kesey completed *Sometimes a Great Notion*, he felt a change in the air. And in the water and in the earth. It seemed universal. It seemed that the forces of evil he had observed in the VA hospital were now doing battle against an international conspiracy of heroes—musicians, writers, intellectuals. All they needed to round out the troops were a few Pranksters. Kesey began to feel it was time to redirect his energies, to "leave literature behind." There would be no third jewel, no triple crown. More serious matters were at hand.

"All of the people that were hanging around together were already talking 'revolution' in kind of vague terms. We were educated enough to know that the beatnik kind of revolution just wouldn't work. It was going to take a revolution of consciousness. I don't think anybody *invented* this; I just think a bunch of people realized it at the same time and joined forces without even knowing that there was an army.

"When we got into acid as a group of people, we felt like we were dealing with the end of time. I don't feel the same way now, but then I felt that writing was done for the future, and suddenly we were *cut off* from the future. I did not feel that *Cuckoo's Nest* was going to be read in three or four hundred years. It was a different consciousness than writing. I could not do the same kind of writing I had been doing. We got into what I would call Rorschachian art. Tim Leary, Bobby Dylan, John Lennon, Bill Burroughs—we were all reaching in to wrench the language apart. It was as if the syntax were anchoring us to something older—something ancient, something staid—and we were trying to tear it out. The slate was ours. We wrote on it what we wanted. We felt that the consciousness revolution was going to take us off physically—like *Childhood's End.*"

THE REAL MEANING BEHIND Kesey's squadron in the revolutionary army—the Merry Pranksters—was lost on many because of their utter looniness. Herb Caen's column in the *San Francisco Chronicle* would report on the meanderings and public sneak attacks of *Further* and its Day-Glo passengers. Around San Francisco, where the standards for behavior are slightly skewed from the national average, they were seen as harmless entertainers, a concentrated extension of the mimes, musicians, jugglers, and magicians that appeared every night on Union Street or by Fisherman's Wharf. This bunch just had their own transportation.

To truly invade the American Consciousness, Kesey decided it was necessary to embark on a cross-country crusade to meet the Infidels of the East. Who *was* this "Doctor Timothy Leary" anyway—a Harvard professor, living off the fat of the Gulf Oil heir's estate?

In the early days, there was an almost academic snobbishness to drug experimentation. As the movement grew, there developed an East-West schism. Kesey saw Leary as an elitist Harvard professor, washing down his LSD with Chardonnnay from a wicker picnic basket. "They were the beautiful people," he remembers. "They had mansions. They had money. I remember a picture of Peggy Hitchcock in her million-dollar bikini."

Out West, Kesey, the Pranksters, and the Hell's Angels blasted back their drug capsules with cheap beer from an iron bucket. "We were the scruffiest," he says. In Cambridge, Leary had organized IFIF—the International Federation for Internal Freedom—with Aldous Huxley and a group of well-known academicians. In La Honda, Kesey countered by painting a green-striped star on his front tooth, hanging out with the baby-raping, barbarian Hell's Angels, and founding ISIS—the Intrepid Search for Inner Space.

While they remain close friends today, the basic differences in the two most visible counterculture heroes remain.

"One of the things with power," says Kesey, "is that you don't want to draw attention to yourself. I think that's one of the mistakes that Leary made, and when it started happening with me, I always tried to back away from it."

In the summer of 1964, arriving unannounced at Millbrook (after a party in Manhattan where Kerouac, invited by Cassady, had solemnly taken an American flag being used as a Prankster's serape, folded it neatly, and disappeared), they had to wait three days before Leary would see them.

They waited and enjoyed themselves; the estate during the summer is idyllic. Then Owsley made a fleeting appearance, leaving behind chemicals so that Leary, Kesey, Cassady, and Ken Babbs could all have a "session" in the small meditation house. With the passage of time, Kesey has gained a better feel for Leary's initial aloofness at Millbrook, especially when he later found himself in a situation similar to Leary's.

"I have often thought of that," Kesey says now. "A few years later, strange painted buses with kids fifteen or twenty years younger than me came rolling in here, and I was trying to deal with calves being born, and I was strung out from writing all night. And these kids wanted me to *respond!* I have become very sympathetic to the whole Millbrook scene, because we were a nuisance."

The elitism and pseudoscientific nature of the early days at Millbrook left their impact on the Western outlaws, too. "At one point at Millbrook I remember there was a dog walking by. Cassady was sitting there and when he saw this dog go by, he said, 'Look at this! Another wisenheimer!' We didn't feel snubbed exactly; we were disappointed."

Back on home territory, the man who always "tried to back off" when too much attention came his way was getting more attention than he could handle. The worst came from the law; after two drug busts, he had had enough and took off to Mexico, after having someone drive his van off a cliff north of San Francisco and leaving behind his sky-blue cowboy boots and a suicide note. The prank failed; in the *San Jose Mercury*, a headline read, KESEY'S CORPSE HAVING A BALL IN PUERTO VALLARTA.

He came back, still a fugitive, but gave interviews on local radio, just to get the establishment's goat. Then he was spotted and caught in rush-hour traffic. Because he had fled the country, the case belonged to the FBI.

"I came back from Mexico in 1966, and the FBI caught me. All of the San Francisco revolutionaries were waiting to see what I would do. My metaphor is this: There were guys on either side of me, each with a gun at my head. There was someone in front of me with a microphone wanting me to say something so that he would be able to record the sounds of the shots. Anybody who had been through that situation knows you have to cooperate to survive. But still, through this, you are sending a message to the people, saying, 'If you are paying attention, you know I have to do this.'

"I finally really came to hate those people who wanted me to sacrifice myself and wanted me to stand up and say, 'Everybody take dope and overthrow the government,' even though they knew the government had me. I was in the mouth of the wolf."

SINCE RETURNING TO OREGON, Kesey has in many ways become a flaming traditionalist. He ended his own psychedelic world because he felt "unconnected, like a boat out to sea, drifting around. You reach for the tiller, which is the past, to try and steer toward the future, and it isn't there." It was an overdose of Fritz Perls's and Baba Ram Dass's "Be Here Now" Gestaltian world.

"When you have kids," he says, "thinking of the future is a primal thing and rings a primal bell. All of the other stuff is just so many old ladies talking about the future. When you actually have a child, you want your sons and grandsons yet unborn to have at least as good a world as you had."

Kesey is proud of his family. Like a homesick businessman stuck at a week-long convention in Cincinnati, he unfurls photos of his kids and excitedly chatters about each one. He wears his emotions on his coveralls. The fact that one teenage daughter, Sunshine, is the daughter of his Prankster paramour, Mountain Girl, who lives nearby, seems merely an honest extension of family responsibilities.

Kesey has spent ten years writing about the experiences of the 1960s, filling an entire wing at the University of Oregon, but he has published very little in recent years. He writes nearly every night, however, often all night long. Volumes of work lie unpublished and unproofed. He is sensitive about his writing skills and his inability to produce another novel. When pressed about the public's yearning for a third novel, he retorts, "Piss on 'em." In the event of his death, he has instructed Faye not to give interviews or show any written material.

AS WE SIT AROUND his wooden table, Kesey pumps an exercise spring with his right hand. Behind him on a table littered with piles of books and an old "Grateful Dead '82" poster a telephone rings unnoticed. Outside, the lame macaw shrieks. A teenage boy comes in, sits down, silently eats a baloney sandwich, then leaves. Two chickens fight for their lives on the porch. A spaniel, Mary, noses crotches excitedly, then chases the chickens away. All this is a backdrop for Kesey as he *click-clicks* his hand strengthener, eats guacamole, sips wine, and begins to talk for five hours, almost nonstop.

He looks back on some of the social growth of the 1960s and '70s with a jaundiced eye. He lumps Eastern religion, est, Scientology, Weight Watchers, and "amoebic" dancing into a selfish cop-out bundle, ways of avoiding the realities of twentieth-century living. A Valium in your back pocket, a way of sliding by peacefully and, in the process, cheating society of your possible contributions. He disdains shirking, and jokingly shakes a finger at some of his former sidekicks' alternative life-styles.

"Alpert is a Jew. Ginsberg is a Jew. I'll say, 'Ginsberg, you're a Jew; never mind all this Buddhist baloney. You're a Jew and you'll never shake it. It is who you are; it is the card God dealt you. All of a sudden, if you don't like being a Jew, you can't throw the card away and try and draw some cards from India or from China.' "

Kesey admires Leary for his toughness and consistency over the long haul. Although he would likely draw some opposition to his comment that Leary "never did any wrong and spent a lot of jail time for just two joints," he paints an interesting distinction between Alpert and Leary.

"At one point, God says to all the angels, 'I am going to have to deal this acid. I am going to have to have a run. How about that Jew and that Irishman? Okay, that's perfect; they make a great vaudeville team!' "

Kesey wonders aloud what would have happened if both Leary and Alpert had been put in prison. "Alpert," he says, "would have sat in prison and meditated. He would have lit incense and given everyone a great sense of peace and tranquillity. He would have gotten out early for Buddhist-like behavior. At his going-away party, braless little girls in long dresses would have brought him mung beans, garlands, and carob cakes. With flowing eyes and turbaned heads, everyone would have 'Omed' their way into the night.

"But that shit is oil on the waters. Leary escaped. He went hand-over-hand on the wires out of the prison at San Luis Obispo and left the country so that he could continue saying what he felt he had to say. Leary is going to drink Irish whiskey, get into trouble with the women, and tell enormous lies, but his energy, his spirit, is indicative of his direction. His logic, like all our logic, leaves a lot to be desired, but logic is the cheapest stuff. Spirit is the right stuff. It really is.

"I feel superior to him in familial ways. I don't believe you can sacrifice the crew of your ship just to keep the ship afloat. Leary may have done that a time or two. That's where Leary and I disagree. You cannot abandon your crew. Either we all go or nobody goes."

To Kesey, the future seems embedded in the present; he is excited by space exploration. "It is a very American feeling; it has to do with our destiny as a nation. Our destiny is different from other people's destiny; you can't deny it. Our destiny is off the planet. We know what space is. Every American knows this. Even the most downtrodden black guy knows that all he has to do if he really wants to get away is to drive for an hour and a half and he'll be in an empty place. That is the frontier consciousness that is part of our culture. You don't have that in Amsterdam.

"I was in Amsterdam once. What a contrast. Beautiful Dutch women with eye makeup, no bras, best hash in the world. But wonderful as it was, you knew they were on the cutting edge of awareness when Vermeer was painting. They were big-time four hundred years ago, when they were putting in dikes and running their shipping and trading lanes around the world. They *had* their crack at civilization."

———— ◇◆◇ ————

THE ESSENCE OF KEN KESEY is clearly western American heterosexual. The literary critics who saw a contradiction between the alternative life-style of the acid-dropping Prankster and the brawny, Hemingwayesque lumberjacks who tromped heavy-footed through his books had merely failed to inspect the author. He admires strength, in a gentlemanly and Christian way. He still chuckles over the length of time it took people to realize that *One Flew Over the Cuckoo's Nest* was at its heart a Christian allegory.

McMurphy was the Christian character, the Western Hero who was willing to sacrifice himself for his fellow man, putting his life on the line for the downtrodden. Kesey gets exercised when the topic of the movie version of *Cuckoo's Nest* is brought up. He sold the movie rights, as a kid in his twenties, for a mere twenty thousand dollars; he had a wife, two kids, and the Pranksters to support. The money aspect still angers him, but his greatest frustration is with the fact that the moviemakers missed the point of the whole book by making Big Nurse the villain. He has never seen the movie and vows he never will, but he knows clearly who had the Academy Award–winning starring role, and he doesn't like it one bit.

He jumps up from the table as if spring-loaded, guacamole and wine slopping all around. He spins to his desk and grabs two brand-new foreign-language editions of *Cuckoo's Nest*. On the cover of each is a large photograph, from the movie, of a slightly deranged-looking Jack Nicholson. Kesey slams them on the table in front of us. "How would *you* like it if your best book was plastered with a picture of this five-foot, six-inch *wimp!*"

I cautiously inquire whom he would have preferred. "Gene Hackman would have been great!" he says.

Regardless of how well his two books have sold, without the typically fat movie rights, Kesey lives lean, selling chickens and shearing sheep. He is hard at work on a new book, and one suspects that if it is made into a movie, the rights will go for considerably more than twenty thousand dollars. It deals with Alaska, the last earthly American Frontier.

Kesey is keenly interested in the Eskimo and Aleut Indians. They exist on the edge of civilization, with a blend of intellect and physical ability that assures survival if you have it and seals your doom if it is lacking. When Darwin talks, Eskimos listen. It is the perfect backdrop for Kesey's favorite theme, a place where man stands alone, doing battle with the forces of Nature, Good, and Evil. Kesey is still looking, digging deep, for that imaginative spark that will again ignite the consciousness of a nation as *Cuckoo's Nest* did twenty-five years ago.

———————— ◇◆◇ ————————

TOWARD THE END OF the day I ask Kesey what about himself puzzles him the most. He loses eye contact, looks distant, and repeats the question, half-mumbling to himself. He pauses, looking down at the small kitchen matchbox filled with a few wooden matches and half a poorly rolled joint.

"*Interests* is better than puzzles," he says.

He hovers there for a while, knowing full well what he is going to say, never wondering for a second which of the many experiences in his complex life has been most interesting. A matchstick in one hand, he idly cleans an already immaculate thumbnail on his ham-sized wrestler's hand, too huge and functional for an artist, nowhere graceful enough for a mystic. He looks just like a kid who had done something bad and knows full well he will be punished.

"I know. Sure. It's, 'Why me?' What was it about *me*, my family, my father, about this part of the country, that it just happened to be *me* who wrote *Cuckoo's Nest*. It is not something you set out to do. It's like all the angels got together and said, 'Okay, here's the message that America desperately needs; now let's pick *him* to do it.'

"Hell, why an Indian? When I wrote that book, I'd never known a single damned Indian. It's strange, like magic. You just have to be prepared—like this fifty-cent piece"—he rolls a half-dollar between his wurstlike fingers, smooth as mercury down a staircase—"you have got to stay nimble, because it might happen again.

"I can go into that back room night after night and sit at that typewriter, and nothing comes. I can't push the buttons or pull the levers to make it happen. I can do every drug imaginable, and they still don't pull those levers that make for creative release. It is something bigger, more mysterious, a far more abstract force that dictates that. And if it happens again, a third time, then I have just got to be prepared. And I'll know when it happens.

"It's like the 1963 Rose Bowl. A guy named Vanderkelen was quarterbacking Wisconsin, and they were getting whipped by Southern Cal, who was the number-one team in the country. Wisconsin was ranked second. They were down by about thirty points late in the game. All of a sudden something happened. Vanderkelen started to connect on every pass. Suddenly *he* knew it. Then his backfield sensed it. Then his linemen felt it. Then his whole team. They just clicked in perfect synchronicity for that short period in time. There was an eerie kind of silence in the one hundred thousand people at the Rose Bowl. No one knew what it was, but everyone knew something special was happening. Vanderkelen threw for four-hundred-some yards, one long one was called back, and at the gun, USC won forty-two to thirty-seven, but the Trojans were running *backward* with the ball to kill the clock! That game was *Cuckoo's Nest* all over again. It is a state of grace that simply defies articulation; when that special thing touches you, you know it. I knew it with *Cuckoo's Nest* and with *Notion*. And I am beginning to feel it with *Alaska*."

———◇◆◇———

IN TAKING LEAVE, I ask Kesey to autograph my copy of *Cuckoo's Nest*. He first looks in the front and notes that it is a thirty-third printing. Then he starts thumbing through the pages, stopping at random two or three times, picking out shards of sentences and stringing them together into a non sequitur that reads, "I squirm unconscious through a disturbed administration—Ken Kesey."

He hands the book back, and his laugh rolls out from deep within his wrestler's torso. "Someday people are going to look at my autograph and say, 'Now just what in the hell did he mean by that?' "

As we walk to my car, he gives me some advice on writing about the 1960s. "Treat it like Tolkien did his hobbits. Just wander around, bumping into interesting people and tell it like it was . . . Magic!"

He picks up a stone to toss in the direction of a few farm animals that are evidently encroaching on the wrong territory, something that always seems to be happening. "I feel like I've done something real bad, and life on this farm all these years is my punishment," he says. "Work, work, work. Animals, electricity, and we just got the insulation in. Maybe next year we can afford to put fiberboard *over* the insulation." He waves good-bye, turns, and chases a wandering cow through the wet grass.

———◇◆◇———

IN LATE JANUARY 1984, Kesey's son, Jed, was killed in, of all things, a bus accident. The vehicle skidded off the road and down a hundred feet. Like his dad, he had been a wrestler for the University of Oregon; the bus was on its way to a match. He was hospitalized for two days in Spokane. A split second before Jed died, Kesey saw his son's legs shake, his jaws clench, and a flash of consciousness pass over his face.

Kesey helped make Jed's casket; two days of effort that restored a semblance of order after the irreversible chaos of death. The ceremonies were held out back by the fish pond. The casket was lined with some Tibetan brocade that Owsley had given Mountain Girl years before, a pattern of phoenix birds rising from flames. Ken put in his silver whistle with the Hopi cross he used to wear during the Trips Festivals and a photo of Ken and Faye in front of *Further*. A fraternity brother of Jed's put in a symbolic piece of the future: a quartz watch that would "beep" every fifteen minutes for the next five years.

The Whole-Earth Emperor:
Counterculture in the 1980s?

IN THE EARLY DAYS, the darkest fear for people living in the Oregon Territory was hostile Indians. At Rajneeshpuram, history seems to be repeating itself.

The music is contagious, and even at 7:30 A.M. the driving guitars and drums prod you to movement. The sound system features state-of-the-art speakers the size of U-Haul trailers, and the noise goes right into you. It is inescapable, thoroughly compelling. It is so loud it surrounds you, blocking out any possibility of thought, yet, somehow it is not annoying. It is perfectly fitting. To a good, solid rock beat, the faithful are chanting, "Living in a Buddhafield, playing in a Buddhafield, living in a Buddhafield, playing in a Buddhafield," over and over again.

Almost every single person is dancing, or sitting on the floor rocking back and forth and clapping. It's a scene very much like the last time I saw Chuck Berry just before they closed the Fillmore West. Those not propelled by the music stand out like statues: two men stock-still with their Uzi submachine guns loaded, cocked, barrels straight up and down.

The machinegunner on the left of the elevated podium is left-handed; the gunner to the right is right-handed. Together they can spray this entire room of six hundred people within a split second of manifest danger.

Beyond the machinegunners, to each side of the stage with the large empty chair in the center, are men with headsets, earphones, and crackling walkie-talkies. A woman further to one side just looks out over the crowd, still writhing in religious rock-and-roll joy, and watches.

The pulse of the music accelerates as the volume increases. The acoustics inside this 2.2-acre hall of worship are good, and no echoes disrupt the rhythm and lyrics; it's music that lulls the cerebrum while sensitizing the body.

The crescendo grows, but does not yet reach an orgasmic peak. Above the noise of the rock chant comes the *slap slap* sound of a helicopter, very close overhead. This is a sound to which these people have become conditioned, and like a huge kennel of Pavlov's dogs sensing their reward is near, they all raise their hands higher and sing with even more energy. It is a concentrated frenzy of expectation that seems capable of lifting the huge roof right off the walls.

To the side of the big chair, behind the left-handed Uzi guard, fifteen feet in front of where I sit in the VIP area, Bhagwan Shree Rajneesh appears from behind a partition. Thunderous clapping erupts as expectations meet reality.

The rock band, its U-Haul speakers pummelling us like bad surf, surges forward into an even faster tempo and a greater volume. The white-bearded five-foot-five-inch Indian phenomenon, dressed in sand-colored robes, sand-colored knit cap, and sand-colored sandals comes dancing, shuffling, hands rhythmically pumping the air, eyes smiling mischievously, his feet doing a slow rumba toward his chair—his regal throne— at center stage. He turns from one side to the other, continuously dancing, his robes swaying, his hands held chest-high like a surgeon after scrubbing up, moving, always moving, until he reaches his chair and sits, right leg over left, and the entire audience becomes silent. One thousand and two hundred eyes stare into his two.

Suddenly, from far across the immense room, comes a screeching of tires, a smashing of glass, and piercing screams of profanity. Twelve hundred eyes remain glued to Bhagwan. No head turns except my own.

The scene is violent and acted out in silhouette against the floor-to-ceiling windows of this indoor cavern. One man, dressed in boots, Levi's, and flannel shirt, runs from his pickup truck, still partly obscured by the dust storm it kicked up, into the building. He is roll-blocked by one guard, then gang-tackled immediately by five others. He is hammered, pummeled, and half-Nelsoned to the ground by a swarming, reflexive defense that would warm the heart of any pro-football coach.

The screams of the uninvited guest rattle off the walls, and it seems clear from his soon-muffled comments that he did not come to worship at the morning dialogue. "You motherfucking bigoted god-damned phony asshole . . . I'm gonna . . . I'm gonna . . . I'm gonna . . ." We never get a chance to learn what he was "gonna" do, as he is immediately trundled off presumably to Wasco County jail.

All this is in supreme contrast to the serenity of Bhagwan Shree Rajneesh and his audience. The leader of four hundred thousand world-wide New Age cultural revisionists sits motionless at center stage in what looks like the Western World's fanciest Lazy-Boy recliner.

Bombings, threats, arson, wayward rifle shots, and actual assassination attempts are not unusual here. In fact, they form an important part of the psychological glue that binds them all together. What better confirmation of one's way of life than to have it attacked by some foul-mouthed, gin-fueled redneck in a four-wheel-drive pickup? The tangible presence of an external enemy has always been a vital dimension in the crystallizing of any countercultural group. The role played by conservative parents, local police, and various arms of the federal government during the 1960s is played here, in Rajneeshpuram, Oregon, by conservative ranchers and state officials. Welcome to counterculture 1985!

After nearly a minute of deafening silence, perhaps a test of the announcement made earlier to the crowd to "not cough in Bhagwan's presence," the morning dialogue is opened by the true power behind the throne, Sheela. An attractive, thirty-five-year-old woman, Sheela has recently revealed that her father, a former political adviser to Gandhi and a disciple (*sannyasin*) of Bhagwan Shree Rajneesh's for fifteen years, had adopted Bhagwan, thus making them siblings with a twenty-year age difference.

Sheela, lotused on the floor in front of the Lazy-Boy, speaks through the microphone, which blasts through the same U-Haul speakers, and asks a question: "Bhagwan, why don't you address your audience?"

Bhagwan Shree Rajneesh seizes upon this helpless little inquiry and with truly miraculous oratory momentum, proceeds to talk nonstop for an hour and fifteen minutes. One does not interview Bhagwan Shree Rajneesh; one asks a question, then goes along for Mr. Toad's Wild Ride. He is not the past all-India debating champion for nothing. His Amazing Orality.

He uses Sheela's entry card to state, one more time, his own designer brand of Buddhism—and what it will feel like if you drop your ties to your past and work real hard at "being with Bhagwan now."

"It is a natural feeling—an orgasmic experience—you will be a totally New Man. A New Woman. All boredom disappearsssss." The S's slither away like a satiated cobra back into the jungle. They sooth the ear. "The world will be full of rejoicingsssss, laughtersssss, dancesssss, songsssss, music . . . *and* . . . experience how God makes everybody clear."

He pauses at the end of each sentence and in between each word. His "dialogue"—better termed a monologue—is being taped, and its transcription will be available later in the day, but he talks slowly enough for it to be chiseled into stone as he speaks.

"Because you have experienced so much, you would like to sing this song, compose poetry, play on your guitarshhhh . . . *or just dance!!!* Existence has been such a benediction. . . . So there are reasons why I don't address you as 'ladies and gentlemen.' Those are dirty words!"

With that punch line, the crowd goes into a berserk eruption of snorts, hoots, hollers, and belly laughs, accompanied by wild applause. His point is this: If you are a Rajneeshi, you *are* God, and therefore to address you as a lady or a gentleman would be denigrating, if not downright insulting. But this has taken half an hour for him to say. He shuffles his words and thoughts just like he shuffled his sandals to the music, and my lower back doesn't like the lotus position one bit. I use the raucous interlude to do some shuffling of my spine.

Finding no question to field from his docile audience, he rolls on toward what is becoming a hallmark of his daily proclamations (which, once transcribed, are made into books and video tapes and will be sold worldwide tax-free to the tune of two million dollars per year), that time-honored issue that lies somewhere at the bottom of the caldron out of which humanity bubbles: sex.

"Homosexuality is a religious phenomenon, born in monasteries where women are prevented. Man is creative and will find some other sexual release." And then comes the ultimate insult to the past lives of the gathered Rajneeshis, sixty percent of whom came from strict Jewish or Catholic backgrounds: "God himself is gay! In the Christian Trinity there is no space for a woman! This God is hanging with two gay fellows!" A new eruption of belly laughs and squeals of hysteria, "How could he be so *delightfully* irreverent?" they seem to be saying. It's like Johnny Carson playing Las Vegas. Yessiree, if Bhagwan has said this is his circus, as he did recently on the Australian *60 Minutes* show, then this is clearly the Greatest Show on Mirth.

"And do you think God would not like once in a while a sexual sneeze?" Laughter comes in wave after wave, with a touch of astonishment at Bhagwan Shree Rajneesh's boldness. He finishes with a message that was the essence behind the origins of Buddhism in 500 B.C. and still holds an allure to many, some twenty-five hundred years later: "Civilization has created zoos. In the wild there is no homosexuality, no masturbation; only in zoos. *Come back to nature!*"

THE NEAREST TOWN, OF any size, to Rajneeshpuram is fifty-two miles away, the last eighteen of which are unpaved and tough as nails. It gives one a sense of appreciation for the effort of the early-morning gate-crasher; he had to have his own sense of mission just to get here.

Curiously, the town has a very Indian name: Madras. In Madras, the concept of "cow" may be nearly sacred, but its interpretation is much closer to "ground round" than to a holy heifer. The biggest structure around is the Central Oregon Livestock Auction Grounds, just south of town. On Main Street, which is also U.S. Route 97, are indications that the town is in the very thick of contemporary Western life: video rental clubs, a Major Muffler franchise, and a Dairy Queen.

Entering the No Name Bar at three o'clock in the afternoon the day before, I was spotted as an outsider from the moment I stepped inside. After I had downed a couple of bites of my Angus Burger ("Half a Pound of Pure Bull"), I noticed an assortment of bumper stickers and T-shirts for sale behind the bar. One sticker showed the grill of a Rolls-Royce, dead-center in a rifle's cross hairs. Above was printed "Open Season," below was "No Bhag Limit," an obvious reference to the fact that Bhagwan Shree Rajneesh owns ninety Rolls-Royces.

A T-shirt, printed with the slogan "Better Dead Than Red," showed a likeness of a mountain man, a .306 resting on his shoulder, carrying a bearded, sandaled man dressed in shades of red, with a string of beads around his limp neck. (The Rajneeshi dress in reddish colors of the sunrise, to symbolize their "awakening," and all wear a 108-bead necklace, or mala, with a photo of Bhagwan at the bottom.)

Waiting until the third bite of my Angus Burger was half-chewed, I turned to a man communing with a full mug of beer and pointed to the anti-Rajneeshi material. "That stuff must work," I said, "I don't see a single one in here."

The beer worshipper looked at me carefully, then said something about how pleased he was that I was wearing the color blue; otherwise I might be spending the evening looking for my derriere in another location. As I recall, his *exact* words were "You'd best fucking believe they work, son. If you'd come in here wearing red, yer ass woulda been buckshotted right outa Jefferson County. One hundred years ago my great-grandfather helped put the Indians on their reservations, now *these* fucking Indians are tryin' to put a cage on us!"

The bar contained an atmosphere not unlike a Ku Klux Klan meeting house the day after the signing of the 1964 Civil Rights Act. The cause for this siege mentality was a recent ruling—just days before—by the Oregon Court of Appeals. The decision, which followed an Oregon Supreme Court decision, was the latest in the four-year-long legal range war between the Rajneeshi and the People of Oregon.

The most recent edict stated that there is no basic contradiction between building a city—while using the land with a keen eye to conservation—and the state of Oregon's incredibly complex land-use laws. The town of Rajneeshpuram could remain intact.

In July 1981, the Rajneeshi Investment Corporation paid a little less than six million dollars to a Texas investment company for a sixty-four-thousand-acre ranch, called the Big Muddy. Its only claim to fame was the fact that it was the location where John Wayne filmed *Rooster Cog-*

burn. The name, which changes during the summer to the Big Dusty, tells you something about the place. The land was overgrazed. Much of the soil was graded Class VIII by the U.S. Soil Conservation Service. This means, quite bluntly, "unrecoverable." The 2,100 acres where the incorporated city of Rajneeshpuram now sits supports around 5,000 people, 550 head of beef cattle, 140 milk cows, 2,800 chickens, and produces about 400 tons of truck farm vegetables per year. It had been projected by the Bureau of Land Management as adequate grazing acreage for nine cows and a calf.

When the Rajneeshis began buying land in the town of Antelope, 80 percent of that lunar landscape was for sale. The cattlemen here in the No Name Bar had simply missed out on the biggest multimillion-dollar land boom ever to hit north-central Oregon. Then, to add insult to injury, a bunch of women and city slickers who had never had a blister or a callous on their hands in their lives came out to this lava pit at the end of the earth—and turned it green!

The first reports filtered back to No Name, brought in by a horseman with a pair of powerful binoculars trying to discover if it really was an immense nudist colony (only a small part was). The voyeuristic cowboy reported a strange phenomenon: The women were driving bulldozers and the men were planting beansprouts and flowers! "Lesbos and twinkletoes" quickly became yet another rallying cry. The T-shirt and bumpersticker business soared.

The most organized counterattack to any expansion or development by the Rajneeshi centers on the significant issue, in this primarily agrarian state, of conservation and land use. It is spearheaded by an organization known as the Thousand Friends of Oregon and its past director, Henry Richmond. Someone once referred to this group as "the Sierra Club North, with a Hell's Angels mentality." They appear noticeably less Neanderthal, however, when dealing with the press. Richmond, an attorney who has been labeled a bigot by the Rajneeshi, felt their development of the land should be right up his conservational alley.

The ironies in the series of legal assaults by the Thousand Friends against the Rajneeshi are numerous. The group's original intentions were to preserve two areas in Oregon: the Oregon coastline and the fertile farmlands of Willamette Valley. Their enforcement of the state's complex land-use laws has put eighteen million acres under Exclusive Farm Use, more than the other forty-nine states combined. It is the equivalent of twenty-three Rhode Islands. In fact, the community at Rajneeshpuram has become a model example of the land-use laws the Thousand Friends were formed to enforce. Not one state politician has yet taken the Rajneeshis' offer to come and visit the town.

No one in the No Name Bar had been down into Rajneeshpuram either. Some had been to the town of Antelope, now renamed Rajneesh.

This was the town of one hundred that in 1982 played municipal Russian roulette—and lost—by voting (unsuccessfully) to disincorporate in order to block the Rajneeshi from constructing a printing shop, allowable only on incorporated land. The only reason the Rajneeshi had for stepping a single sandaled foot into the town of Antelope in the first place was that the development, eighteen miles down in the valley, had no phone service. So, they bought two commercial lots and brought in a trailer of telecommunications equipment. When you have four hundred thousand followers worldwide, you need a lot of technology to reach out and touch them.

The rumors that were Ping-Ponging around the No Name were truly incredible. The Great Guru, as they called him, ran a sex shop that made Hugh Hefner look like a reject from a Masters and Johnson clinic. There was nudity, screwing in the open, orgies all night long. There were no children on the ranch due to cannibalism. "They just *eat* the little fuckers," one said, as I took the last bite of my Angus Burger.

The most heinous crime of all had come about a year before, when the commune had opened their gates and bused in street people from all over the country. This was the ill-fated "Share-a-Home" project, the failure of which had spilled hundreds of inner-city adolescents, who could not cope with the rules of the ranch, let alone the world from which they had come, onto the streets of Portland.

A great deal of attention was brought to this influx of people and to the people who had moved into Antelope just weeks before the April 15, 1982, disincorporation vote. Were the Rajneeshis simply busing in walking, talking pro-Rajneeshi votes? The answer comes in two parts: Yes, they were; and yes, it was all very legal, because Oregon's same-day voter registration laws required no more than a sleeping bag to be eligible to cast a ballot.

The experiment brought attention from press around the world—another public-relations coup. Live global television coverage into one hundred million living rooms sure beats sending out little glossy flyers to travel agents and chambers of commerce. Soon the 145-bed Rajneesh Hotel was booming. Air Rajneesh and its aerial tag team of DC-3s, Twin Otters, and Howard Hughes's old Convair, are kept busy shuttling people to and from Portland, taking off on a 4,500-foot runway in the very bottom of this overgrazed lava bed, turned counterculture hub of the universe.

MY DECISION TO STAY at the hotel precipitated a cascade of detailed procedures. Spending a night at the commune was tougher than getting into mainland China. Forms were everywhere. After I filled in my name and address, the desk woman started to repeat my name, saying, "Aren't you an 'expected guest?' " Looking through a well-organized binder, she found my name and expected time of arrival. A sense of paranoia washed over me, until I remembered I had written weeks before, then forgotten about it. The second form was a stiff, legalistic statement that affirmed I was not carrying firearms, explosives, or "dangerous drugs." "This means Valium and speed are okay?" I asked, thumping the form with my pen and grinning. They all grinned back and said, "As long as it's prescription!" I wondered about the three full cans of beer in my trunk, knowing that many Eastern sects ban intoxicants.

Next, I signed a form agreeing to allow them to search my car. The only male working the desk brought out Sloane, the Wonder Sniffer, a playful German shepherd. He dove into my car, puffing like an overweight jogger, then jumped into the backseat, stuffing his furry head under the back of the passenger side. He leaped out in front of me and dropped an empty beer can at my feet.

"What's the policy on beer?" I sheepishly asked. "Oh, it's fine," I was told. "We have two discos and a restaurant with a fine wine selection. As a matter of fact, we'll be bottling twenty-two thousand bottles of wine grown right here." I was relieved, since my plans here included a good, long run in the desert heat to work out the cramps that can only come from driving all day. And any run, for me, must be followed by a beer, just like night follows day. Next came the forms for my baggage search, then the search itself. It was thorough. The woman searching was polite and official. Afterward, she directed me to watch the in-house VCR while waiting for the tour bus to arrive.

The building that houses the visitors bureau and the chamber of commerce is, like every other building in the valley, pleasant, efficient, and very utilitarian in design. All are prefab, a fact of construction that was necessitated, back in the fall of 1981, by an impending winter.

The cassettes being shown on television were from opposite sides of the journalistic coin. *Fifty-seventh Street* kicked things off and made a big deal about the daughter of Congressman Leo Ryan—the man whose murder precipitated the Jonestown, Guyana, mass suicide—being a member of the Rajneesh commune. "I just like living here, it's that simple," she said, matter-of-factly.

Next up was the Australian *60 Minutes*, which proceeded to show the interviewer being lulled into a kind of trance state by Bhagwan's monologue. The high point of the show was an interview with Sheela, the Rajneesh Foundation International's chief spokeswoman and *agent provocateur*. When asked about public resistance to the Rajneeshi buying land in Western Australia for a school, she put on her best evil-eyed, hooded-cobra look, gazed straight into the cameras, and hissed, "Tough titties." The slogan has become a rallying cry here, a simple phrase that buoys them when they feel the Oregon Supreme Court is trying to eradicate their species. In the boutiques here, on proud display, are red and magenta T-shirts emblazoned across the front with "Tough Titties!!"

The bus arrived, and our guide, Rosie, was as bright, gracious, and good at crowd control ("I'm *really* sorry, sir, but we are running late, and there just *isn't* time for a cigarette"), as a tour guide at the Hearst Castle in San Simeon. She was entertaining, informative, and fielded questions about compost recovery as well as she did those on spiritual awakening.

After the desk crew discovered that I was doing a book, I was given the front seat, next to the driver, for the tour. During the first stops our guide explained that different work here carries no difference in status; one's labor is termed *worship*. Hence, on the left, are people worshiping in the Temple of Used Tires. Just down the road was the Temple of Changing Oil, which doubles as the Temple for Fixing Broken Buses. (The commune has the second largest transportation fleet in the state: Rajneesh Buddhafield Transport.) The used oil is removed, emptied into underground containers, then burned to heat the floors of the buildings during the winter months. The floor where mechanical work is done, our guide pointed out, is absolutely spotless. Everything here is absolutely spotless. On entering the university I found a woman cleaning the telephone receiver with rubbing alcohol and a Q-tip to get into each of the little holes. Their interpretation of cleanliness borders on compulsiveness.

The commune is said to be more than 70 percent self-sufficient, and the produce under cultivation on the eighty-acre truck farm, the drip irrigation in the vinyards, and the sewage reclamation plant all bear this out. The only real expense is in importing electricity through Wasco County from Bonneville Dam, and there are plans for wind-generated electricity, our guide said.

Outside each cafeteria, where everyone eats who doesn't dine at Zorba the Buddha restaurant, are separately labeled trash bins: "Food," "Paper," "Metal." Even the glass is separated and recycled according to color.

As we circled the compost field, it quickly became clear why the Rajneeshis, who are exclusively vegetarian, are as proud of their shit as the French are of their wine: This pile makes everything grow. Another touch of symbolism—the never-ending, never-beginning cycle of reprocessing the garbanzo beans and yogurt that made up last night's dinner is here in front of your very eyes . . . and nose.

One last oddity came in the form of a lone coyote that appeared in the early-evening shadows, evidently on its way toward the chicken coop. The driver, surprisingly, turned off the ignition and said, "Okay, here's a special treat. Now . . . just watch this!"

I didn't really know what to expect. Was this going to be a scene entitled "Gruesome Death at the Temple of Poultry?" Perhaps it could be used as a lovely parable about how nice and natural death is, a favorite topic of Bhagwan's.

Instead, the coyote eyed us, hangdog, and trotted upwind toward the unsuspecting hens. Suddenly, over the crest of the hill came a ten-foot-high dust devil, a thick brown sponge of desert sand churned up by something headed right for the coyote at the speed of a race car in second gear. The coyote left his own token deposit on the compost dump and headed, wild-eyed for the hills. Sprinting out of the dust cloud came a pair of trained attack emus. Emus are, next to the ostrich, the world's largest flightless bird. They can run like the wind and kick like a punter. They are mean as hell, five feet tall, weigh a hundred pounds, and hate coyotes. (They probably don't really like chickens, either, but train them right and it's another living example, down here on the Big Muddy, of nature in harmony.)

The tour included the showcase hotel. All the room keys are part of a Rajneeshi Tarot deck, so you don't get stuck remembering just a number, you remember an emotion and then look up the parable in a handy reference book. On the counter was an entire deck of cards with room keys attached, laid out in a semicircle. The desk clerk—a woman in her forties from Santiago, Chile—knew all the parables. She recited the various stories, telling how to make productive use of the cards when feeling angry, rejected, or loving.

Later, back at the main office I was granted an interview with Paul Lowe, a former Esalen therapist who had joined the Rajneeshi and become "awakened." I tried to talk to Lowe, who now calls himself Teertha, as one psychologist to another. I had read that Gestalt techniques (made so popular at Esalen by Fritz Perls), which incorporated methods of focusing on the here and now and interpretations of non-verbal body language as keys to neurotic behavior, were employed here. Traeger and Feldenkrais techniques, also used at Esalen, are mentioned in the Rajneeshi literature. There was a two-year indoctrination program for therapists, to give them all a common approach, so I asked Teertha what that common denominator was. While I asked this question and explained to him that we could speak in professional vernacular, he had been looking right into my eyes as if the rest of the world did not exist. Some people call this concentration. Gestalt and Rajneeshi therapists call it being "centered" and "cloudless." Both have a pleasant ring to them. It's nice to have someone's full attention.

When my question was finished, the former Paul Lowe "centered" on his left kneecap. The only moving object was the second hand on his fifteen-thousand-dollar diamond-studded Piaget polo watch. His stomach gave off a rumble. My stomach answered back, even louder. He stayed centered. I stayed centered. I stayed cloudless, focusing on his eyes. It became a contest. I wanted to check his pulse.

At long last, he turned to me and said, slowly and as peacefully as a wind-blown lotus petal, "From the way you ask your question, it seems clear that we come from very different places. I am uncertain as to what knowledge you seek."

What really irked me was not so much that he didn't answer an obvious question, and not really that it took him ten minutes of silence to figure out that, he, in his fuzzy, scarlet velour jumpsuit with Bhagwan's photo nuzzling in his crotch, and I, in my Levi's and 1984 "The World Returns" Los Angeles Olympics T-shirt, came from "different places." What really pissed me off was that he actually got me to talk in *his* language! Figuring that it *was* his territory, I began asking some silly open-ended question like "In your position as spiritual therapist at the Meditation University, please help me to be more aware of the uses of 'Rajneesh Primal: Cleaning Up the Past' and especially," pointing to the course offering booklet in my hand, "especially the 'Rajneesh Rebalancing Course.' " That last one had really caught my curiosity. It cost $7,500, enough to make you assume that part of the "Rebalancing" included your checkbook.

Teertha took less time to answer this one. He began describing the process of finding, then using, an internal, psychologically constructed Witness, or spiritual guide, who will allow you to get back to your "center" in times of need. "You can be dead drunk, and your Witness will be right there, sober as a judge. You can be angry, and all you must do to remove the cloud of anger is seek out your Witness. As spiritual therapists, we first must find our Witness; then we can assist others."

"What about with mental illness, or under medication?" I asked, trying to look for some obvious limits to what I perceived as a valuable yet only situationally useful concept.

"Oh yes," Teertha replied. "You can be insane or filled with Thorazine; just find your Witness and he will get you centered!" He smiled a smile as soft as his velour jumpsuit.

At that, my head snapped back and my eyes started searching from corner to corner on the ceiling of the room. "You have become clouded, Dr. Whitmer, this is obvious to me," he said.

My knee-jerk reaction was to reply, "You bet your Buddhistic *butt* I'm clouded. You go into a locked back ward and tell some guy in a florid psychosis that he'd better find his Witness, and you're likely to get your fucking head ripped off." Instead I outcentered him, looked straight into his pellucid eyes, and said, "Oh, just momentary; a slight difference in views, but nothing essential.

"Teertha," I asked, "what professional journals or books have you read recently that you have found most useful?" The reason for this question was partly naive curiosity and partly recognition of the fact that the world of psychotherapy is as fractionated as the world of Buddhism—or any old religion, for that matter—and I wondered if he had found something in the professional literature that was particularly provocative or helpful. No such luck. "I do not read anything," he said, and stared at me with cloudless eyes and the same soft-as-the-desert-breeze smile that I now understood to mean, "I know it all. Why waste my time reading?"

———————◇◆◇———————

TAKING MY EVENING RUN turned out to be difficult. I was told that even though I was now wearing a hospital name-band with my name, ID number, and "privilege code" on it, security was tough. My car had been sniffed, my bags had been thoroughly inspected, and it's tough to carry a bomb or submachine gun while running in a T-shirt and nylon shorts. Could there be something they did not want me to see? Were there people here I should not contact? It was all very . . . cloudy.

The tour guide gave me a map and finally said, "Go out of the hotel and turn left. That'll be fine."

One-half mile into the warm dusk of the desert valley, running by the side of the greenest stream east of the Cascades, I began to feel human again. A sense of harmony descended slowly. The crescent moon was at my back, and the dark-purple hills in front began to blend together into thick velvet folds. In the midst of this reverie, a young woman's voice came quietly out of the dark, calling my name. I pulled up to find a uniformed young Rajneeshi with a walkie-talkie, standing, nearly invisible, in the shadows of a tree.

Another wave of paranoia came over me, but I learned that she had been alerted by Rosie, the tour bus guide, that I would be along. The guard was polite and wished me good running with such a depth of honesty that I didn't even care if I was being watched.

Three-guards-popping-out-of-the-darkness later, one of whom actually checked my hospital ID bracelet, I made it back to the hotel, through the hot tub and shower, and was headed to the disco for a beer before meeting my escorts, who were helping a British Columbian talk-show host film an interview with Bhagwan.

Leaving my bathroom, a sign stuck up near the mirror caught my eye. The sign said, in big, red, sunrise colors, Avoid AIDS—Use Condoms and Rubber Gloves. Nearby was a pamphlet with Rajneesh's own words, telling why no kissing is allowed ("a skin-sucking addiction") and that two-thirds of the world is coming down with AIDS. The Rajneesh ashram's explicit-sex policy existed no more.

In order to keep a small group of people intact and working with clear, "centered" energy, a sense of urgency and the concept of a goal are essential. But, both "urgency" and "goals" are antithetical to Bhagwan Shree Rajneesh's world of "be-here-now" existence. However, precisely the same psychological tension can be injected into the system by creating clearly defined enemies.

There is nothing like an external bogeyman to unify the troops, make them forget about past existences, and put their faith in their leader.

Whether that enemy is the Land-Use Board of Appeals or a Bible-thumping, right-wing rancher with an itchy trigger finger, a good leader can use any and all signs of aggression from the outside. It is just simple logic that anyone who enjoys his Monday-night football, eats roast beef, and relies on the local all-night 7-eleven store for impulse buying, is never going to want to live in an isolated vegetarian commune in the bottom of a desert.

But Rajneesh and his lawyers have been scoring success after success in the Oregon State courtrooms, and there are a lot of people in the commune who could afford to *buy* a Monday-night football team: the heiress to the Lear jet and Baskin Robbins fortunes as well as a primary financial backer of the *Godfather* movies. So, when the clothing came off and the parties back in the hills began, attendance at Meditation University and at the Morning Discourses began to drop. Many of the Rajneeshi were using the splendid isolation of the Big Muddy to act more like Zorba and less like Buddha.

What better way to bring the *sannyasin* back to their "center" than to fill the *Rajneesh Times* with reprints from the *Time* and *Newsweek* cover stories about AIDS? A purely brilliant bit of psychological cattle herding by Bhagwan himself. We have met the enemy, and he is us!! Rumors, all unsubstantiated, quickened the pulse of concern within the commune. One rumor, heard all the way back in Los Angeles (Rajneesh has many Hollywood followers), said there was an AIDS leper colony hidden somewhere on the Ranch. Another said that the commune's cafeteria food, where everyone but visiting VIP's eat, was laced with sodium nitrite, or saltpeter. Regardless of hearsay, there is a minireligious war being waged within the walls, and the outcome will be to select the most ardent followers and weed out the pure hedonists.

On the way out of the hotel I picked a Rajneeshi Tarot card and got "Rejection."

The disco was playing some music on an expensive, and excellent, sound system. The dance floor was the size of half a football field. The ratio of women to men was about five to one, but no one was dancing with anyone else. The people looked like a rerun of one of Kesey's Acid Tests. They moved in loose free form, just letting themselves be blown by the musical breeze.

Outside there were two bars, one for real money, one for those with Rajneesh Credit Cards. As I gulped down a beer and began to feel that amniotic floating sensation that comes a half hour after running, a helicopter, searchlight glancing over the black hills like a man with a flashlight lost in a storm, circled again and again. The bartender, who seemed utterly unconcerned, said, "Probably Channel Two News." Everyone around, all of whom were *sannyasin*, laughed at the joke. I believed him.

The music played on. The dancers wriggled, and the helicopter circled. I felt for my extra car keys and found them. If this was some Bhag-wan-Darwinian test for "How well do you stand up under gunfire?" I wanted to be the first to flunk out.

In a moment a new Ford Bronco (all vehicles here, like everything else, are new and expensive) with a blue strobe light on top came slowly by the disco. I asked the bartender, "What does *that* mean?" and grabbed for my car keys a second time. The memory of the videotaped interview with Shannon Ryan, which included footage of her father's assassination, was in my mind. The bartender, nonchalantly pouring another glass, seemed unmoved and said, cryptically, "It means that there's something behind him."

At that, all the dancers stopped, all the drinkers stopped, and all the conversation stopped, as if on silent command. Everyone went toward the corner of the indoor-outdoor disco and began a slow clap, all in unison. They had known since the first *thwap-thwap* of the helicopter the timing and choreography of this procession.

Following the Peace Force Bronco by two hundred yards and traveling the speed of a slow walk was a customized six-door, gold-colored Rolls-Royce with a little red-and-white Rajneeshi flag on the hood ornament. The whole thing was festooned with streamers of flowers like the Beverly Hills entry in the Rose Bowl parade. Inside, under the dome light, was Bhagwan Shree Rajneesh, former all-India debating champ and professor of philosophy, dressed in a gold-and-red lamé caftan, wearing a sparkling biretta, and waving to the masses, each wrist adorned with three-inch-wide silver-and-diamond-studded watches. He was on parade—sheer opulence being driven through the throng of clap-clapping worshippers, most of them barefoot—right past us, at the dusty, prefab intersection of Nirvana Drive and Yoga Road, just like some Whole-Earth Emperor.

———————— ◇◆◇ ————————

ALL THE WEALTH AND materialism fit in perfectly with Bhagwan's grand plan. He'll tell you that the Rolls limo, which costs as much as a three-acre manse in central New Hampshire, is just one of a fleet of eighty-nine others; that if he drives a different Rolls on each day's drive, it will take 208 years before the five-thousand-mile oil change; that he has lost track of all his jewelry; that he rarely wears the same caftan twice; and that he loves every second of it. That's Zorba speaking. What the little Buddha in him then says is that he is the poorest man on earth. *He* does not own anything. He just borrows a Rolls from the Rajneesh Classic Car Trust or a plane from Rajneesh Travel Corporation, or has Rajneesh Investment Corporation lease some more land, after Rajneesh Legal Services Corporation does a thorough title search. The incredible Yuppie truth of it all is that Bhagwan Shree Rajneesh sits firmly on top of a legally defined, interlocking, Subchapter S, airtight principality, run by an internal staff of four hundred attorneys, paralegals, and assistants. If his vision is of "enlightenment," rest assured that it has a stringer of subclauses and disclaimers that could only make sense to T. Boone Pickens.

Many of the Rajneeshi attorneys hit it big on the outside in their former lives. They put their money into a trust fund, sold the Mercedes, leased the house, and signed on for a new power trip: fighting for all the publicity in the state of Oregon, if not the greater Northwest. The legal competition within Rajneesh Legal Services Corporation doesn't involve winning a large award or becoming a partner. It involves winning or losing each step in their case, and to date they have done an exemplary job. Like a crack hit-squad, they have given the political bodies of Oregon fits.

After witnessing the passage of the Whole-Earth Emperor—a "drive-by," as they like to call it—I met my escorts at the hotel. The man was a former attorney with a firm in Los Angeles that was "growing too quickly." After a brief chat, he left. His wife was an articulate Chilean from an upper-class Catholic family, who related stories of dropping LSD at age sixteen and living in a hut on Easter Island for six weeks with twenty men. She felt that marriage was too confining and that her husband was too jealous, but Bhagwan liked seeing them together. She had been an inner-circle member, a veteran from the days in Poona.

Dinner at the Magdalena Cafeteria was far better than the vegetarian offerings at Esalen. The vegetarian stroganoff really had me fooled.

My escort was keen on having me meet the only other outsider then at the commune, Frances FitzGerald, the Pulitzer Prize–winning author of *Fire in the Lake*. She was completing a book that was to reveal something about American culture by looking at a retirement community; the followers of Jerry Falwell, a gay community, and Rajneeshpuram. We found FitzGerald and her escort in the regal dining room of the Zorba the Buddha restaurant. The waitresses wore silk, purple, and mauve floor-length dresses, and silver cobra belts.

Frances FitzGerald asked a lot of questions about my book and the characters in it. I ordered a pot of black coffee on her bill, but she said Simon and Schuster wouldn't mind.

Frances's male escort, called Subhuti in this incarnation, was a former London journalist; he was dead drunk and had no idea where his Witness was. As we began discussing the 1960s and the people about whom I was writing, Subhuti had definite opinions.

"Ken Kesey is *fucked*," he shouted to the nearly empty restaurant, turning a few heads. "Ken Kesey wrote one book and still lives off of it."

I tossed out a few more names for the scrutiny of the drunken journalist. "Timothy Leary is *fucked*," came the next judgment. I reminded him that the title of a Bhagwan book, *Turn On, Tune In and Drop the Lot* was Bhagwan's, by way of Leary. Continuing on his profane course,

Subhuti then shouted, "Tom Robbins is *fucked.* He doesn't know how to end a book. They are *all fucked,* because they haven't the guts to drop those lives and find enlightenment!" After his anger had run its course, I finally found a quiet moment to speak. Ever so gently, I put my hand on Subhuti's forearm, gazed cloudlessly into his bloodshot, wobbly eyes, and told him my final analysis.

"Subhuti . . . I truly appreciate your comments, and I assure you that your words will stay in my memory." I paused for a Bhagwan-like length of time, then continued. "But there is one thing that perhaps you could do for me." Subhuti uncrossed his eyes and actually managed to get the wine bottle back into its cooler, which for him was the equivalent of a three-point, off-balance shot in the NBA. FitzGerald and my escort looked on.

"Subhuti, please shove your attitudes up your ass. I don't care what you think. I think there are about forty thousand people outside this valley who will thoroughly enjoy reading about the people you think are *fucked.*" Frances FitzGerald, smirking the whole time, clapped softly and said, "Hear, hear. Hear, hear!"

Subhuti and I made our peace, but what registered most was not that one of Bhagwan's inner circle, escort to an important American writer, had gotten ripped and mouthed off in the middle of the classiest restaurant on the commune. He may do that with predictable regularity. The striking part was his display of anger. All of his psychological past was supposed to have been deconditioned, *dropped,* and replaced by the powers of love. This *sannyasin* was as loving as a caged Java rat, and if there is an official ban here on sex, the ban on the fruits of the vine may not be long in coming.

I spoke with FitzGerald in the lobby of the hotel for an hour or so, surrounded by stone carvings for sale at prices well over my credit-card limit. Our conversation had to compete with a tape of reverberating sitar music.

We agreed that Bhagwan was a charismatic leader in a classic sense, but that this whole place was a balancing act. The clearest explanation of the Howard Hughes–like compulsion for cleanliness (they did own Hughes's airplane) is simply that it's the most effective way for Bhagwan Shree Rajneesh to keep out potential rivals. Creative thought does not come from procedural thinking, from form filling and cleaning out the holes in a telephone receiver with a Q-tip. Nor does it come from closing one's eyes and meditating for entertainment. The terrain for intellectual brainstorming here, the real source of cultural advancement, is as bleak as the Oregon landscape, and is meant to be so.

On the wall at the hotel reception desk, where I got my Tarot-card key ("Anger"), was some kind of work of art. It looked like the grille of a 1952 Buick that had been abandoned at a nuclear test site—charred, twisted, painful attempts at vertical and horizontal lines, about three feet high and six feet wide. Upon inquiry, I learned that it was an artistic rendering of Bhagwan Shree Rajneesh's signature.

Heading to my room, the 1952 Buick signature weighing heavily on my mind, the idea occurred that perhaps Bhagwan Shree Rajneesh is functionally illiterate. His handwriting is so awful that it passes for bad modern art. His books are mere transcriptions of his spoken word. His entire philosophical staff at the university educates and entertains itself with their eyes closed, and the whole one hundred-square-mile, multi-million-dollar enterprise is held together by a crew of escapee attorneys. Closing the door in my room, I felt as if someone had already snuck in ahead of me. Ravi Shankar was spilling out of the speaker on the TV, and it took some serious moving of heavy furniture to unplug the cross-legged little bastard.

I looked out of my window, over the valley, and thought of all the people, snug in their four-families-to-a-building prefab houses. The melding of Indian philosophy, American money, and honest-sweat equity had changed this landscape immeasurably. The darkness was dotted by yellow streetlights, white porch lights, and the neon-blue of the bug lights. The silence was overwhelming.

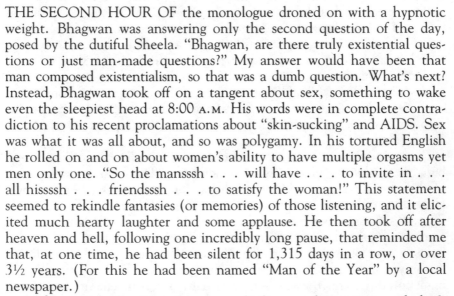

THE SECOND HOUR OF the monologue droned on with a hypnotic weight. Bhagwan was answering only the second question of the day, posed by the dutiful Sheela. "Bhagwan, are there truly existential questions or just man-made questions?" My answer would have been that man composed existentialism, so that was a dumb question. What's next? Instead, Bhagwan took off on a tangent about sex, something to wake even the sleepiest head at 8:00 A.M. His words were in complete contradiction to his recent proclamations about "skin-sucking" and AIDS. Sex was what it was all about, and so was polygamy. In his tortured English he rolled on and on about women's ability to have multiple orgasms yet men only one. "So the mansssh . . . will have . . . to invite in . . . all hissssh . . . friendssss . . . to satisfy the woman!" This statement seemed to rekindle fantasies (or memories) of those listening, and it elicited much hearty laughter and some applause. He then took off after heaven and hell, following one incredibly long pause, that reminded me that, at one time, he had been silent for 1,315 days in a row, or over 3½ years. (For this he had been named "Man of the Year" by a local newspaper.)

Making up for lost time, he wove a little story the intention of which was to remind his followers always to doubt, to question authority, and to rebel against structure in an attempt to discover truth.

"Heaven must be boring to death . . . Hell must be more exciting because there is so much work to be done. You will find all the colorful peoplesssh . . . you will find in Hell . . . because they never believesssh . . . in religion or dogma. They live spontaneously."

Then, nearly in midsentence, he called it quits and got up from his silver-and-white Lazy-Boy with the built-in microphones. To the tune of a new rock chant, he reversed his sandal-stomping, hand-waving, robe-flowing shuffle back past the machinegunner (he had been changed every fifteen minutes, to maintain optimal vigilance) and was gone. Some people chanted and sang, while others lay prostrate—perhaps sleeping—on the floor.

Going to pick up my car keys, I quizzed my guide on what appeared to be a discourse, and a philosophy, replete with contradictions. She agreed. The doubting of authority did not fit well with the unintellectual, close-eyed meditation. The existence of rules, dress codes, and behavior codes did not fit with the theme of spontaneity. Polygamy did not fit with his anti-skin-sucking campaign.

She seemed most concerned with the last issue and pointed out valleys and sun-drenched rocks where she had enjoyed some amount of orgiastic spontaneity in the old days. A sad look clouded her eyes, but she shook it off, saying, "That silly old man. You just never know what he is going to say. He is so amazing, so totally unpredictable." An inner-circle member, she was reacting like the parent of a child prodigy. This kind of acceptance of the unpredictable and the contradictory is something they all know, accept, and laugh at here in the valley. It is as if they are all living out the life of an inscrutable Zen koan, a puzzle that cannot be answered, yet no one cares.

LEAVING THE VALLEY, YOU climb, long and dusty, past the guardhouses with waving uniformed Rajneeshi. Through the town of Rajneesh, the road is paved with oil and gravel, and it twists like a desert snake up the hill.

At the junction of routes 218 and 97, is a town that is the last—or first—outpost of the true-blooded Oregonian civilization. On some maps it is labeled as a ghost town, but people still live there. The town is called Shaniko.

At the city limits, the town sign shows that Shaniko's altitude (1,250 feet) far exceeds its population (thirty). At two o'clock in the afternoon, one sees the essence of a town that time has trashed. The Historic Shaniko Hotel still stands on crippled wooden legs, its sign apparently unpainted since it was first hung sixty years ago. The windows are broken, the front door unhinged. The slat sidewalks reek of tetanus. The hills beyond are too parched to support a goat.

Though the population is listed as thirty, the number seems absurdly bloated. Four teenagers, shirts off in the afternoon heat, are the only indications of life. The three on one side of the street stare at me as I drive by with my out-of-state license plates. The looks on their faces run the gamut from sullen to surly to churlish. The teenager across the street, older and taller, has a menacing look in his eyes that says he'd love to pick a fight with someone twice his size, just to help make the day move a little faster.

When your world consists of a town that has been shunned by progress, that has been forgotten by its closest neighbors, that is simply a curve in the road for speeding tourists, your life has reached the dusty bottom of the barrel. There is no place to go . . . or is there?

The Big Empty

OH! SOMEWHERE IN THIS promised land, sunrise colors shine bright. The disco's playing somewhere and *sannyasin's* hearts are light. And somewhere swamis are laughing, and somewhere children are glad. But there's no joy in Big Muddy, the Bhagwan has gone mad.

Had the Rajneeshi not relied so heavily on a common external enemy—the rest of Oregon—to define their own identity, it seems theoretically possible that they all could have carried on, pretty much ignored. Had they achieved total self-reliance (and they were quite close), one might envision a future *National Geographic Special* entitled "New Civilization Uncovered in Parched Central Oregon: Families Thrive Where Cows Died." But getting out of Rajneeshpuram has become more popular than getting in, and the whole world witnessed the fall on nightly news.

First, Sheela left in September 1985, for Zurich and then West Germany. She took with her some key people; the mayor, the judge, the head of the bank, and a doctor. Bhagwan and the *sannyasin* seemed caught off-base, and he publicly called her entourage "a gang of fascists." Initial probes into "the gang's" misdoings were vague, and it took quite a while before anything specific was produced; but Bhagwan always was a slow speaker. "I cannot say anything precisely," he told the FBI, in one of his all-time most precise statements.

Then the lid came off Pandora's box, and some specifics, and a whole lot of allegations, crawled out. Sheela was to have appeared as a grand-jury witness regarding a salmonella outbreak in the Oregon town of The

231

Dalles; she was not a willing witness. Before leaving, "the gang" wrote letters of resignation from their respective positions in the Rajneesh Foundation International, but did not process the necessary documents to cancel their ability to draw on Rajneesh bank accounts, many of which were believed to be in—where else?—Zurich, Switzerland. Bhagwan was enraged. He accused Sheela of a wiretapping scheme; underground bunkers and escape tunnels to the outside were discovered. She allegedly secretly monitored community activities; plotted attempts to murder Bhagwan's personal physician, dentist, and caretaker; instructed an Air Rajneesh pilot to dive-bomb the Wasco County Courthouse in The Dalles (he refused and was exiled to Europe); and experimented with poison. (Manuals entitled "How to Murder Mice" were turned over to the FBI, along with hollowed-out books and electronic surveillance gear.)

From the Black Forest, Sheela countered these allegations in an interview in *Der Stern,* saying that the sect's leaders were using the drug Ecstasy to control the disciples' minds. ("I don't need Ecstasy. I'm twenty-four hours on the real thing," Bhagwan hissed in retort.) Sheela complained of Bhagwan's petulant demands for "one more Rolls-Royce," and a two-and-a-half-million-dollar diamond watch. "I never thought Sheela to be so stupid," said Bhagwan. "Where there is [sic] ninety Rolls-Royces available, what difference does it make if there is one more or less?"

The trans-world shouting match went on for weeks, and none of it went unreported by the press. Everyone had expected the battle lines to be drawn between Rajneeshpuram and the state of Oregon; this internal schism added a whole new dimension. Was it possible that Bhagwan was putting on another one-guru floor show, throwing the hounds off his scent while he left in the middle of the night to join Sheela and a Swiss bank account fat enough to purchase *another* ninety Rolls-Royces? Or was Sheela truly "a spiritual thug," who had kept Bhagwan isolated from decision making during the two biggest media events in the Oregon outback—the takeover of the town of Antelope and the busing in of street people. Bhagwan had maintained his silence through both incidents and Sheela could conceivably have grown power hungry. One piece of evidence discovered in the underground bunker seemed to put the black hat on Sheela's head: a bullet-proof bra. "Tough Titties," indeed.

Catching some by surprise, Bhagwan then began to dismantle the "religion that isn't a religion." First, he appointed as his new aide Françoise Ruddy, former wife of Al Ruddy, producer of *The Godfather.* Seeing another human barrier installed between them and their nonleader, the lines of devotees at pay phones soon stretched down Nirvana Drive nearly as far as Allan Watts Canyon. The ranks of sunrise colors were now diluted with drab brown and navy blue as hordes of FBI agents rummaged through the commune looking for evidence. You couldn't even float on your rubber raft on Krishnamurti Lake without having a government frogman, diving for discarded weapons, pop up beside you.

Bhagwan decided a rally was in order; spirits were diving lower than the frogmen. On September 30, all the books in Rajneeshism and Sheela's long red robes were piled in the crematorium and burned. (The bulletproof bra was ported off by a dutiful FBI agent, no doubt to reappear in Portland's federal court as one of the more bizarre pieces of evidence ever judged.)

"Rajneeshism was created by Sheela," Bhagwan told those around the crematorium. "It ishh nesheshary to deshhstroy it."

(He added a one-liner that lent credence to my own hypothesis about his illiteracy. Waving a robed arm toward the burning books he said slowly, "I never read them anyhow.")

Then, on October 28, the Enlightened One took off in the middle of the night in a Lear jet, refueled at Salt Lake City, and landed in the middle of a cordon of armed U.S. marshalls at the Charlotte-Douglass International Airport in North Carolina. They deposited Bhagwan in the Mecklenberg county jail, then sent him back to Portland a week later. He faced Immigration and Naturalization Services (INS) charges of arranging four hundred sham marriages of aliens to U.S. citizens and lying about his intent to remain permanently in the United States.

"Fleeing Oregon was against Bhagwan Shree Rajneesh's teachings of taking responsibility for one's actions," pleaded defense attorney Swami Niren, evidently forgetting that with the book-burning also went Rajneesh's teachings. "There was no crime committed. There was no proof he was going anywhere . . . except on vacation." (The swami avoided questions concerning the timing of Bhagwan's late departure Sunday, and the thirty-five grand-jury indictments to be issued the next day.) In prison, the Bhagwan was given vegetarian food, but his Lazy-Boy throne was not allowed.

The wheels of justice turned quickly for Bhagwan. Less than ten days after his return to Portland and his release on $500,000 bail he pleaded guilty to two of the thirty-five charges involving sham marriages and lying to the INS. The fine was $400,000, which meant he got $100,000 in change on his bail bond. He also agreed to stay out of the United States until 1990. "I never want to return again," he snarled to the judge. "You may never be *permitted* to return again," snapped U.S. District Judge Edward Levy.

Meanwhile, the Big Muddy has been renicknamed: the Big Empty. About one hundred Rajneeshi toil trying to unload to anyone with cash in hand anything not tied down. The town name of Rajneesh has been changed back to Antelope (by a 34 to 0 vote).

When the Bhagwan left for India in November, there was an immediate run on the bank, where several accounts over $100,000 were frozen after allowing a 10 percent withdrawal. Angry "investors" then piled their BMW's full of anything of value they could find. "Everything is both a beginning and an end," they quoted, as they packed their rucksacks. "Life is its own meaning," they said, as they carefully embraced good-bye (still no kissing). "He told us to wake up, and this is his way of making us," another explained.

On the other hand, some grumblings were heard. One man in his midtwenties moaned, "What do I do for a résumé? What do I say in a job interview? That I've been working as a cult member the past four years??" Another ex-commune member, a woman, said she was heading back to New Mexico and her old job as a waitress/masseuse in what must be the only massage parlor with room service. "Before I left to come here, if I'd done the sex stuff, I would have made a lot of money. Then I was too shy. Now, I'm *not* shy but I'm too afraid of disease."

The ranch itself is for sale; forty million dollars takes everything, including forty-five hundred used sleeping bags and a free demonstration on how to operate the crematorium. The land and mineral rights go along with it. But there is as much irony as gold in those hills. The town of Madras has lost the best money-making tourist attraction it ever had. For months on end, when the legal battles began to brew, long before Sheela even left, Madras was literally jammed with FBI, INS, and other government security personnel. Motels were jammed, and at the No Name Bar, they did ten thousand dollars' worth of business in lunches alone. "That's a lot of mayonnaise," they say, looking back on the boom. "A lot of mayonnaise."

The Post-Modernist Outlaw
Intellectual

. . . all a person can do with his life is to gather about him his integrity, his imagination and his individuality—and with these ever with him, out in front and sharp in focus, leap into the dance of experience.

"Be your own master!

"Be your own Jesus!

"Be your own flying saucer! Rescue yourself.

"Be your own valentine! Free the heart."

—Tom Robbins

Even Cowgirls Get the Blues

A LONG, THIN STRIP of water separates the tiny town of La Conner, Washington, from the Swinomish Indian Reservation. It's as if some force larger than either was still enforcing a white-man/red-man standoff. On the reservation side, the darkness is almost total. The only lights are from a few fireworks stands, open long before and long after July Fourth. The feathery white noise of the wind through the cedars and the water through the channel is rudely spiked by the explosion of a Moon-and-Air Cracker and two Chinese Red Dragons. Then nature takes over again, and the Skagit Valley fog fuzzes up the row of lights from the bars and stores on First Street. The breeze off the Japan Current swirls and twists the sound of someone's huge wind chimes, and the sound bounces through the fog like some distant cosmic xylophone.

This place, with its nearly total isolation, is perfect for someone whose vocation requires spending quiet days at a desk. Distractions are at a minimum here.

La Conner is about as far from Hollywood as you can get. The closest touch of sun and swaying palms I found was in the men's room of the La Conner Tavern, where a dispensing machine advertised, "Silky Samoa— In Tropical Colors—the Condom with the Polynesian Touch."

Over at the pool table between the bar and jukebox, only a seven ball separated one of the locals from victory. As the seven ball disappeared into a corner pocket and the two began another game, I slid off my bar stool, walked around the pool table, and put three quarters into the music machine. Perversely, I plugged in the numbers to play Carly Simon's "Jesse" four times in a row, followed by "Mamas Don't Let Your Babies Grow Up to Be Cowboys," then "Jesse" one more time for the road. Not only do I like "Jesse," I like to see the reaction this repetition gets. It is a good finger on the pulse of a community.

The pool ace was, in many ways, a typical La Conner resident. He appeared to have just gotten out of his VW bus after the drive up from Haight-Ashbury. He pushed the cue stick with the expertise of someone whose avocation may earn him more money than his vocation.

"Yep, I musta set the land speed record, Seattle to Ketchum—fourteen hours—and it burned out me and my car. But my old lady slept like a redwood the whole damn way." He shot a puzzled glance at the jukebox behind him as "Jesse" caught its second wind.

Skinny as his cue stick, he had a ponytail down to the middle of his back, and red suspendered Levi's tucked into over-the-calf, yellow-striped athletic socks that disappeared inside a pair of well-worn logger's boots. He looked like an anorexic winger from the all-1960s Lumberjack Soccer Squad. His John Lennon rimless specs shot back twin glints from the pool-table lamp as he related his most recent plight. "I was supposed to go to Alaska, but the guy with the boat ran it up on the rocks, so he got fired. Shit-canned my job, so here I am . . ." At "Jesse's" third appearance he hollered at the waitress, "This damned thing's stuck—it's driving me nuts," to which she paid no attention. I acted rather uninvolved and bought three chances to win fifty dollars on a punch board— a sort of honeycomb of fortune, where you use a tiny metal rod to push out a rolled-up piece of paper that holds your financial future. Each of mine turned up worthless.

The fourth round between "Jesse" and the pool player proved decisive, although those scoring the event might have given it a split decision. After becoming rigidly catatonic at the all-too familiar first notes, he took off after Carly Simon's voice. He attacked with the thick end of his pool cue and nearly knocked the juke out of the box before the waitress ran over, unplugged the machine, and bought the poor guy a beer to calm his "Jesse"-jangled nerves. No one else in the bar even seemed to notice. This was indeed a laid-back place.

The waitress fiddled with the back of the jukebox, plugged it in, and to the soothing three-four time, *plunk-plunk-a-plunk* of "Mamas Don't Let Your Babies Grow Up to Be Cowboys," the sapling-skinny version of Minnesota Fats began banging at balls again.

As the song wound down, I paid my bill, closed my notebook and headed out into the quiet, cool night, just as all hell broke loose. "Jesse" was back, but I was gone.

———— ◇◆◇ ————

THE NEXT DAY, AT Tom Robbins's suggestion, I somewhat hesitantly returned with him to the scene of the crime. The same waitress was back on duty, and I wondered if she had any idea . . .

It is a rare clear day in La Conner; the sun has burned off the Skagit fog that hung so tightly last night and early this morning. It has gone quickly from a Pendleton-and-boots morning to a T-shirt-and-sandals afternoon, as Robbins and I sip beers out back of the tavern, on the waterway. He looks as I expected he would—a slightly older and wiser version of the face on the back cover of *Still Life with Woodpecker*. The crow's-feet from the 1980 photo have deepened slightly. He has the hesitant smile of a self-proclaimed "recluse," a perpetually tousled head of once-red hair, and an outlaw twinkle in his eyes.

As the waitress approaches, he says, "I'd like a large order of french fries, with a side of mayo, extra ketchup, lots of tartar sauce, and a pocket map of Venezuela." It all comes out in a quiet molasses-slow monotone, as if he didn't want to let the sea gulls know food was coming.

The waitress fires back, never looking up from her pad, using the same laser-straight monotone, "Okay, but you *know* the map of Venezuela doesn't come with the fries. It's extra." She knows how to deal with the prattle that has sold millions of copies of paperbacks.

———— ◇◆◇ ————

IT TAKES A SPECIAL environment to nurture Robbins's creativity. When he first stepped his tennis-shoed foot into La Conner, he immediately understood this was the place to set up practice.

His intuitive feel for the area, he quips, is partly because Jack Kerouac used to hitchhike through here. He did, too, in the summer of 1956, to and from an eight-week summer job as a fire-watcher in the Cascade Mountains. Robbins elaborates on his affinity for this part of the country in more realistic terms. "Rain is ideal for writers. It reduces temptation. During the rainy months you're forced to stay indoors. You turn inside. It's a cozy feeling, very comfortable and introspective. In life as in literature, I prefer wet to dry. And, of course, living out here in Monsoon Central, I can be as secluded as I need to be."

He sees life in this tiny fishing village as a necessity for maintaining a clear artistic view and a sense of purity in his work. "I think it's important to live far from the centers of ambition, to keep away from literary politics, and the sort of social contacts that can put the wrong emphasis on one's work."

He bought his recently renovated, century-old frame house on April Fool's Day 1970. "I always make important decisions on the first of April," he explains. "That way, if anything gets screwed up, I have something to blame it on."

Jesus: Hey dad.

God: Yes, son?

Jesus: Western Civilization followed me home this morning. Can I keep it?

God: Certainly not boy. And put it down this minute. You don't know where it's been.

—Tom Robbins
Another Roadside Attraction

"I get depressed talking about myself, and believe me, I don't get depressed easily," Robbins admits as we discuss the origins of his spirituality. "When I wrote the last sentence in *Woodpecker*, 'It's never too late to have a happy childhood,' some critics looked at that and saw an endorsement of frivolity, but that was not the intention. I think you can cut loose from the past. The past can be a prison. I view my books as cakes with files in them. You can eat the cake and lick the frosting, but inside there is a file that you can chop through the bars with, if you are so moved. I really believe we do not have to be weighed down by the past." But past influences spring eternal in his works. He grew up in North Carolina. His mother, who was a nurse, wrote children's stories for Southern Baptist magazines. His father moved up the corporate ladder, becoming an executive with a regional power company. Robbins had a younger sister, who died in childhood; his mother prayed for twins and had them—two girls. "I believe in prayer," Tom says, matter-of-factly.

His family was steeped in religion. "Both my grandfathers were Southern Baptist ministers. One was ordained. The other was not, and he traveled back into the 'hollers' of Appalachia on a mule to preach. I've been accused of preaching, even before my first book. I say 'Okay, what's wrong with that? We have the epistolary novel, journalism as a novel, the diary as novel. What is wrong with the sermon as novel?' Whatever works, works. Instead of trying to cut that out of my work, I have decided to perfect it, refine it, but go ahead and preach and make it work in the context of the book.

"My characters suffer. They are killed. They die. They have all the griefs and sorrows that characters in so-called realistic novels have. But in the end, they insist on joy in spite of everything."

Robbins recalls that as a child, "Johnny Weissmuller—Tarzan—was my big hero. I sort of grew up going to the Southern Baptist Sunday school and felt that Jesus *should* be my hero. But, somehow, he never measured up to Tarzan. I would go to Sunday school every Sunday and really try to get excited about Jesus, but he didn't move me. The latest Tarzan film would come around and I was 'up' for months. So I dealt with that in my first book, *Another Roadside Attraction*. I actually had a meeting between Tarzan and Jesus, trying to work that out."

Poking fun at religion and man's mortality is a time-honored practice, yet few can carry it off with Robbins's incisiveness:

Wiggs: One last thing about death.

Pris: What's that?

Wiggs: After you die, your hair and your nails continue to grow.

Pris: I've heard that.

Wiggs: Yes. But your phone calls taper off.

—Tom Robbins
Jitterbug Perfume

For nine months of the year, Blowing Point, North Carolina, was "like Dogpatch. It was Appalachia all the way—impoverished, ignorant, populated by men who beat their wives and drank too much—a rather *mean* place, abounding with natural beauty and colorful characters, but violent, snake-bit and sorrowful all over."

During the summer months, however, the town of seven hundred people became a country resort for the wealthy, who came to take the mountain air. The streets were lined with Rolls-Royces; glamorous men and women played golf and tennis, and a theater played first-run films. Then after Labor Day, everything shut down again.

"The dichotomy between the rich, sophisticated scene and the hillbilly scene affected me very much," Robbins says. "It showed me how the ordinary suddenly could be changed into the extraordinary. And back again. It toughened me to harsh realities while instilling in me the romantic idea of another life. And it left me with an affinity for both sides of the tracks."

The "other" side of the tracks was represented by a roadhouse just outside of town, called The Bark. There, hard drinking, cigar smoking, tatooed men, and their women, roared through the red clay parking lot on Harley-Davidsons. "At The Bark, folks drank beer and danced," Robbins remembers. "Can you appreciate the fact that among fundamentalist Southern Baptists, drinking and dancing were major sins? My mother taught a Baptist Sunday School class for people aged sixteen to twenty-three, and once a week, Wednesday night, this class would meet at our house. It was partly religious, parly social, but they did a lot of gossiping, and the hottest items of gossip always involved The Bark. 'So-and-so was seen leaving The Bark Saturday night,' and so forth. Now I was a little kid—seven, eight, nine—while this was going on, but they made The Bark sound so attractive, so fascinating! I just loved eavesdropping on those shocked conversations about the evils of that roadhouse. All I wanted to do was grow up and go to The Bark, to drink beer, squeeze floozies, dance, get tattooed, smoke cigars and ride a motorcycle."

Before he was old enough to sample the pleasures of The Bark, Robbins's family moved to Burnsville, North Carolina, where they lived on the edge of the campus of a vacant private school. Tom's introduction to magic—a theme that permeates his writings—came first with the overnight transformation of the vacant schoolyard into an oasis of flapping canvas tents, strange odors, weird animals, and exotic people: the Barnes and Beers Traveling Circus had slipped into Burnsville in the middle of the night.

"I was an eleven-year-old with an active imagination and went over right away to get a job so that I could get in free." He watered the llamas, set up the menagerie, and scraped moss off the back of a six-foot alligator. But something else really caught his attention: "I met Bobbie and just fell totally in love. She was the most exotic thing I had ever seen. She had waist-length, brilliantly blond hair. She wore black, pat-ent-leather riding boots and riding britches. She had this pet black snake and scars on her arm where it had bitten her. I have always been a romantic, one of those people who believes that a woman in pink circus tights contains all of the secrets of the universe."

Whether it's Amanda setting up the flea circus in *Another Roadside Attraction,* Sissy Hankshaw thumbing rides on passing clouds in *Even Cowgirls Get the Blues,* Princess Leigh-Cheri contemplating "how to make love stay" in *Still Life with Woodpecker,* or *Jitterbug Perfume*'s Kudra mixing the potent potion of life, the theme of feminine insight to heavenly delight runs deep: Tom Robbins is a heroine addict.

Robbins's fascination with the circus put him in touch with something at the core of human existence. "The circus is a real metaphor for society at large. What appeals to me in particular is the wire-walkers. They are totally unnecessary. Society does not *need* aerialists in any literal sense. What role is fulfilled by a man risking his life walking on a wire? It is a Zen act not only to risk your life but to devote your life to these curious obsessions.

"Carl Wallenda, another of my heroes, once said, 'On the wire is living—everything else is only waiting.' During the time it happens, you are in contact in a primitive way with 'that which of which there is no whicher'—a God-force—the essence of the universe."

Somewhat irreverent as an adolescent, he was sent to a military school, then entered college at Washington and Lee University in Lexington, Virginia, as a sixteen-year-old. He pledged Pi Kappa Phi, wore a coat and tie to class, and worked as a cub sports reporter under T. K. Wolfe III. "Tom Wolfe was a senior when I was a freshman. He was the editor of the campus newspaper, the *Ring Tum Phi*. Ridiculous name. It was kind of a ridiculous school. I didn't last long.

"One of my friends was sitting at the fraternity housemother's table, and I tried hitting him with a pea. It went off to the side, hit her in the chest, and ran down her cleavage." Some of the fraternity brothers began berating Robbins, questioning his parentage among other things. "I just reached over, picked up some biscuits, and started lobbing them at her. Not to hurt her, but I sent this whole shower of biscuits. *That* was the end of my days there."

His next experiment landed him in the air force. He lasted two weeks in officer-candidate school then was assigned to study meteorology at the University of Illinois before being shipped off to teach in Korea. "Korean pilots had very little interest in meteorology. They would not circumnavigate storm systems. They would fly right into them—it was just their style. They were bored and I was bored, so we operated a black-market ring instead. Small stuff—cigarettes, cosmetics, and Colgate toothpaste—which I found out later were going into China. I had this fantasy that I was supplying Mao Zedong with his Colgate toothpaste."

Working shifts of four days on and four days off, Robbins would hitch rides on air force planes to Tokyo, where his interest in Eastern thought blossomed. He had enough time there to take a course in Japanese culture and aesthetics, an interest he would later pursue briefly at the University of Washington. The Orient was a heady experience for a twenty-year-old from the Carolina hills. "I became enamored with the romance of solitude. I love waking up in strange cities, where I know no one and don't know what the next move is going to be. I used to wander around Tokyo for hours and hours, knowing very little Japanese. *All* those strange sights and smells . . ."

Even after winning the enlisted men's Scrabble championship, Robbins was still the only member of his outfit not to receive a reenlistment lecture. He came back to the States, got a degree in art at Richmond Professional Institute, and began work in the *Richmond Times-Dispatch*.

Given his interest in travel, he harbored thoughts of becoming foreign correspondent and ended up the international-news specialist on the copy desk. One of his other duties was to edit the syndicated Earl Wilson celebrity gossip column, pick out one of the people mentioned, and get his or her photo from the newspaper morgue. "One time without even thinking, I put in Louis Armstrong. 'Satchmo.' Well, they got letters! They suggested to me that I should not put a 'gentleman of color' in the column. Of course it really annoyed me. Some months later I was feeling ornery. The column mentioned Nat King Cole, and I slapped ol' Nat in there." The managing editor warned him that a repeat performance would be his finale.

About two weeks later, Robbins sensed it was time for one of life's moments of decision. "It was one of those synchronistic things. On that particular day Earl Wilson mentioned Sammy Davis, Jr. He was one of the most hated black celebrities because he had married a white woman. So I put ol' Sammy in there and just walked out. I didn't give them a chance to fire me. I turned in my resignation."

The road headed west and slightly north—Seattle was as far as he could get from Richmond. Accepted at the Far East Institute of the University of Washington, Tom arrived early in 1962 and got a job at the *Seattle Times* to pay his tuition. This time around, his editing brought more positive attention; he wrote the headlines for the "Dear Abby" column, and nurtured an appreciation for her concise blend of wit and wisdom.

"She came by the *Seattle Times* and asked if she could meet the person who was writing her headlines. She was syndicated in about one hundred and fifty newspapers and none of them had headlines like the ones in Seattle. Someone had written in about Tarzan books being banned in California because Tarzan and Jane were not married. So my headline read, "Did Tarzan Live Too High in Tree?"

An opportunity arose to actually put his academic training to work when the *Seattle Times* art critic quit. Robbins felt the position was a chance for him to get into something where his "voice" might materialize. It worked for a while. He did some good work. He got a feel for the power of a critic and, predictably, tried to approach his role from "an educational standpoint. Not to try to punish people."

Then, on the way to becoming an art critic, lightning struck. Usually vague on dates, Tom remembers the day precisely: "July 19, 1963. I was given LSD from an enlightened physician in Seattle. I did not know a single other person who had had it. It was the most profound experience of my life, and it suddenly gave me a new culture. It was like being a Southern Baptist one day and a Russian Jew the next, so you don't relate to Southern Baptists anymore. I went looking for my people."

He called in "well" one day and left for New York City, ostensibly to write a biography of painter Jackson Pollock (he actually did a lot of the research but never wrote the book).

"At that point in my life I had dabbled in the major world religions, the systems of philosophical liberation, a great deal of Zen and Taoism. But it was abstract. In one eight-hour session with LSD all this became totally real. My life was never the same after that."

In 1964, he lived two blocks from Allen Ginsberg in the East Village and, that fall, marched side by side with him in a LEMAR (Legalize

Marijuana) demonstration. Robbins then went to hear a lecture by Timothy Leary at Cooper Union. The message that evening could be stated in one sentence: "You have to go out of your mind to use your head." The hall was packed, but Robbins got a seat close enough to see that the color-blind Leary was wearing red socks with his tweed suit. From that point on, Robbins wore red socks for years. (Later he began to wear mismatched socks, a personal eccentricity he uses as a constant reminder of the "clarity of vision" that can only come from swimming against the stream.) Being far too shy to approach Leary, Robbins recalls actually meeting him shortly after the lecture.

"I ran into Tim on the street after the talk he gave at Cooper Union. We were both at a vegetable stand, and I was buying brussels sprouts. He said, 'How can you tell the good ones?' I told him, 'You pick the ones that are smiling.' "

The 1960s, in New York City, later in San Francisco and then Seattle, were a potent time for Robbins. He is an artist irrevocably rooted in that decade, and he tracked the evolution of consciousness expansion like a dog lost and wandering in the forest, listening for his master's whistle.

"I followed it all, and in a certain sense I participated in it, right at a very core level, but I was never really a part of that scene. It was just not in my nature to be part of a scene."

———————— ◇◆◇ ————————

THE SUN IS DIPPING low across the waterway, and the evening chill begins to sink in. In this part of the country one changes clothing according to the time of day rather than the time of year. Robbins and I head out of the La Conner tavern and hitch a ride up the hill to his place. We had to catch his Seattle Seahawks drubbing the Minnesota Vikings.

As we approach the house, all that is visible is the fence. "The original house was built in 1873, the same year *your* Sigmund Freud"—and he turned to me as if to indicate some proprietary relationship—"dropped out of law school." (At the time I said nothing, but made a quick mental note. Later I verified the accuracy of his statement. Indeed, his research is inevitably thorough, if sometimes unorthodox. For *Another Roadside Attraction*, he read seventeen books on the life of Christ; for *Still Life with Woodpecker* he meditated for days on a pack of Camels.)

His literary successes have allowed Robbins to build some additions onto his house, though he admits, "It is built against all architectural concepts of open space. Its density—all these nooks and crannies—are just the way I write."

The humor evident in his books is here, too. In the glassed-in hot-tub area, as the steam dissipates, an eerie, etched UFO can be seen to materialize slowly from under the condensation. It's another reminder of his playfulness, like the framed *National Enquirer* pages here and there.

Sitting in his living room, Robbins talks about the long road back to the West Coast after his year in New York City. (Above him, Warhol's twin portraits of Mao look down sternly.) He spent a pivotal period in the San Francisco area—at Berkeley and in the Haight-Ashbury.

"In June 1966 I went to the Avalon Ballroom, and it occurred to me that things would never be the same. I really thought that we were in for a full renaissance. It was so mind-boggling. Cooper Union in New York was liberation on an intellectual level. But I walked into the Avalon Ballroom in San Francisco and there were people in costume and the first light show I had ever seen. There were children running around, rock bands playing, people dancing free-form, which was the beginning of dance for me. I had never really liked to dance before because I didn't like learning the steps. That night I started to dance. Children, dogs, everybody had a smile and a hug for everyone else. It was like Utopia. It was so totally different from any of my experiences in American culture. This was the *end* of the old world and the beginning of the new."

Back in Seattle, Robbins found an outlet in the underground newspaper *The Helix.* By now the tides of change had washed all the way to Seattle. Robbins demonstrated the beginnings of his "voice" in the summer of 1967 in a review of a Doors concert:

> The Doors. Their style is early cunnilingual with overtones of the Massacre of the Innocents. An electrified sex slaughter. A musical bloodbath. . . . The Doors are carnivores in a land of musical vegetarians. . . . their talons, fangs, and folded wings are seldom out of view, but if they leave us crotch-raw and exhausted, at least they leave us aware of our aliveness. And of our destiny. The Doors scream into the darkened auditorium what all of us in the underground are whispering more softly in our hearts: we want the world and we want it . . . NOW!

He became a disc jockey for a radio show, *Rock and Roll for Big Boys and Girls.* (He politely refused a guitar audition by Charles Manson.) He began reviewing art for *Seattle Magazine.* Finally, in 1967, he was contacted by an editor from Doubleday. Like Dear Abby before him, the editor saw something unique in Tom's writing. He asked if Robbins wanted to write a book, which he did, but not about West Coast art, which the editor wanted. Initially both were disappointed, but then the editor asked what Robbins's book was about.

"I said, 'Oh, it's about the discovery of the mummified body of Jesus Christ in the catacombs of the Vatican, its subsequent theft and reappearance in America in a roadside zoo.'

"I'd had that particular idea kicking around in my head for six or seven years. Well, his eyes kind of lit up and he said, 'Tell me more.' I didn't know any more, so I started making it up then, to keep his interest. When he had finished his coffee, he asked when he could see it. I said it was in pretty rough form—I hadn't written a word. So I went home that day and told my girlfriend, 'I've got to start writing a novel.' "

The novel was begun in 1968, while Robbins was living in a three-dollar-a-night hotel on then-sleazy First Avenue. It became *Another Roadside Attraction*, the book *Rolling Stone* called "the quintessential '60s novel." A prodigious reader, Robbins cites as his literary influences Henry Miller, Jack Kerouac, and Nelson Algren. "I have always admired them tremendously, yet in my finally realized style I don't think they had much to do with it. Many books about the 1960s failed because they used old novelistic techniques. I went from the inside out and tried to *evoke* the experience of the 1960s. The whole book is structured psychedelically. It doesn't move from minor climax to minor climax up a slowly inclining plane to a major climax. It actually develops in the way that a drug experience would. There are a lot of flashes of illumination strung together like beads. Some illuminate the plot, others merely illuminate the reader."

The idea behind the book had been in Robbins's mind since child-hood. He was intrigued by the extent to which Western civilization—from its cultural myths to individual behavior—was predicated on the divinity of Christ. "So I wondered, what would happen if we were to learn conclusively that Christ was not divine? What would this say about Western civilization, about the future of Western civilization? Could we continue to lead moral and ethical lives if Christ was proved to have died and stayed dead?"

Robbins had never made a serious attempt to write fiction before he began his first book. "I'd been writing stories off and on since I was five years old, but nothing I wanted to show anyone, and I'd never begun a novel or anything like that. I concentrated on non-fiction. I was waiting to find my voice. Once I found it, I was off and running."

Robbins is quick to add an important point concerning the relation between the psychedelic experience and his unusual writing style. "Drugs did not make me more creative. I don't think they gave me any talent I didn't already have. What they did was free me to make connections that one doesn't normally make. A more multidimensional relation to reality."

When *Another Roadside Attraction* was finished, Robbins felt he *had* found his voice. Unfortunately, few readers found his *book*—at first. "I was making one and a half cents a copy, and at that price you have to sell a lot of books to make any money. I had a bad contract because I was an unknown first novelist and didn't have an agent."

Like his characters, always insisting on joy, he pushed himself into a second novel. When *Even Cowgirls Get the Blues* was published in 1976, its instant popularity pulled sales of his first book in its wake; there are now over two million copies of *Another Roadside Attraction* in print. It became an underground classic, passed conspiratorially from hand to hand to hand, like a never-ending joint of the best grass. Critics were puzzled; most reviews were negative.

Typically, Robbins answers with a story. "*Another Roadside Attraction,* was the Hell's Angels' all-time favorite book. Also, did you know that Elvis Presley was reading *Another Roadside Attraction* the night he died? True. A copy of it was lying beside him on the bathroom floor. With the Hell's Angels and Elvis on your side, who the hell needs the *New York Review of Books?*"

From his study of Jackson Pollock, Robbins emerged with a perspective on creativity that, once understood, illuminates his writing, as well as the ongoing lack of respect afforded him by most reviewers. "I consider Jackson Pollock a realistic painter and Andrew Wyeth an abstract painter," he says. "Wyeth's paintings are two-dimensional reductions of the three-dimensional world. Thus, they're abstracted from the external world. They are pictures *of* things. Pollock's paintings don't refer to things, they *are* things: independent, intrinsic, internal, holistic, *real.* Now, in a sense, books are abstractions in that they refer to countless things outside of themselves. In my books, when I interrupt the narrative flow and call attention to the book itself, it's not cuteness or self-consciousness but an attempt to make the novel less abstract, more of a real thing.

> This sentence has a crush on Norman Mailer. This sentence is a wino and doesn't care who knows it. *Like many italic sentences, this one has Mafia connections.* This sentence is a double Cancer with Pisces rising. This sentence lost its mind searching for the perfect paragraph. This sentence leaks. This sentence doesn't *look* Jewish . . . This sentence has accepted Jesus Christ as its personal savior. This sentence once spit in a book reviewer's eye. This sentence can do the funky chicken. This sentence is called "Speedo" but its real name is Mr. Earl. This sentence may be pregnant, it missed its period. This sentence went to jail with Clifford Irving. This sentence went to Woodstock. And this little sentence went wee wee wee all the way home. This sentence is proud to be a part of the team here at Even Cowgirls Get the Blues. This sentence is rather confounded by the whole damn thing.

> —Tom Robbins
> *Even Cowgirls Get the Blues*

Robbins's irreverence is also carefully crafted, and here he makes an "important" distinction. "Important humor is liberating and maybe even transformative. Important humor is also always inappropriate—if a joke is appropriate, you can rest assured it is unimportant. But a joke in the *wrong* place at the *wrong* time can cause a leap in consciousness that is liberating to the human spirit.

"Have you ever noticed that nothing upsets an intellectual as much as discovering that a plumber is enjoying the same book he is? The literati are too insecure to ever admit to liking a book that isn't inaccesible or esoteric."

After his third book, *Still Life with Woodpecker,* Robbins's success was assured. Ironically, it also reintroduced him to the man with whom he had once discussed brussels sprouts. Robbins was in the parking lot behind Papa Bach's, a Santa Monica paperback bookstore, autographing copies of his new book for a long line of fans. It was night, and searchlights were set up in typical L.A. fashion to hype the event. A rock band played as Robbins talked to the people coming to have their books signed. Behind a cyclone fence at the edge of the parking lot some Chicanos took note of this strange spectacle.

"Pretty soon," Robbins remembers, "there were fifteen or twenty Mexicans standing against the fence, drinking beer, watching this whole scene, trying to figure out if I was some renegade pope. It really did look religious the way the people had to kneel before me at this little low table. Every once in a while I would look over and kind of bless them. About halfway through I looked over and standing against the fence was Tim Leary."

The two have remained close friends ever since. In *Jitterbug Perfume,* the character Dr. Wiggs Dannyboy, the defrocked Irish ex-Harvard anthropologist, is partly modeled on Leary.

In Robbins's view, the 1960s were an aborted evolutionary leap. He disagrees with Leary regarding the democratization of consciousness-expanding chemicals. It should not have been so egalitarian, Robbins contends, but used, as Huxley suggested, only by an elite few, "an enlightened minority, like in the Eleusinian Mysteries in the Golden Age of Greece, where one was condemned to death if he revealed the secrets." He feels that the stream was further polluted at the source by sloganeering and extensive media coverage. A throng of mutant imitators was created, out just to be part of the party, rather than seeking enlightenment. In a recent letter, written to me on his Sidd Finch Fan Club stationery, he expanded on this theory:

> It boils down to this: what happened in the Sixties was only secondarily political. First and foremost it was a *spiritual* phenomenon.
>
> And I believe it proved my thesis that if we work on changing spiritually, philosophically, then the political changes will naturally and automatically follow. For centuries, we've been putting the cart before the horse.
>
> The magic of the Sixties, the triumph of the Sixties, began to dissipate when we took our eyes off the spiritual ball and shifted our focus to the political fallout from our spiritual advances.
>
> Next time, I want us to get it right.

Robbins's thoughts on any subject are never written in haste. He writes in longhand from 10:00 A.M. until 4:00 P.M. each day. The density of his work is a sign of his craftsmanlike approach: A half hour might be spent on a single sentence; two pages a day is his goal.

"My method of writing is to paint myself into corners," and then, he says, "see if I can reach into my pocket and find suction cups to put on the bottom of my feet and walk up the wall, across the ceiling, and out of the room. That is a terrifying way to work. I would not recommend it to anyone. It sort of keeps you on the edge of terror all the time, but for me that's salubrious. It adds something to the work."

He then scurries over to a pile of magazines in his living room, pulls out a copy of *Fiction International,* and reads me his most recent contribution. It is clearly the definitive statement of his attitude toward his craft.

"Some of these are long-winded," he says with disdain. "Mine is quite short. 'A writer's first obligation is not to the many-bellied beast, but to the many-tongued beast. Not to society but to language. Everyone has a stake in the husbandry of society, but language is the writer's special charge—and a grandiose animal it is, too! If it weren't for language, there wouldn't be society. Once writers have established their basic commitment to language and are taking the blue guitar-sized risk that that relationship demands, they are free to promote social betterment . . . but let me tell you this: Social action on a political, economic level is wee potatoes. Our great human adventure is evolution of consciousness. We are in this life to enlarge the soul and light up the brain. How many writers of fiction do you think are committed to that?' " He snaps the magazine down and looks at me with a challenging smile.

Mentioning a many-tongued beast was a piece of synchronous timing. Ka Ka Ka ZAP, Robbins's five-foot-long Sumatran thunder lizard, a souvenir of an Indonesian raft trip, enters the kitchen and begins eating with a horrendous crunching-belching-ripping sound. I turn toward the creature as it looks toward me, emitting a long, menacing hiss, eyes glowing like electric tangerine Life Savers.

"Why the three *Kas* in her name?" I ask, disconcerted.

"Birth defect," Robbins says quietly. "She has an extra fork in her tongue and can't even hiss properly. I've heard better third-grade piccolo sections. But for God's sake, do not pity the poor bastard. With equipment like that, she is simply hell on flies."

"Don't you ever lock her out?"

"I'm just too nice a guy," he says sheepishly, tossing more chickens into the huge ceramic bowl in the corner.

———————◇◆◇———————

I LEAVE TOM ROBBINS feeding Ka Ka Ka ZAP. The Buick, at the end of a long and hazardous trip, now sounds like a McCormick reaper on a rocky field. Leaving La Conner, I cross the steel bridge to the reservation side, in search of something I had seen years ago as a child, driving through here to visit relatives in British Columbia. As a child it was a curiosity; as an adult it would hold deep significance.

For many years, there was a unique totem pole in front of the Swinomish tribal headquarters. Unique, in that very few people—except the Swinomish, and maybe Tom Robbins—understood and appreciated its profundity. A heraldic reminder of the clan's ancestry, carved with dignified restraint, it portrayed the guardian spirit figures of key importance to this coastal tribe's survival and it placed them in an order that reflected the biological food chain. Near the bottom were stylized ocean waves with a salmon curling above. Then came the beak of a fish hawk, then the great fanged bear. On top, complete with monocle and cigarette holder, was carved, with paramount reverence, the head of Franklin Delano Roosevelt.

Any understanding of Tom Robbins, and indeed, the entire decade that was the sixties must include a rather thorough amount of empathy for the magical and the mystic. In the heraldic, carved fir trunk, the power of the ocean at the base and the power of the president of the United States on top would have been joined, had Indians had the ability to carve "totem wheels" instead of totem poles. It is only to white man's separate reality that FDR seems more powerful than the ocean waves. In Tom Robbins's view the full circle of the world is seen from a different perspective, one that disdains the tyranny of power of anything except the power of the individual over himself.

Somewhere in America

I'M STRAPPED IN SO tight to my seat that all I can move is my head. Up front a video shows where oxygen, flotation devices, and exit slides are in case of the Big Emergency. Noise and movement begin simultaneously. The mechanical growl emerges victorious over a chorus of ear-piercing whines; the acceleration squeezes me back into my seat. The DC-10 shakes like a wet mutt and sounds like a junkyard during an earthquake. Suddenly I am no longer a prisoner of gravity. The buildings of Seattle shrink to tiny toys; in the noon sun, the snow-covered top of Mount Rainier shimmers and flashes as if it has been secretly scrubbed clean and polished by the gods during the night.

Looking around the plane, I realize that I am not only in first class, I *am* first class; the other seats are empty. For the six hours to Boston there will be no distractions, only my thoughts. It's a run-from-the-sun, jet-short day, skimming the entire curved, flexed muscle of America. A polite flight attendant honors my desire for privacy while keeping an attentive eye on the level of my champagne glass. It never goes dry.

Below me, Tom Robbins sleeps late ("I never get out of bed until I hear the number twenty-three") and Kesey, off to the south, beyond Mount Hood, has finished another long night writing under the ever-watchful eyes of *Further*.

The phenomenon of seeing America nonstop from coast to coast is simultaneously inspiring and depressing. The ceaselessly changing immensity of it all—people going to work in Seattle, farmers tilling their fields in the Iowa afternoon, the electric glow of East Coast villages warding off the night. There is comfort in knowing the sense of unity we share. On the other hand, from thirty-seven thousand feet there is an oddly sad sense of detachment, a hollow place inside that comes from seeing all those highways, back roads, secret lakes, and tiny cabin roofs reflecting the summer's sun. I will never know them or the people that bring them alive. The jet in which I streak overhead near sound's barrier is a mirror snap of light for those few on the ground who see it; a silver pinhead leaving a chalk-line contrail that disappears in seconds, like a tiny, distant water-skier on the pale-blue sky.

From my view on the wing, the sun begins to slant back now, and the plane begins to bump. The captain's voice crackles through the PA system, interrupting the in-flight stereo playing James Taylor's "So Far Away." He calmly announces the turbulence and orders seat belts to be fastened, ". . . just like we do here in the cockpit; this won't last long. It's perfectly clear, but those Rocky Mountains down there do kick up a fuss now and then." I know better; it is turbulent because we are right over Woody Creek, Colorado, and Hunter Thompson has probably returned from Florida. He's in his backyard. I can almost see him; sunglasses on, rifle in hand, he squeezes off a few rounds at the Chinese gongs he has hung from the trees as targets. Surely if the DC-10 makes too much noise, he'll pop a few up at us, but I take heart and remember his words: "I never kill more than I can eat."

———————◇◆◇———————

WHEN I WAS INTRODUCED to psychology at Berkeley, reading Henry Murray's personology and Robert White's *Lives in Progress,* all I wanted to do was dig in and explore the endless labyrinths that make up people's lives. Ernest Hemingway once remarked to F. Scott Fitzgerald that the rich are different from us; they have more money. Likewise, I found that the human icons of a generation are different from us; they lead slightly larger lives, on a broader scale of existence. Their actions are a source of inspiration. Their message is, "Push harder. Ask questions. Don't conform. Look for different answers in strange places, and *don't slow down!*"

In these individuals I found a full gamut of life forces at work, from the purely random to the seemingly predestined. Allen Ginsberg went to Columbia as a callow, confused seventeen-year-old, with a vague notion of becoming a labor attorney. And in a sense, after his accidental meeting with Kerouac and Burroughs, after his San Francisco therapist, and after *Howl,* he has become one. For three decades, he has been a self-appointed spokesperson for the common man against a Pandora's box of antagonists. Timothy Leary stood in line to register as a philosophy major at the University of Alabama, only to be told that the next and much shorter line wasn't such a bad major, either—psychology. His "Milk of Human Kindness" letter, written as a twenty-year-old from West Point, became an amazingly accurate blueprint for his life.

THE LEVEL OF THE champagne bottle is sliding quickly below the *A* of *Almaden;* the sun is sliding quickly behind the Rockies; and I wonder just where in the world I am. One of the cockpit crew emerges, and I ask him our location and, in particular, where Lawrence, Kansas, was.

"Well, if you look way off the leading edge of the right wing," he says, stooping to see into the thickening midwestern gloam and squinting a bit, "there is a dull glow. That could be it. Hard to tell. Is that home for you?" he asks.

"No," I answer, "that's not home for me. Just an old acquaintance of mine. He's been everywhere, knows everyone, done everything. Now he's in Lawrence."

Perhaps my inquiry goaded the pilot into a heightened sense of geographic awareness; as the plane invaded the night, few lights on the ground went unidentified. "Kansas City on the right; Saint Louis on the right; Pittsburgh straight ahead," came the announcements as we zipped toward Boston. "New York City *way* off the right wing," was the last marker. A ruddy glow elbowed its way skyward through East Coast smog, marking the city where Ginsberg and Mailer toil "like scientists who are each working on the same problem."

Lower down now, on the final approach to Logan International, seatbacks "in their upright position," tray tables and safety belts fastened, I could pick out the bend in the Merrimack River and a greenish light, diffused into a soft cotton candy over Kerouac's Lowell, now marked not by textile mills, but the towers of Wang Computer. We've come full circle back to Boston, where I live, where Timmyball had spun Harvard, and then the country, on its ear a quarter century ago. What a road, what a flight, what a long, strange trip it has been.

Things in the 1980s hum. The times don't crackle with volcanic force or exude the smell of ozone as they did in the 1960s. Is this a lull before yet another cultural storm, or has the country "grown up," becoming boring and spiritually flaccid in the process? I'm not sure, but somewhere in America that old witch's caldron must be bubbling. Somewhere in America an old Jefferson Airplane album spins. Somewhere in America, youth is asking simple questions and getting complex answers. Somewhere in America, the future is happening right now . . . somewhere in America . . .

Index

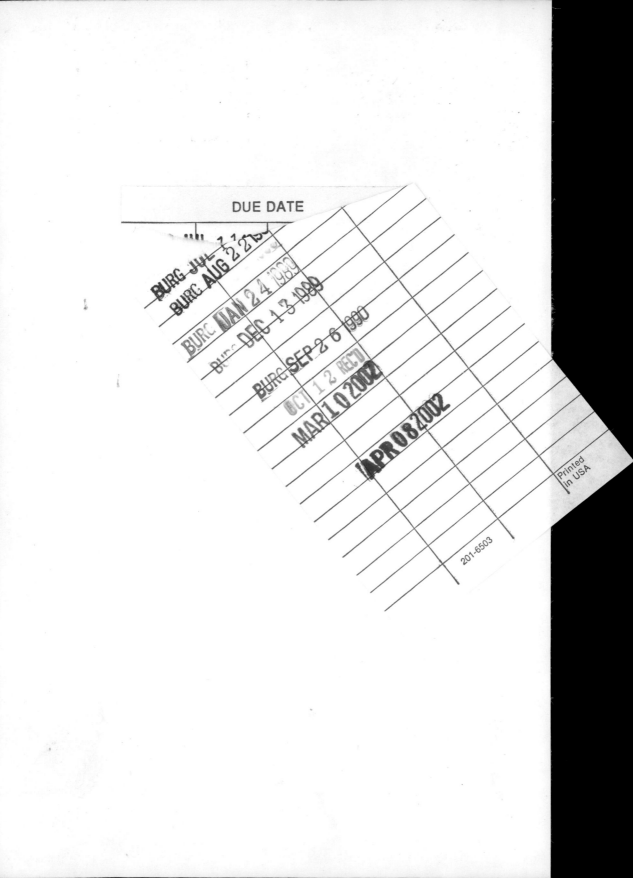